Understanding Our Story

Understanding Our Story

The Life's Work and Legacy of Adrian van Kaam in the Field of Formative Spirituality

REBECCA LETTERMAN
AND SUSAN MUTO

WIPF & STOCK · Eugene, Oregon

UNDERSTANDING OUR STORY
The Life's Work and Legacy of Adrian van Kaam in the Field of Formative Spirituality

Copyright © 2017 Rebecca Letterman and Susan Muto. All rights reserved. Except for brief quotations in critical publications or reviews, no part of this book may be reproduced in any manner without prior written permission from the publisher. Write: Permissions, Wipf and Stock Publishers, 199 W. 8th Ave., Suite 3, Eugene, OR 97401.

Wipf & Stock
An Imprint of Wipf and Stock Publishers
199 W. 8th Ave., Suite 3
Eugene, OR 97401

www.wipfandstock.com

PAPERBACK ISBN: 978-1-5326-0179-8
HARDCOVER ISBN: 978-1-5326-0181-1
EBOOK ISBN: 978-1-5326-0180-4

Manufactured in the U.S.A. FEBRUARY 13, 2017

Dynamics of Spiritual Direction by Adrian van Kaam and Susan Muto, Epiphany Association, 2003. Used by permission. All rights reserved.

Epiphany Manual on the Art and Discipline of Formation-in-Common: A Fresh Approach to the Ancient Practice of Spiritual Direction by Adrian van Kaam and Susan Muto, Epiphany Association, 1998. Used by permission. All rights reserved.

Essential Elements of Formation Anthropology and Formation Theology: A Compilation of Complementary Considerations by Adrian van Kaam and Susan Muto, Epiphany Association, 2008. Used by permission. All rights reserved.

Formative Spirituality series by Adrian van Kaam, Epiphany Association, 1989–1991. Used by permission. All rights reserved.

Formative Theology series by Adrian van Kaam and Susan Muto, Epiphany Association, 2004–2007. Used by permission. All rights reserved.

The Life Journey of a Joyful Man of God: The Autobiographical Memoirs of Adrian van Kaam by Adrian van Kaam, edited by Susan Muto, Epiphany Association, 2010. Used by permission. All rights reserved.

New Revised Standard Version of the Bible, copyright 1952 [2nd edition, 1971] by the Division of Christian Education of the National Council of the Churches of Christ in the United States of America. Used by permission. All rights reserved.

Contents

Illustrations | *vi*
Acknowledgments | *vii*
Introduction | *1*

Chapter 1	Spherical Facets of the van Kaamian Formation Field Model	10
Chapter 2	Dimensional Facets of the Formation Field Model	25
Chapter 3	Integrating Structures	41
Chapter 4	Dispositions	62
Chapter 5	Faith and Formation Traditions	82
Chapter 6	Dynamics of Conscience and Consciousness	95
Chapter 7	The Appraisal Process	120
Chapter 8	Modes of Direction	132
Chapter 9	Transcendence Crisis	147
Chapter 10	Phases of Human and Christian Formation	160

Epilogue | *177*
Glossary | *183*
Bibliography | *217*
Index | *229*

Illustrations

Figures

Figure 1: The van Kaamian Formation Field Model | 14
Figure 2: Integrating Structures of the Human Life Form | 42
Figure 3: Exemplary Form Tradition Pyramid | 89
Figure 4: Formative Regions of Consciousness | 104
Figure 5: Appraisal Process | 122

Tables

Table 1: Dimensions, Dynamics, Expressions of the Human Life Form | 27
Table 2: Introspection vs Transcendent Self-Presence | 116
Table 3: Six Components of a Direction-in-Common Session | 138

Acknowledgments

WE ACKNOWLEDGE WITH HUMBLE gratitude the help we have received from our friends, family members, and colleagues at both Northeastern Seminary in Rochester, New York, and at the Epiphany Academy of Formative Spirituality in Pittsburgh, Pennsylvania, all of whom have made this publication possible. At the Epiphany Academy we thank in particular our expert publication manager Mary Lou Perez and our graphics coordinator Lori Mitchell McMahon. We are also grateful to our friend and colleague Rev. Dr. Ruth Correll, who promoted the writing of this book and assisted us in its early design. We owe an immense debt of gratitude to the expert readers of our text in its various draft forms, including Dr. Paul Livermore, Dr. William Roth, Elizabeth Guckenbiehl-Lang, and Pamela Curtis. We are grateful, too, for our publisher, Wipf & Stock, and its outstanding editors and staff, thanks to whose help we were able to bring this text to final publication. May those named and unnamed sense the depth of our appreciation and our promise of continued prayer.

Our debt to Adrian van Kaam and his formative thinking will be clear to all who read these pages. It has been our privilege to know him as our colleague, mentor, friend, and fellow sojourner with Christ. And, of course, we are most thankful to the Triune God, without whose guidance and help this project would never have been completed.

Introduction

The Unfolding Project of Formative Spirituality

SHEER OBSERVATION REVEALS THAT we live in an era of transition and change far too rapid for most of us to grasp. Is it any wonder that humanity and Christianity are in need of a theoretical-integrational framework to accommodate the growing hunger for spiritual formation that is at once experientially meaningful and theologically sound? The need to integrate understanding and experience, theory and practice, what we know about the Divine from revealed teachings and how to live these beliefs in daily life, is the basis of this book on the science, anthropology, and theology of formation. It presents a comprehensive view of the life's work of Adrian van Kaam, CSSp, PhD (1920–2007) and addresses in detail his integrative approach to formative spirituality, including the visionary guidance he offers to all Christians and to sincere seekers in all walks of life.

The Journey Begins

Father Adrian, as he was fondly called by both his colleagues and students, was born in The Hague, Netherlands, on April 19, 1920. He began his studies at the Preparatory Academy of the Holy Ghost Fathers in Weert in 1932 and graduated with highest honors six years later. In 1939, the future priest and member of the Spiritans entered their novitiate in Gennep and from there advanced to the senior seminary in Gemert to complete the required six years of study in theology and philosophy prior to ordination. He stood among the first in his class. Though he anticipated being ordained in 1945, he found himself caught behind enemy lines during the infamous Dutch Hunger Winter of 1944–45, which lasted until the liberation of his country in May of 1945. Following that momentous occasion, he returned to the seminary.

His transcript reads that he took two semesters of classes in psychology, metaphysics, natural theology, ethics, cosmology, and the history of philosophy, as well as six to eight semesters in dogmatics, moral theology, psychological pastoral theology, biblical theology, canon law, and church history. This was the standard curriculum for seminary students of his time. Although his experience of study was interrupted in the summer of 1944, this break would prove to be a life-changing experience. As he frequently observed, "I would be catapulted from the ivory tower of the seminary to endure with countless others the Hunger Winter, but the lessons this year away from the seminary taught me would forever change my understanding of learning and formation." Once the war was over he returned to Gemert, completed his studies, and was ordained on July 21, 1946.

This crucial experience of starvation and endless threats of deportation in occupied Holland gave him an unprecedented chance to forge his main ideas about how to minister to people in crisis situations. Raised to new heights was his respect for the fullness of their humanity and his compassion for the inner emptiness occasioned by the devastating changes all the victims of Nazism experienced. What he learned and what continued to fascinate him was the discovery that when all else has been stripped away, what remains in each soul is a profound longing for transcendent reality. He observed that this quest for the More Than was unquenchable. It prevailed in the most oppressive circumstances—in the face of physical debilitation and emotional stripping—exacerbated by the tragic repercussions occasioned by the culture of death shadowing the continent.

Throughout the Hunger Winter, van Kaam encountered individuals representing a variety of faith groupings, who came to him for solace and spiritual counseling. Could not this "man of the cloth" help them to cope with everything from episodes of cold-blooded murder to the abject misery caused by food and fuel shortages? Meeting in secret with van Kaam as their facilitator, these broken people expressed the heart-wrenching events they had to face in their lives without losing hope. What other chance did they have but to learn from experience how to trust and respect one another despite their diverse belief systems?

In relatively short order, van Kaam began to integrate his experiences of counseling these victims of war into a unique, ecumenically sensitive paradigm of formation, reformation, and transformation. He brought their narratives into dialogue with his extensive reading of the classic literature of spirituality, balanced by the theology and philosophy he had to master in the seminary. Both in the city of his birth and in Nieuwkoop, the village in the countryside where he went into hiding, he kept extensive journals of his experiences. Always a writer, he took the chance to publish an underground journal to inspire not only the members of his own congregation but also fugitives of diverse backgrounds and stations in life. He saw the triumph of the human spirit, which enabled so many to move from fear and demoralization, through seeking consolation from one another, to dreams of once again being a free people. Under cover of darkness, in barns and sheds where they could reflect on the meaning of their solitude and suffering, their heartfelt accounts provided the experiential basis van Kaam would need to craft his narrative-based approach to formative spirituality.

Following the war and his ordination to the priesthood, van Kaam was appointed professor of philosophical anthropology at his seminary in Gemert. An unprecedented opportunity came his way in 1947 to join the founder and faculty of the government-sponsored Dutch Life Schools of Formation for Young Adults, whose teaching took place in local mills and factories. This nationwide program, initiated during the war by the Belgian school supervisor Dr. Maria Schouwenaars, was devoted to the social and spiritual formation of young laborers. The methodology for van Kaam's emerging theory of human and Christian formation can be traced in part to his expertise in the companion fields in which he specialized for his Dutch degrees, namely pedagogy and andragogy, covering the education of children and adults.

In this capacity, van Kaam was able to take his ideas beyond the seminary into the highways and byways of post-war Holland. He modified his theory to fit the unique individual and communal situation of his students. He honed his practical counseling and spiritual guidance skills in the Dutch Governmental Psychological Observation Center for Juvenile Delinquents at Kamp Overberg, Veenendaal, Holland.

Having been freed by his congregation to pursue these formational and transformational ideals, van Kaam published his findings in prestigious Dutch journals and gained a reputation for experiential thinking and practice in various educational and counseling settings. In 1952, he was assigned by his congregation to go to Paris for a year to conduct research and write a biography of the founder of his religious order, the Venerable Francis Libermann. This outstanding work, which first appeared in Holland, was published in English in 1954 under the title, *A Light to the Gentiles*. Shortly after completing his research in Paris and his teaching and other assignments in the Netherlands, van Kaam met the then president of Duquesne University in Pittsburgh. Impressed by the young Spiritan's work, the president invited him to join the faculty, not, as he had expected, in the school of education, but in the department of psychology. Van Kaam arrived in the United States in August of 1954 and, shortly thereafter, became an American citizen. Although he had hoped to continue on a full-time basis the work he had begun in Holland, he accepted the challenge to develop a new program at Duquesne, which he named "psychology as a human science."

Much to his credit as a scholar open to new fields of thinking, he became both a student of and an expert in the relatively new field of "humanistic psychology." Drawing upon his earlier Dutch degrees in educational psychology and phenomenology, he agreed to pursue a PhD in psychology while developing a uniquely holistic or existential approach to this endeavor. From a life of quiet study, adult education, and ecclesiastical commitment, he threw himself with his usual enthusiasm into the midst of a major turning point in thinking and practice, captured in breakthrough books of his like *Existential Foundations of Psychology*, *The Art of Existential Counseling*, and *Religion and Personality*. In short order, he found himself becoming a figure of significant influence and renown. Due to his seminal works on the nature of personality, existence, religion, and the human sciences, van Kaam was sought out by theorists and practitioners like himself who saw that psychology was in the process of advancing beyond both behavioristic and positivistic models, which seemed to reduce the human condition to stimulus-response mechanisms or statistically proven measurements only.

In the light of his illuminating views, original works, and personal friendships, van Kaam was able to produce a body of literature that put the movement of humanistic psychology in the forefront of counselor and counselee concerns throughout the 1960s and 1970s. Further thinking on his part would serve over time to bolster these advancements while addressing some of the shortcomings associated with "self-actualizing" psychology, which lingers on today. What was evident to van Kaam even then was the danger of placing the self at the center of reality with consequences like moral relativism, secular humanism, and sheer narcissism.

Van Kaam's contact with many of the brilliant minds affiliated with the inception of this new wave in psychology helped to shape his own comprehensive view of the human condition as sociohistorical, vital, functional, and transcendent. In other words, we are "more than" our family of origin, our physical makeup, our set of skills. We are spirit through and through.

From the 1980s until the eve of his death, he continued to develop a research methodology and metalanguage in service of his original science of formation, with its complementary anthropology. It came into being in relation to, yet distinct from, the science of psychology, for which he maintained the greatest respect. He devoted the latter part of his life to perfecting his thinking and teaching in formation theology. This crowning phase of his work was accomplished under the auspices of the Epiphany Academy in Pittsburgh, Pennsylvania.

Seeding of van Kaam's Body of Work in Academic and Ministerial Settings

Students in van Kaam's classes on phenomenological psychology in the 1960s witnessed the ease with which he drew upon European thinkers like Jacques Maritain, Max Scheler, Gabriel Marcel, Maurice Merleau-Ponty, and William Luijpen. Like him, they felt the need to focus on "the acting person." Who are we most deeply? How does our situation affect us? Why do some people maintain hope and others despair in the same circumstances?

Van Kaam encouraged his students to read widely from the works of psychologists like William James and novelists like Graham Greene to seek answers to these existential questions. He himself entered creatively and critically into ways of thinking that centered on formation of the human heart and its matching character. Interests of this sort were inherent to his thinking and helped to guide him when he completed his doctoral dissertation on "The Experience of Really Feeling Understood by a Person" and graduated from Case Western Reserve University in Cleveland, Ohio, in 1958. The methodology he used to evaluate the narrative-based psychological experiences of 365 subjects was unique among research methods popular at the time. His phenomenological method of qualitative analysis influenced other researchers after him at Duquesne University and elsewhere.

Particularly after World War II, a dilemma faced Catholic psychologists like himself. He was a meticulous scientist of the human spirit, yet the climate of the times saw a beginning separation between science and religion. He himself saw the distinction, not separation, between the "sciences of measurement" (behavioral) and the "sciences of meaning" (existential). He never doubted the need to link psychology to the search for ultimate answers to the crises we face. By the same token, he saw where the dynamics of ego-psychology left off and those of transcendent spirituality began. Such interests explain why he joined with a number of colleagues to found and support Division 36 of the American Psychological Association, named Psychologists Interested in Religious Issues. By 1975, this division was granted APA status and van Kaam, one of its first members, was the first to receive the prestigious William C. Bier award.

A bit of historical contextualizing is in order at this juncture of van Kaam's story. At this time new psychotherapeutic approaches (gestalt, client-centered, group therapy) broke the old molds of strict psychoanalysis. Side by side with this development, there seemed to be more awareness of the bridge between psychology and spirituality insofar as the life of the spirit started to be recognized as part of the healing process.

Client-centered approaches began to flourish, notably under the influence of Carl Rogers and Gordon Allport, colleagues of van Kaam, who, like him, chose to pursue a humanistic view of counseling that was more encounter-oriented. Van Kaam welcomed every opportunity to become acquainted with this and other happenings in the field of psychology. He benefitted from his collaboration with a number of practitioners and theorists. He participated in training programs at the Alfred Adler Institute under Drs. Rudolf Dreikurs and Heinz Ansbacher. He studied personality theory under Abraham Maslow and Kurt Goldstein at Brandeis University. He honed his skills in psychotherapy under Carl Rogers at the University of Chicago. He consulted with existential thinkers like Henry Elkin, Rollo May, and Erik Erikson, not only to be apprised of their work but also to keep his students informed of rapid developments in the field at that time. He complemented his own teaching, writing, and speaking by becoming consulting editor for the *Journal of Humanistic Psychology,* the *Journal of Individual Psychology,* and the *Review of Existential Psychology and Psychiatry.* He served as a visiting professor at Brandeis University, taking the place of Abraham Maslow while he was on sabbatical leave. Having collaborated with him and others on several peer-reviewed and respected ventures in research and publication, he traveled in the United States and abroad to share the expertise he had gained. For example, he was invited to be a guest professor at the University of Heidelberg, Germany, where he lectured for an entire summer on his theoretical and practical approach to character and personality formation. To widen his knowledge of "the transcendent self" (the title of one of his later books), he spent several months at a Zen-Buddhist monastery in Japan. Though this event provided van Kaam with a broader view of the challenges he faced, he never deviated from his biblical foundations. He returned in between semesters to Holland to continue investigating the links between education and formation, anthropology and spiritual theology.

While pursuing these contacts and completing the manuscripts he had started in the Netherlands, van Kaam began to formulate at Duquesne his own phenomenological-anthropological approach to psychology. It would influence not only the Duquesne program but also the future direction of this field. At the end of this nine-year effort (1954–63), van Kaam faced one of the most significant "from-through-to" movements of his own life. He knew that the time had come for him to move from the prestigious reputation he had gained in the field of psychology, through the relative obscurity of returning to his original dedication to spiritual formation, to the task of founding in 1963 an independent Institute of Man (later renamed the Institute of Formative Spirituality) under the Graduate School of Arts and

Sciences at Duquesne University. The progress was slow at first, but from 1966 onward, the institute began to attract more students, evolved a fully accredited master's degree program, and grew by 1979 to the point where it was possible to initiate its own doctoral degree in the field of formative spirituality. By the time this phase of van Kaam's work ended, having extended over a thirty-year period from 1963 to 1993, the institute had matriculated approximately eight hundred students from twenty-six different countries, most of whom at the time of this writing still hold leading positions in their religious orders and institutes of higher learning.

During this period, van Kaam published books and articles ranging from psychology and its anthropological foundations to personality theory and spiritual maturity in the lives of laity, clergy, and people in religious orders, including the founding and coediting of such journals as *Studies in Formative Spirituality* (formerly *Humanitas*) and *Envoy*.

Throughout the 1970s and 1980s, amidst his teaching and publishing efforts, van Kaam kept his eyes on the goal of generating a truly integrative paradigm to bring together, under the umbrella of "formative spirituality," the three interweaving facets of the science, anthropology, and theology of formation. These new fields of study would take into account the psychology of human development, but would go beyond it to pursue the meaning of the forming, reforming, and transforming relationship between God and the inner and outer forces that influence our life's journey from conception to natural death. The results of this holistic approach to life underpin every page of this book and the learning opportunity we believe it holds for every reader.

Epiphany Association: Fulfillment of van Kaam's Work

Van Kaam remained the director of the Institute of Formative Spirituality at Duquesne until 1980, when he entered a long recuperation process after a serious heart attack. He asked Susan Muto, PhD, to become its director, a leadership role she accepted for the next eight years. After that she resigned her full-time tenured professorship to accept the position of executive director of the Epiphany Association, a nonprofit center cofounded with van Kaam in 1979 to handle their non-university ministerial work in faith formation. No sooner had she resigned than both of them saw the "writing on the wall" that would lead to the closing of the Institute at Duquesne in the mid-1990s, primarily for budgetary reasons. Thanks to the providence of God, the Epiphany Association with its own board of directors and generous benefactors placed under its auspices what would prove to be the crowning phase of Father Adrian's seminal work. Today, the association and its Epiphany Academy engage in research, publication, and dissemination of the findings of formative spirituality. The academy ministers to people from all walks of life representing many different faith and formation traditions. Father Adrian continued until his death to be actively involved in its nonprofit, ecumenical mission and ministry as a writer, speaker, mentor, researcher-in-residence, and member of the corporation board.

This always joyful and humble man of God died quietly of complications due to pneumonia on November 17, 2007, leaving behind as his legacy a visionary body of work from which countless students, scholars, and those influenced by them continue to benefit, including the coauthors of this book, Rebecca Letterman and Susan Muto.

Understanding Our Story: The Goals of This Book

From his days of listening to the stories of those huddled with him in hiding in Holland during the Hunger Winter, through the writing of his dissertation, "The Experience of Really Feeling Understood by a Person," to the eleven-volume series he wrote articulating his formation science, formation anthropology, and formation theology, Adrian van Kaam exuded a passion to help individuals and groups to understand themselves and each other. Most of all, he wanted people to know that they were understood and loved by God. He did this first and foremost by listening to people, to Christian history and scriptural wisdom, and to fields of study from neuroscience and medicine to physics, from film and art to anthropology, and from music to psychology. Van Kaam's joyful interest in humanity and creation was endless. More than listening, van Kaam had the gifts of insight and appraisal. He detected behind the formation events people shared with him not only their frustration with what occurred but their need to understand its meaning.

As a committed Christian and Catholic priest, van Kaam believed that God's grace illumines and enlightens human nature, never destroys, but redeems and transforms it. He was thoroughly conversant with systematic and doctrinal theology; he drew extensively upon the age-old wisdom of his faith and formation traditions in his teaching and preaching. Experience had taught him that beyond informational thinking, there was a profound need in peoples' lives for a complimentary formational approach. This felt need prompted him to construct a truly holistic theory of personality that he designed from the beginning to be conducive to and compatible with the Christian revelation.

To this end, he wrote his seven-volume Formative Spirituality series and he coauthored with Susan Muto his four-volume Formation Theology series. Essential as it is to read and study this remarkable body of work as a whole, we believe the time has come to introduce it to readers in a single volume. While we hope that this book will inspire everyone who reads it, this book may hold particular interest for Christian pastors, leaders, chaplains, missionaries, seminary scholars, and students. There is no doubt in our mind that it will help persons from every walk of life to know themselves in relation to God and others and to understand the significance not only of major formative events but also of the everyday happenings we experience from birth to death.

In this book we present van Kaam's most salient ideas and the formation science, formation anthropology, and formation theology metalanguage he designed to explain them. We include quotations directly from van Kaam's original work. We clarify his theory by drawing upon examples from his life, from experiences of daily living, and from the treasury of formation wisdom found in Holy Scripture and the writings of well-known spiritual teachers. Each chapter ends with reflection questions designed to help our readers apply formative spirituality to their own lives. We provide a meticulously edited glossary of terminology, along with comprehensive citations, and a bibliography helpful to scholars as well as general readers. May this thorough introduction to the life's work and legacy of Adrian van Kaam confirm what has already formed and informed your journey, while revealing yet-to-be-disclosed insights and findings intended to help you understand your story in all its richness.

Chapter 1

Spherical Facets of the van Kaamian Formation Field Model

It was from a fundamental conviction of the ultimate meaningfulness of life that Adrian van Kaam began his quest for truth. The rich texture of the Genesis story, with its account of the creation, fallenness, and promised redemption of humankind, was fascinating to him. For him, this many-splendored narrative held insights pertaining to human formation, deformation by sinful disobedience, and ultimate hope for reformation and redemption. The "fall" into an arrogant, me-centered orientation to disobedient control may have marred the outcome of the Genesis story God intended for humankind, but it marked the beginning of a redemptive Christian story, grounded in the all-encompassing love of God that is beyond words. Van Kaam sought to develop a truly holistic model of spiritual formation, wherein this whole story could be told, retold, and processed in every detail.[1] He named this model the formation field.[2] The idea for it came to him at the most trying time of his young life, when, as he narrates in his memoirs, he was catapulted out of the ivory tower of his seminary into the infamous Dutch Hunger Winter of 1944–45. He wrote,

> In the light of these experiences, I thought again of our life as a field of formation, consisting of five intertwining spheres: our ongoing formation by the mystery at the center of our existence (*centrale vorming*); our intraformation (*innerlijke vorming*); our interformation (*wederzijdse vorming*); our situational formation

---

1. van Kaam, *Fundamental Formation*, 13–14, 243. Note that for van Kaam, human formation was synonymous with spiritual formation. He argued that the spirit as a gift of God was the unique, defining characteristic of being human.

2. Throughout this book, we will refer to the van Kaamian Formation Field Model simply as van Kaam did, as the formation field. Further reflection on the van Kaamian full field model of formation can be found in van Kaam and Muto, *Living Our Christian Faith*, 176–79.

(*situatie vorming*); and our formation in the wider world (*wereld vorming*).³

He characterized our lifelong unfolding as a multifaceted and multidimensional participation in a field of formation (in Dutch, *vorming veld*), rooted in what he called the Divine Forming and Preforming Mystery. For Christian believers like himself, he understood this Mystery in terms of his faith and formation tradition as the Most Holy Trinity.⁴

Underlying this original insight and use of a full field model were two basic motivations. First, van Kaam sought to represent a fully integrational approach to human spirituality. His model would offer a way to represent myriad dynamics, dimensions, and expressions of various spheres of formation. The always integrated and yet distinguishable influences of the spheres of his field model picture at one and the same time the dynamic complexity of the development of the spiritual life of persons in community, and the processes by which they are being formed, reformed, and transformed ultimately by the grace of God.

Second, the choice of a field model for spiritual formation with the Mystery at the center was an intentional move on his part. He sought to develop a theory of personality holistic enough to honor insights of formation from many different fields of study, while at the same time enabling a Christian critique of contemporary approaches to human development that were becoming as highly influential as secular humanism and neo-gnosticism. Van Kaam not only critiqued humanistically centered theories of development; he creatively initiated an alternative theory of personality (in fact, a new science and anthropology of formation) designed from the beginning to be conducive to and compatible with biblical revelation historically guarded by the Christian church. His integrative full field model provides a framework open to tracing and integrating insights relevant to human and spiritual formation from multiple fields of research, while remaining faithful to biblical revelation.

The Mystery as Source and Center of the Formation Field

At the center of van Kaam's full field model, scientifically speaking, is the Mystery of all formation.⁵ In his use of the term "mystery," van Kaam was

3. van Kaam, *Life Journey*, 143.
4. van Kaam, *Fundamental Formation*, 212.
5. Van Kaam used the term "mystery" in his composition of formation science and formation anthropology with intentional precision and as a reminder of the ultimate transcendence of God. In his formation theology writings, he referred to the mystery formally as either the Holy Trinity or as the Divine Forming and Preforming Mystery (see

seeking to emphasize his awareness of our limited human perspective in relation to God. He sought to affirm both the wonder of divine revelation and to acknowledge the limits of our human understanding of God. In his model of the formation field, the Mystery interacts dynamically with the essence and empirical expression of who we are as distinctively human, both personally and relationally. While revealed in all its multispheric splendor throughout our formation field, the Mystery is always in some respects transcending us, "hidden from" or "mysterious to" us.[6] The Mystery is the radical ground of the formation field, the foundational, transcendent, omnipresent source and sustainer of all formation.[7]

According to van Kaam, the Mystery of formation is not an indifferent force that sets the universe in motion and subsequently has nothing to do with it. Rather, in keeping with his location of the Mystery at the center of our formation field, he said that the Mystery is always in relation to us and truly cares about us. In form theological terms, the loving and caring nature of the Mystery is revealed to us most clearly in Jesus Christ, "God's mystery, that is, Christ himself."[8]

Van Kaam noted that the Mystery discloses itself to humanity in three main ways: the cosmic epiphany, the human epiphany, and the transhuman (transcosmic) epiphany.[9] The cosmic epiphany points to "the atomic and subatomic cosmic dance of the ongoing formation and reformation occurring at

---

van Kaam and Muto, *Foundations of Christian Formation*, 263). He used this language out of a respect for the transcendent nature of God, coupled with his own modeling of resisting the human tendency to control God by defining God too succinctly. At the same time, van Kaam resisted the contemporary urge to conceive of God in a nebulous, vague way, for he was committed to the truths of the Christian revelation of God revealed to us through cosmos, through history, through Scripture, through the person of Jesus Christ, and through the ongoing work of the Holy Spirit. Throughout this text, which is written primarily for a Christian audience, the term "Mystery" will be capitalized to signal to the reader its connection with formation theology, even when it is being used in the context of formation science and formation anthropology. The same rationale will be used for the capitalization of "the More Than," another phrase that van Kaam used for the Mystery.

6. van Kaam, *Transcendent Formation*, 44–45; van Kaam and Muto, *Essential Elements*, s.v. "Consonance in Relation to Our Transcendence Dynamic." The terms "mysterious" or "hidden," in this sense referring to our formation being hidden in God, occur hundreds of times throughout van Kaam's writings.

7. van Kaam and Muto, *Essential Elements*, s.v. "Mystery of Formation as Radical and Epiphanic."

8. "I want . . . hearts to be encouraged and united in love, so that they may have all the riches of assured understanding and have the knowledge of *God's mystery, that is, Christ himself*, in whom are hidden all the treasures of wisdom and knowledge" (Col 2:2 NRSV, emphasis added); and "Without any doubt, the mystery of our religion is great: He was revealed in the flesh, vindicated in spirit, seen by angels, proclaimed among Gentiles, believed in throughout the world, taken up in glory" (1 Tim 3:16).

9. van Kaam, *Fundamental Formation*, 187.

every moment in the universe."[10] Openness to this disclosure of the Mystery fills us with awe. For example, is it not awesome to meditate on the fact that we live on a planet in perfectly calibrated orbit around the sun? Van Kaam went on to say that the Mystery of formation "gives rise to a subtle and complicated web of forming interactions between changing forms with a variety of life spans that appear briefly in cosmos, history, and humanity."[11]

The Mystery also discloses itself in a privileged way in each human life.[12] Whether we realize it or not, each of us is a human epiphany of the Mystery by whom we have been created. We are servants of the Mystery; we are not and never can be the Mystery itself. As caretakers of the cosmos, the Mystery invites us to respond to the beauty and order revealed to us in creation.[13] Unfortunately, instead of celebrating these cosmic patterns of formation, we can despoil, deface, and destroy them.

The transhuman epiphany of the Mystery opens us to that which is beyond any cosmic or human expression we may experience. It represents the highest disclosure of the Mystery, the self-communication of God to us, in what van Kaam described as "transcosmic consonance, or love."[14] In summary:

> The three epiphanies of the formation mystery are manifestations of the same forming source. They do not exclude but complement each other. The main difference [of the human epiphany] is that human freedom enables us to disobey the directive patterns communicated by the formation mystery in all its epiphanies. Perfect consonance in cosmic formation means that all forms fall into place within this network of forming relations without excess or deficiency.[15]

A grounding assumption of formative spirituality in Christian terms is that the Holy Trinity is "at the root of all formation in universe, world, and history," for in God "we live, move, and have our being."[16] By placing the Mystery (whom we call God or Triune God) at the very center of our formation field, van Kaam countered the tendency of all forms of secular humanism to place the self, my experience, or human consciousness, as the definitive source and definer of who we most deeply are. No human being

10. Ibid.
11. Ibid.
12. Ibid., 202–3.
13. Ibid., 206.
14. Ibid., 211.
15. Ibid., 206.
16. Ibid., 6; Acts 17:28.

can control, manipulate, or exhaustively understand spiritual formation in such a reductionistic fashion.[17] Independent self-actualization is incompatible with the Christian faith and formation tradition. Our spiritual formation is a gift from our Divine Source to humanity.

The formation field model relationally positions the Triune God at the center of our experiential, everyday living. The Holy Trinity is both transcendent and immanent. God is other than and always transcending human experience, while at the same time being intimately involved with the life and world of every person and community. The empirical realization of our true essence in God the Father is possible in its fullness only through the reformational and transformational power of the Spirit, disclosed to us through the life, death, resurrection, and ascension of Jesus Christ. The personal relationship of God with us means that while there are common themes in our human stories, each one of them is at the same time unique. Van Kaam and Dietrich Bonhoeffer, Etty Hillesum and Corrie ten Boom—all suffered under Nazi occupation in the Netherlands and elsewhere; yet each of them has their own story of survival or martyrdom to tell.[18]

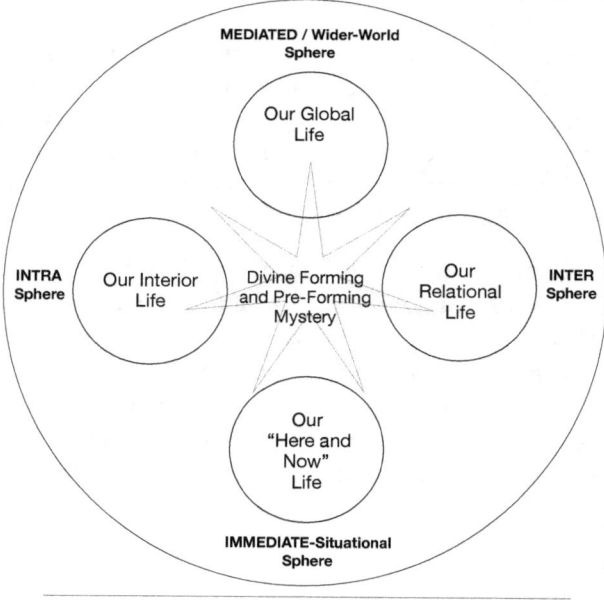

© Epiphany Association / The van Kaamian Model of Full Field Formation
All Rights Reserved. Not for Duplication. Used with Permission.

---

17. Ibid., 7–8; van Kaam, *Human Formation*, 244–45.

18. See Bonhoeffer, *Cost of Discipleship*; Hillesum, *An Interrupted Life*; and ten Boom, Sherrill, and Sherrill, *The Hiding Place*.

Spheres of the van Kaamian Formation Field

Van Kaam observed that from the moment of our conception until the end of our life on earth, we are being formed and are forming the world around us. Consider the effects of pregnancy on a woman. Before a child is born, that child in her womb is being formed and shaped by God and by the woman's body and environment. At the same time, that child is literally forming and shaping her mother. Once born, a child not only receives sustenance and nurture from her parents and others around her, but at the same time, she is shaping the lives of those she encounters, whether those encounters with her are through her demanding cries or her adorable smiles. On it goes through life: human beings are constantly being formed by and are forming the world around them. Van Kaam referred to this human potency to give form (form donation) and receive form (form reception) as formability, and noted that there is a basic human striving to maintain this potency throughout our lives.[19] Formability is ongoing and is never static, but it is one of the dynamics of spiritual formation always present throughout our lives.[20]

The spheres of this holistic model express the empirical-experiential nature of spiritual formation and articulate the ways we both give form to and receive form from life as we know it.[21] The spheres in the van Kaamian Formation Field Model represent the pathways by which we process directives coming to us and through us throughout the course of our existence.[22] Each of the spheres interforms or interacts with, and influences, all the others. Though distinguishable, all the spheres are always and forever wholly integrated, with the Mystery at the center of them. The formation field model with its spheres and dimensions represents a snapshot in time of who we are. In that sense, "I am my formation field" at any given moment.

---

19. van Kaam, *Fundamental Formation*, 17, 244, 247–48. Note that formability is one of five dynamics of formation that van Kaam referred to as infrastructural principles. All five principles (formability, transcendence-ability, the formation field model, formation traditions, and the maintenance of form potency) will be touched on in this text. For a succinct summary of these principles, see van Kaam and Muto, *Christian Articulation of the Mystery*, 73–76.

20. van Kaam, *Fundamental Formation*, 66; van Kaam and Muto, *Christian Articulation of the Mystery*, 73.

21. The concept of giving and receiving form (meaning, shape, existence) as part of human spirituality was one of van Kaam's basic working principles (see van Kaam, *Fundamental Formation*, 17, 166 for further discussion of this dynamic).

22. van Kaam, *Fundamental Formation*, 244–45. Note that a synonym throughout van Kaam's writing for the term sphere is the term pole. He used pole to "indicate that there exists a certain tension between these interrelated spheres of formation and their contrasting and expanding influence on each other" (van Kaam, *Formation of the Human Heart*, 126).

According to van Kaam, what makes us distinctively human is our spirit, our openness to the Trinity, in what he called our transcendence dynamic. We are enfleshed spirit. Van Kaam took great care to avoid any form of spirit-body dualism. Instead, he emphasized the essential unity between human spirit and body.[23] We are preformed not only transcendentally but also sociohistorically (we do not choose where to be born); vitally (our DNA is, so to speak, given to us with no possibility of choice on our part); and functionally (with a set of skills and aptitudes we will unfold over a lifetime). The center of the formation field posits the reality of our spirit's constant expression of itself in and through our physical presence, through our "vital-reactive . . . substratum" of life.[24] We do not, and indeed we cannot, choose the underlying aspects of our formation, because they are preconscious and prepersonal.[25] There are facets of our vital life that are not accessible to our conscious mind. While the human will is a significant aspect of who we are, there are sensate, physical facets to our formation that initially and in an ongoing way occur without our recognition of them.[26] Van Kaam wrote,

> We are always in some kind of formation on the vital level. Here we are neither conscious of our preformation nor are we its free subjects. Life-directing sensate experiences and images of color, taste, sound, smell, and touch result from a preformative, vital interaction with our surroundings. This occurs at such a depth of our organismic vital presence to reality that we are unable to penetrate it with our appraising mind. Neither are we able to influence this preformation directly by means of free *formation decisions*.
>
> Below us, as transcendent-functional persons, is a vital substratum that forms our formation field in preconscious, prepersonal ways. This substratum is our vital life dimension itself at the point where it is still undifferentiated from its organismic structures. All preformative life directives, which emerge on this level, appear to be related to the vital structure of our body. We should thus not identify our life formation and the formation of our formation field with conscious or free formation only. Vital preformation is formation, too. It is one of the foundational sources of the forming orientations of our life.[27]

23. van Kaam, *Fundamental Formation*, 63–64.
24. Ibid., 72–73. This includes our basic given temperament (van Kaam, *Fundamental Formation*, 130).
25. Ibid., 70–73.
26. See chapter 6 of this book where formative will and its role are discussed.
27. van Kaam, *Fundamental Formation*, 72–73. Van Kaam held that we are not only

Our preconscious reactions may be reoriented and reorganized in such a way that they become responsive to what transpires in our overall field of presence and action. Although certain aspects of our vital, bodily formation may be relatively autonomous or even reflexive, in van Kaam's model, all facets of our human life are potentially open to the ongoing influence of the Spirit of God, which, in van Kaam's language, is the forming and preforming Mystery.[28]

Intrasphere

According to van Kaam, the intrasphere is "the area of life where we [receive and] give form to our personal directives, thoughts, feelings, modes, and decisions."[29] It is the interface between who we are created and called to be, and how we live out who we are in our everyday world. The differentiation of our intrasphere from the other spheres in our formation field represents our unique gift as humans to create "a kind of inviolate inner sanctum . . . [that] prevents us from being wholly outer directed."[30] That is, humans are not simply or even primarily instinct driven. In addition to external dynamics that may trigger instinctual responses, human behavior is affected by internal dynamics as well. The constellation of intraspheric dynamics will be explored throughout this book, but here we note on a general overview of the central dynamics of the spirit, what van Kaam identified as the heart, the mind, and the will.[31] A powerful dynamic of the intrasphere, which van Kaam referred to as the defining motif of our distinctively human spirit, is the transcendence dynamic.[32] This dynamic integrates all levels of our being in the light of the Mystery in the center of our formation field as experienced and expressed through our heart, mind, and will.

Van Kaam conceived of the human heart, which he termed the core form, as a relatively stable configuration of character dispositions.[33] For ex-

---

preformed vitally or biogenetically but also sociohistorically, functionally, and most important, transcendently. These preformed givens constitute a potent influence on us throughout our lives.

28. van Kaam, *Transcendent Formation*, 250–54.

29. van Kaam, *Scientific Formation*, 204.

30. van Kaam, *Formation of the Human Heart*, 157.

31. van Kaam, *Human Formation*, 167, 170..

32. For van Kaam, the human spirit, or the incarnation of the transcendence dynamic, is the foundation of all spiritual, human formation (for this claim, see van Kaam, *Fundamental Formation*, 13–14). For a further overview of the transcendence dynamic, see chapter 9 of this book.

33. Here, van Kaam built on the French term for heart (*le coeur*; van Kaam,

ample, if we adopt a deformative disposition of impatience in our core form, it will manifest itself as a matching impatient character that demonstrates its presence throughout many facets of our lives, from the way we drive to the way we posture ourselves as we wait in a grocery store line that is moving slowly. Our core form, he said, functions in two ways. First, it is the primary integrating dynamic of our lives. One of the most important examples of this for van Kaam is that our heart, our core form, strives to integrate who we are most deeply called to be with all the empirical spheres and dimensions of our lives as they unfold.[34] Think of how many references to the word "heart" there are in the Bible. A sampling would be:

> God is my shield, who saves the upright in heart. (Ps 7:10)

> O Lord, you will hear the desire of the meek; you will strengthen their heart, you will incline your ear. (Ps 10:17)

> Therefore my heart is glad, and my soul rejoices; my body also rests secure. (Ps 16:9)

> Blessed are the pure in heart, for they will see God. (Matt 5:8)

> For they all saw him and were terrified. But immediately he spoke to them and said, "Take heart, it is I; do not be afraid." (Mark 6:50)

> For where your treasure is, there your heart will be also. (Luke 12:34)

> Do not let your hearts be troubled. Believe in God, believe also in me. (John 14:1)

In this sense, our hearts as integrative express who we most deeply are in the various circumstances in which we find ourselves.

Second, the core form serves as the symbolic center of our emotions and their many dynamics of formation. Everyday language proves this point in such expressions as "my heart longs for you" (between lovers); "my heart aches" (with loss of a loved one); "my heart leaps up" (at a surprisingly good

---

Transcendence Therapy, 251). He defined the heart, or what he termed the core form, as the primary integrating structure of human life. He viewed the human heart as so central to spiritual formation that not only does it appear throughout all seven volumes of his Formative Spirituality series, nearly eight hundred times, but one of the seven volumes is, in fact, dedicated entirely to an exploration of its formational dynamics. See van Kaam, *Formation of the Human Heart*.

34. van Kaam, *Human Formation*, 172; van Kaam, *Transcendent Formation*, 28. The founding form, the ground of who we are called most deeply to be, will be discussed in chapter 3.

outcome of a plan). While our emotions and their dynamics do not wholly define us, as significant facets of our ongoing formation they, too, need to be acknowledged and appraised in light of who the Mystery calls us to be as expressed throughout our formation field.[35]

The intrasphere is also the locus of internal dynamics of the human mind, including such aspects as attention and appraisal.[36] Related to and supporting these formative facets of the mind are memory, imagination, and anticipation, what van Kaam termed incarnational sources.[37] These auxiliary sources of our mind's formation increase our powers of attention, alert us to compatible symbols and images, and affect our ability to recall the past and to anticipate to some degree the future. The formative effects of these three sources cannot be missed when we read a good historical novel, watch the interactions of characters in a film like *The Mission* or *Babette's Feast* (two of van Kaam's favorites), or hear an exquisite song that enables us to recall a host of events from an engagement party to a requiem service. We find our attention riveted and may recall for a lifetime memories of the ways our hearts were moved by them.

Another facet of the intrasphere in relation to the spirit is the dynamic of the human will.[38] Van Kaam highlighted throughout his writings the formative dynamics of willfulness, will-lessness, and willingness. He linked the human will in both its orientation and its implementation phases with dynamics related to trust.[39] By orientation of our will, he means our openness to the transcendent meaningfulness of life, as in the expression, "I will try to fulfill my calling." By implementation, he referred to how we intend to live such meaningfulness, as in the expression, "I will go to law school."

So crucial is the intrasphere to spiritual formation that throughout much of human history, to say nothing of the history of Christianity, one's

---

35. van Kaam, *Transcendent Formation*, 28–29. Dynamics of the human heart will be discussed in more detail in upcoming sections of this book, including the sections on integrating structures and dispositional formation.

36. What van Kaam meant by the human intellect, especially in his nuancing of both transcendent and functional facets of the will and mind, will be explored in detail in chapter 6 of this book.

37. van Kaam, *Fundamental Formation*, 252–53. The dynamics of attention, regions of consciousness, and memory, imagination, and anticipation as incarnational sources will all be discussed in chapter 6 of this book.

38. van Kaam posited that the human will, especially in its spiritual transformation to become the will to love, is grounded by the Holy Trinity's will that first loved us. See chapter 6 of this book for further discussion of van Kaam's nuancing of different types of human willing.

39. van Kaam, *Transcendent Formation*, 21; van Kaam and Muto, *Essential Elements*, s.vv. "Mind-Will Dialectic in Formation," "Role of Mind in Decision-Making."

inner life had been considered the most relevant sphere of maturation. While acknowledging its foundational importance, van Kaam felt obliged to complement this emphasis on interiority by positing the following outer spheres as part of his formation field model.

Intersphere

Identifying the intersphere as part of his formation field model was van Kaam's way of acknowledging the influence of human traditions on spiritual formation, whether our encounter with them is direct or indirect. In doing so, he first avoided the error of privatizing ("God and I") spirituality as only an internal affair. Second, he noted that for the influences of people to be the most formative spiritually, such influences need to be in dialogue with the entirety of their formation field.[40]

The intersphere represents the ways in which people relate with one another, directly as in the case of family, friends, or foes, and indirectly or even symbolically, as in the case of a community of people within a particular culture who influence one another through their communal or cultural traditions across time.[41] Van Kaam used the term horizontal interformation to point to the influence of people on one another in the here-and-now moment, and the complementary term vertical interformation to point to the influence of people on one another from the past and into the future.[42]

To aid our reflection, van Kaam reminded us that the role of community is not only important in initial formation, as between parents and children; its influence is ongoing over a lifetime.

> Traditional formation will continue only if it is somehow expressed at times by ourselves or by others. Otherwise it may lose for us its solidity and credibility. It would become shadowy and unreal. The formative power and credibility of traditional texts, symbols, and rituals would dissipate if they were not shared in some measure with a like-minded community. Absence of any communication and the cessation of all public expression of form traditions would leave them open to forgetfulness or to idiosyncratic interpretations.... Subjectivistic interpretation by intraformative powers would make the link with inter and outer reality tenuous. Therefore, it is my contention that some form

---

40. van Kaam, *Transcendence Therapy*, 29.
41. van Kaam, *Transcendent Formation*, 122.
42. van Kaam, *Traditional Formation*, 269–70. For a further exposition of horizontal and vertical formation, see van Kaam and Muto, *Living Our Christian Faith*, 60–62.

of interformative communication is necessary between people who presently strive to stay faithful to their own form traditions in daily life as lived in a pluritraditional society. Vertical interformation with the masters of formation of the past should be complemented by horizontal interformation with those who live the tradition in the present.[43]

Situational Sphere

Not only do the internal dynamics of our intrasphere and the interformative dynamics of our intersphere influence the emergence and unfolding of our character and personality, but so, too, do the dynamics of our immediate environments. All people live in and are influenced by setting—urban or rural, advantaged or impoverished, tropical or temperate. Van Kaam designated these environmental influences as our situational sphere. It represents the ways in which directives from our setting are given and received in the here-and-now.

Of special interest to van Kaam in reference to this sphere was what he called formation traditions, which express themselves in our everyday world.[44] Such formatively significant "situational symbols" end up being "carried by events and acts, by the media, the arts, demonstrations, movies, plays, books, heroic and criminal events, [and] news . . . that permeate our everyday environment."[45] Spiritual formation is not esoteric and disconnected from life. It is embedded in the very details of daily life—where we live, our places of employment, our places of worship. Encounters with the people, events, and things around us shape our lives, sometimes subtly and at other times in starkly noticeable ways.

Some of the situations in which we find ourselves are not freely chosen. An obvious example would be the transport of the Jewish people to death camps organized by the Nazi regime. For some, this heinous situation marked the end of hope. For others like Betsie and Corrie ten Boom, Dietrich Bonhoeffer, and Viktor Frankl, this situation had meaning so profound that they were able to interpret it in the light of a deeper belief system they had embraced.

---

43. van Kaam, *Traditional Formation*, 269.

44. Formation traditions and their underlying faith traditions will be explained in chapter 5 of this book.

45. van Kaam, *Transcendent Formation*, 122–23.

World Sphere

Having lived in Holland prior to and during World War II, van Kaam was attuned to the fact that the wider world, though often not initially perceived in our immediate situation, is also connected to us in formational and deformational ways. To represent this less noticed, yet always significant influence, he incorporated into his field model the world sphere.[46] This sphere is mediated to us through a variety of channels. These include, but are not limited to, shared scientific discoveries, education, literature, and especially the media.[47] Van Kaam was cognizant of studies in mathematics and physics that articulated the interconnectedness of the cosmos. The world sphere differs from the immediate situational sphere in its physical remoteness. Whether we watch the evening news or listen to broadcasts from outer space, what happens the world over has an influence on everyone. Though such happenings seem remote to us, they play their part in our formation both uniquely and communally. This facet of formation science challenges the belief that we live in isolation or insulation. It reminds us of our dependence on a Mystery in and beyond us, a Loving Other involved in every iota of creation, ourselves included.[48] In summary, the Mystery at the center of our field at once embraces and redeems the empirical experiences of being human in the universe and in the world in which we find ourselves. Van Kaam's formation field model seeks to articulate the largess of God's redemption.

Conclusion

Ongoing formation, as we have seen, can only be approached in the context of a full field model. To do otherwise fails to account for the breadth of influences involved in our formation. All of humanity, regardless of ethnicity, race, creed, or religion, shares foundational dynamics of formative spirituality, starting with the common experience of receiving and giving form from conception to death in our inner and outer life. The model that has guided this chapter shows that our intrasphere, intersphere, situational sphere, and world sphere cannot be separated from the Mystery at the center of our

---

46. van Kaam, *Fundamental Formation*, 249, and "Appendix 2, Chart V." Synonyms for "world" in relation to this sphere are: wider world, mondial, and global.

47. van Kaam, *Transcendent Formation*, 123. Another synonym that van Kaam used for the world sphere is the "mondial sphere" (van Kaam and Muto, *Essential Elements*, s.vv. "Description of Full-Field Paradigm," "Expansion of Social Conscience through the Media," and "Full-Field Theory of Formation").

48. Rom 8:28–29 NRSV.

formation field, for the entirety of who we are is to be open to the forming, reforming, and transforming work of the Spirit. In the next chapter we shall consider van Kaam's dimensional articulations of this model.

Reflection Questions

1. Understanding Our Story: Reflection on Directives during a Significant Event in Your Life

    Van Kaam observed that the Holy Spirit forms and shapes us throughout various facets of our formation field; we in turn give shape to our lives and world in many ways. The spheres of the formation field provide a framework for reflection, a way to "unpack" significant times of formation in order to help us attend to dynamics at work that we may not have been aware of in the moment.

    Call to mind a specific, and significant, event or time in your life or in the life of your community of faith. Reflect in turn on each of the spheres of your formation field at the time (intrasphere, intersphere, situational sphere, and world sphere). To the extent that you are able to do so, identify specific directives and priorities that came to you from each sphere. Were some spheres of your field more prominent than others in their influence on your experience at the time? Looking back on the situation now, how would you describe the ways the directives from the various spheres shaped you (or your community) in that moment?

    Now pause for a while to be with God and allow God to be present to you as you reflect on this important time in your life. As you do so, gently attend to whether the Holy Spirit has inspired you to identify, in hindsight, any obstacles to living in openness to the will of Holy Trinity during this particular event in your life. Also, note any conditions that facilitated your openness to God's will at that particular time. Consider whether either the obstacles to or facilitating conditions for openness to God that occurred at that time have any relevance to the way you live in openness to God now.

2. Understanding God's Story: Reflection on Directives of a Favorite Bible Character

    Who is one of your favorite Bible characters? Why is this the case?

Select a significant moment in this person's life. Reflect, in turn, on each of the spheres of the person's formation field at the time (intrasphere, intersphere, situational sphere, and world sphere).

To the extent that you are able to do so, identify specific directives and priorities that came to the person from each sphere of their field (for this exercise, you may need to use your imagination in the case of the person's intrasphere). How would you describe the way that these various directives shaped the person at that time? How did each of the spheres contribute to the person's formation personally and relationally?

Describe any ways that you find yourself responding to or perhaps resisting God's communications to this character in this significant moment.

Chapter 2

Dimensional Facets of the Formation Field Model

THE FORMATION FIELD OUTLINED so far includes distinguishable yet interrelated spheres through which we give form to and are formed by the whole world of meaning in which we live. The spheres represent a snapshot of what occurs during any given moment of our formation story.

Dimensions of the Human Life Form

Added to these spheres are the dimensions of the van Kaamian Formation Field Model. The dimensions permeate all spheres of the field and represent the continuity present in our formation. Perhaps you have seen Michael Apted's British documentary *Up* series. In it, a group of over a dozen British children, from various walks of life, are interviewed every seven years. The series begins in 1964 and ends in 2013, when the children originally interviewed at age seven reach the age of fifty-six. The series is a fascinating example of human formation, as it documents the gradual unfolding of the participants' lives, many of which are filled with unexpected events, both sad and joyful. And yet, in each one of the participants at age fifty-six, you can still see echoes of the persons they were at age seven. In each seven-year episode of the film, the Jesuit maxim is repeated: "Give me a boy until he is seven, and I will give you the man."[1] While our lives often unfold in unexpected ways, they still have a certain continuity to them. It is the recognition of such continuity that van Kaam articulated through the dimensions of his formation field model.

These dimensions model both the human potential for and the empirical actualization of basic modes of human presence and attention in the world.[2] Van Kaam began with the inclusion of four basic dimensions in his

---

1. See Rebecca Mead's summary and reflection on Michael Apted's *Up* series "What 56 Up Reveals," *New Yorker*, January 9, 2013, http://www.newyorker.com.

2. Synonyms for modes of attention that van Kaam used in explaining his concept

model: sociohistorical, vital, functional, and transcendent (later expanded to include the pneumatic-ecclesial).[3] Each dimension embodies facets of our life that are part of our basic givenness, our preformation, as created by God in a particular time and place, unfolding at each phase of the maturation process.[4]

Accompanying each dimension in van Kaam's model is its expression of a specific human striving, understood by him as innate energy involved in our receiving and giving form.[5] Strivings are given different expressions in each dimension. Expressions of human strivings are one of the means by which we give and receive formationally relevant influences. For those exploring human formation, understanding the connection between expressions and their underlying strivings makes us aware of influential formative dynamics. For example, it is well known that eating food has not only to do with strivings of hunger, but may also have to do with a striving to fit in with others around us, or a striving for comfort, or a striving against boredom. The expression of people attending church may be attributable to a desire to worship God, but may also be linked to strivings for socializing with friends, strivings to be recognized as being committed attendees, or strivings to set a good example for children.

Though present in all persons, the dimensions and their related strivings develop at different times with varying degrees of intensity. That is, one dimension or the other may be emphasized at any particular time of life.[6] However, because of the "essentially situated character of human formation," the sociohistorical dimension always plays a markedly formative role.[7] Therefore, it is to this ubiquitous dimension and its strivings and expressions of the human life form that we turn first.

---

of field dimensions include "ranges of alertness" and "directions and corresponding predispositions [of] human formation" (*Fundamental Formation*, 60 and 267); and formation powers (*Fundamental Formation*, 65). Note, too, that van Kaam does differentiate between the innate potential in each dimension and the actual articulation of the potential (see van Kaam, *Transcendent Formation*, 152–153 for his discussion of this distinction).

3. Note that the chart on the next page includes the pneumatic-ecclesial dimension, which is further explained in this chapter and in chapter 10.

4. Phasic maturation is the topic of chapter 10 of this book.

5. Strivings (van Kaam, *Scientific Formation*, 49) are an expression of the universal potency for *formability* (to receive form and to give form; see *Fundamental Formation*, 17). For a more detailed discussion of strivings in the overall context of spiritual formation, see "Appraisal and Formative Strivings for Fulfillment and Exertion," in van Kaam, *Human Formation*, 80–107.

6. van Kaam, *Fundamental Formation*, 66–67.

7. Ibid., 66–67.

Dimensions	Dynamics	Expressions
Pneumatic-Ecclesial 　Inner inspirational source of Christian life formation; the Holy Spirit in the Church	Inspirations	Invitations
Transcendent 　Distinctively human longing for the More Than	Aspirations	Ideals
Functional 　Skills, talents, managerial ability	Ambitions	Projects
Vital 　Genetics, physicality, temperament	Pulsions	Impulses Compulsions
Sociohistorical 　Situated in time, tradition, culture, family	Pulsations	Pressures

Sociohistorical Pulsations and Pressures

We are conceived at a particular time and born into a specific communal setting. This social and historical situatedness of the human condition is acknowledged and represented by the sociohistorical dimension. Van Kaam called the specific strivings of this dimension pulsations, and their related expressions throughout our field of life, pressures.[8] The actual forms that sociohistorical pressures take become "embedded in the customs, symbols, rituals, and resources of our formation fields."[9] As such, this dimension provides as many gifts as it does challenges. The culture and community into which we are born form a kind of "matrix of many directives that emerge in all dimensions and articulations" of life.[10] It bestows on us rich historical resources of formative wisdom that extend far beyond what it would be possible for one person to attain. It also influences with more or less intensity many of the presuppositions we harbor about the way the world works.

---

8. Ibid., 261.

9. Ibid., 95.

10. Ibid., 94. This dimension is closely related to both vertical and horizontal interformation, communicated especially through formation traditions. *Formation traditions* are the habitual empirical forms that we use to express our deeply held *faith traditions*, or beliefs. The van Kaamian constructs of faith traditions and their related formation traditions will be discussed in detail in chapter 5 of this book. For further reading on specific formational dynamics of the sociohistorical dimension in relation to formation traditions, see van Kaam, *Traditional Formation*, chapter 22, "Sociohistorical Freudian and Transcendent Traditions" (203–8); chapter 23 "Sociohistorical, Transcendent, Marxist, and Neo-Freudian Traditions" (209–19); and chapter 24 "Transcendent and Capitalist Traditions" (220–35).

While van Kaam resisted the view that we are defined by our situatedness, he acknowledged the pervasiveness of these social and historical pulsations and pressures on us as we form and are formed as individuals and communities. Aware of the power of unrecognized and unacknowledged sociohistorical strivings and expressions, he was concerned that people engage in appraising and choosing to accept or resist the pulsations in which they are immersed, thereby moving from being mere objects of the strivings in this dimension to being subjects of it, able to dialogue with its pressures.

> It is a lifelong task of formation to help people become the subject instead of only the object of their history. They must face and appraise the historical pulsations that form them. [For example,] certain contemporary pulsations favor the autarchic development of the functional dimension at the expense of the transcendent and the vital [dimensions], to the serious detriment of human spirituality and vitality and the formative imagination nourished by both. This makes it much more difficult for people today [than in some previous eras] to enjoy a harmonious, consonant life formation, to become resilient, joyous, peaceful, and effective (in the best sense of this word).[11]

Van Kaam, therefore, considered the sociohistorical dimension, with its powerful strivings and pressures, to be one of the most influential areas in our field of formation, due to its pervasive impact on the ways in which we receive and give form in the world.

Vital Pulsions and Impulses/Compulsions

During our lifetime we are never separated from the resources, signals, and organic processes of the brain, nerves, breath, muscles, senses, appearances, and emotions that constitute our physical body. Van Kaam conceived of the vital dimension as a combination of both innate (preformed) and acquired potencies of biological-physical energy.[12] Through the vital dimension we acknowledge and integrate the influences of our physicality into our formative spirituality.[13] With wonder, gratitude, and joy, we can explore various

---

11. Van Kaam, *Fundamental Formation*, 94–95.

12. Ibid., 131–32. If the sociohistorical dimension of the van Kaamian Formation Field is thought of as a kind of "external structure" that influences the ways in which we receive and give form in the world, his vital dimension may be thought of as a kind of corresponding "internal structure" that also shapes our formation (for this distinction and its context, see van Kaam, *Fundamental Formation*, 132–33).

13. Ibid., 132.

ways in which our entire embodied existence influences how we concretize the life of the Spirit.[14] Strivings of the vital dimension, van Kaam termed pulsions, which express themselves as impulses and compulsions.[15] When the strivings of the vital dimension are healthy, they lead us to "care for our sensate bodily existence in ways that are biochemically advantageous, vitally pleasant, and conducive to physical wellbeing."[16] When unhealthy, vital strivings can become possibly obsessive and destructive.

It is through this dimension that one experiences the "relative quality, intensity, pace, and excitability of vital impulses."[17] These innate impulses are coformed in earliest infancy by interaction with the rest of our formation field, especially through interformation with other people, notably our parents. They become oriented and "primitively organized" in ways that result in the expression of our basic temperament.[18] Van Kaam viewed the vital dimension as both a source of our temper form (temperament) and as a manifestation of the way we allow it to be expressed.[19] Our biogenetic endowment does not determine us. It is formed by relatively free interactions with internal and external dynamics in our formation field. At the same time, our basic temperament is inseparable from and is coformed by our pre-given (preformed) dispositions.[20]

What are some of the main influences of the vital dimension? The vital dimension both maintains and manifests our basic patterns of physical reactions and responses to the persons and events we encounter.[21] It expresses our actual presence in and to the world. It directs our emotional expressiveness or restraint, and affects thereby our social adaptability.[22] It also influences our preferences for particular expressions of our Christian spirituality as it unfolds, such as our innate preferences for quiet contemplation or vibrantly boisterous praise.[23]

---

14. Ibid., 133.

15. Ibid., 75–76, 261. Van Kaam originally wrote of impulses as expressions of the vital dimension, and later also used the term compulsion as an expression of the vital dimension, especially in regard to coercive dispositions of our neuroform, to be discussed in chapter 3.

16. van Kaam, *Scientific Formation*, 41.

17. van Kaam, *Fundamental Formation*, 75.

18. Ibid.

19. Ibid., 131.

20. Ibid., 132–33.

21. Ibid., 130–31.

22. Ibid., 132.

23. Ibid., 128-29, 132.

Van Kaam also celebrated "the body as the source of energy that empowers human formation and . . . its forming presence" in the world.[24] He posited the gifts of vital energy as inherent to our spiritual formation, be they seen "in business, entertainment, ecological concern, and community organization" or, of course, in the dynamics of human sexuality.[25] His appreciation for the vital dimension had to do with the fact that he viewed it as "one of the main sources of individual limitations and possibilities" as well as the "principle of organismic, spatial, and temporal limitations of one's forming presence."[26]

In summary, the vital dimension is one of the key "sources of the uniqueness of formative life direction, life call, life formation, sensation, and imagination."[27] Through our bodies, we experience and respond to the world around us in formative ways. Van Kaam neither minimized nor ultimized this dimension. Were it to be considered independently of the rest of the field, the vital dimension would more likely than not be viewed as "reactive."[28] However, through healthy interformation with other dimensions, the impulsive strivings of the vital dimension are modulated in such a way that its reactions do not dominate our formation field.

Functional Ambitions and Projects

Also important for human formation is the functional dimension, which articulates our capacity to manage ourselves and our world effectively.[29] This component of spiritual formation enables us to access with relative ease and efficiency the strivings of this dimension, its ambitions, and their ex-

---

24. van Kaam, *Fundamental Formation*, 131. To explore van Kaam's further thinking about the biogenetic energy of the vital dimension as a formative dynamic of formative traditions, see his *Traditional Formation*, chapter 16, "Alignment of Vital Dimension and Form Tradition" (139–51); chapter 17, "Transcendent Form Traditions and the Vital Erotic Facet of Human Love" (152–61); chapter 18, "Transcendent Traditions and Transformation of Eros" (162–71); chapter 19, "Wounded Eros and Transcendent Tradition" (172–79); chapter 20, "Reaffirmation and Transcendence of Eros in the Light of Transcendent Traditions" (180–90); and chapter 21, "Autism, Eros, and the Six Coformants of Love" (191–202).

25. van Kaam, *Traditional Formation*, 73. For van Kaam's extensive reflections on human sexuality and spiritual formation, see, for example, "Spirituality and Sexuality," in van Kaam, *Fundamental Formation*, 103–25; van Kaam, *Transcendent Formation*, 55–56.

26. van Kaam, *Fundamental Formation*, 131.

27. Ibid.

28. Ibid., 75.

29. Ibid., 83.

DIMENSIONAL FACETS OF THE FORMATION FIELD MODEL

pressed projects.[30] It draws upon "imagination, memory, and anticipation, including acts of trial and error" as lived in the challenges presented to us.[31] The functional dimension taps into our preformed collection of gifts and talents, as managed by our organizing and controlling mind and will. This dimension is "marked by individuality, ambition, and control," as well as by "the development of a rational-analytical and functional intelligence."[32]

As the potential of this dimension begins to be expressed, we may develop a functional identity that enables us to acquire and put into motion a realistic sense of what we can and cannot do with the skills we have. We thereby develop "sufficient confidence to allow us to let go of functional activity or intensity when we so desire," while continuing to fulfill worthwhile projects and plans.[33] Provided our functional identity is in dialogue with our deepest transcendent or spiritual identity as sourced in the Trinity, we may find the means by which to appraise and discern our unique-communal life-call.[34] The related results may prove to be formative in many ways, affecting our decisions and actions and the energy and attention we need to execute them, whether it be as a student or a plumber, a cafeteria aide or a surgeon.

The functional dimension, thus, largely contributes to the embodiment of our vital and transcendent presence in the world. Through the translation of the strivings of all the dimensions in our field into functional ambitions and projects, we are able to incarnate them more or less effectively.[35] In this sense, the functional dimension is a bridge between the strivings embedded in our personhood and their articulation in everyday reality.[36] Van Kaam described this bridging characteristic as follows:

> The forming presence of the human spirit can be secondarily attributed to the functional dimension of the life-form. This dimension is so to speak, an in-between area. It is a center of many bridges. It functions as a bridge between the vital and the transcendent dimensions of the life-form. This function enables people to translate their *transcendent aspirations* or form directives into workable *functional ambitions*. Sober ambitions, as practical form directives, take into account the preformative signals of the

---

30. Ibid., 261; van Kaam and Muto, *Essential Elements*, s.v. "Attention as Task-Oriented."
31. Ibid., 90.
32. Ibid.
33. Ibid., 91.
34. Ibid., 90–92.
35. Ibid., 91.
36. Ibid., 93–94.

vital dimension. The functional also provides the bridge between transcendent aspirations and vital impulses of people and the concrete directives of their formation field. People can only effectively give form to the world and to their formation situation if their functional ambitions are compatible with the reality around them. This reality is the necessary point of departure for their formative and reformative presence in the world.[37]

The functional dimension, as the "managing or executive branch" of spiritual formation, is the bridge over which our most important longings are realized in the world.[38] It is the window on reality that enables us to give and receive form, and as such, it is a powerful, incarnating facet of our human and Christian formation.

An important caution of van Kaam's regarding our functional dimension is the danger of falling into functionalism, the tendency to absolutize mere functioning cut off from the transcendent. In this case, we tend to make ambitions and projects our exclusive priority, and one becomes driven by them. The managing me, in forgetfulness of the transcendent dimension it is meant to serve, isolates itself from the other dimensions of the formation field. This aberration occurs when the functional dimension fails to remain open to the limited energy of the vital dimension and the balancing, integrating influences of the human spirit (transcendent dimension), as enlivened and reformed by the Holy Spirit. The defining principle of life becomes what one "does" or "achieves," while ignoring the important "why" or "how" we do things and achieve ends.

Transcendent Aspirations and Ideals

In his comprehensive theory of personality, van Kaam gave primacy of place to the spirit as always "transcending," by which he meant going beyond, or going more deeply into, the sociohistorical, vital and functional strivings of our field. For van Kaam, the human spirit is by no means an add-on part of life. It is integral to the entirety of who we are created to be.[39] The transcendent dimension of the formation field expresses the potential of our human spirit to become all that the Mystery intended us to be, through its strivings or aspirations, and its expressions or ideals.[40] At the same time, by articulat-

37. Ibid. (emphasis his).
38. Ibid., 86.
39. van Kaam, *Traditional Formation*, 79–80; van Kaam, *Human Formation*, 165–68.
40. van Kaam, *Fundamental Formation*, 261; van Kaam and Muto, *Essential Elements*, s.v. "Ideals as Formational."

ing the human spirit as one dimension in his multidimensional formation field, van Kaam acknowledged that it is by no means the only formational dynamic of human life.

Our human spirit is a gift of God, "the ground of each human life and each of its emergent dimensions."[41] At the same time, it is a mystery, not wholly knowable to us. The human spirit as the distinctively human transcendent dimension is preformed in us by God.[42] Over a lifetime, this dimension discloses itself in "dialogue with the other dimensions [of our field] and with successive life experiences."[43] This means that in van Kaamian theory, the sociohistorical, vital, and functional dimensions and their articulations in tandem with the transcendent dimension are essential parts of the emerging human life-form as a whole.[44]

Throughout his work, van Kaam referred to the sociohistorical, the vital, and the functional dimensions as pretranscendent.[45] He called them servant sources in relation to our distinctively human spirit and its unfolding over a lifetime.[46] For healthy formation, these pretranscendent dimensions must neither be ultimized nor minimized, but placed in their proper order in service of the human spirit. Ultimately, our human spirit is itself a servant of the guiding and enlivening Spirit of God.

The spirit interacting with all the spheres and dimensions of our field discloses our deepest identity, which, for believers, is our calling in Christ. According to van Kaam,

---

41. Ibid., 66. Van Kaam's concept of the human spirit as transcendent mind and transcendent will (as distinguished from functional mind and functional will), expressed through transcendent memory, imagination and anticipation, will be discussed in more detail in chapter 6 of this book.

42. Ibid., 6–7, 19. The concept of "distinctively human" formation as spiritual is one of the most distinctive and crucial ideas throughout van Kaam's work in formation science, formation anthropology, and formation theology. He used the phrase "distinctively human" as related to the human spirit over one thousand times throughout his writings.

43. Ibid., 66. Note that van Kaam termed the sociohistorical, vital, and functional dimensions of the formation field "pretranscendent dimensions," and considered their therapeutic interventional purview to fall predominantly within the physical, medical, and social-psychological sciences' treatments and therapies.

44. Ibid. Note again how well this understanding resists any spirit-body dualism.

45. van Kaam and Muto, *Essential Elements*, s.v. "Pretranscendent and Transcendent Integration." Van Kaam extensively utilized the concept of pretranscendent dimensions in his volumes *Transcendence Therapy* and *Transcendent Formation*.

46. van Kaam, *Human Formation*, 5; van Kaam and Muto, *Essential Elements*, s.v. "Bridging Role of Formation Anthropology."

Our spirit discloses gradually what we should strive to become in the future. The human life-form as spirit is an unfolding intuition of what our own fundamental spiritual identity or life direction might be. The manifestations of our everyday pragmatic identity are the signs, shadows, and partial embodiments of a deeper spiritual identity. Without this *spiritual identity* at its core, our vital-functional identity loses its rootedness, stability, and meaningfulness. It becomes a shadow without substance, a phantom self, and we suffer a spiritual identity crisis.

Fidelity to direction disclosures is the basis of the life of formation. Life without the direction of the spirit becomes a paralyzing set of secular or pious routines. . . .

Constant disclosure and appraisal of the emergent direction of our formation is necessary . . . [yet] even the most original intuition of our life direction can happen and develop only in continual dialogue with all other aspects of our life. This dialogue is set in motion by our encounters with people, events, and things in successive life situations that emerge within the formation field. The dialogical nature of human formation, on the basis of transcendent presence, is one of the foundational principles of the science of formation.[47]

Van Kaam observed that the transcendent dimension is, so to speak, the gifted disrupter of what could be a closed system of reactivity caused when the other dimensions of our life-form risk evolving in isolation.[48] This dimension creates a "rupture between impulse and reaction" in such a way that we are freed to listen to that which is beyond our sociohistorical pulsations, our vital pulsions, and our functional ambitions, to that which longs for meaning and fulfillment.[49] The spirit enables humans to experience a certain distancing and perspective, so that life situations can be reflected upon and appraised through the incarnational sources of memory, imagination, and anticipation. Such distancing makes it possible for one to apprehend and affirm life as more than vital-functional reactivity. Through the spirit, we engage the distinctly human dynamic to facilitate a "choice of response" in our formation.[50] Freeing people from lives of reaction based

---

47. van Kaam, *Fundamental Formation*, 62–63 (emphasis his).

48. van Kaam, *Fundamental Formation*, 80–81. Van Kaam noted that "all great form traditions insist on detachment, asceticism, or creative delaying and distancing as an absolute condition for the very possibility of a distinctively human or spiritual life" (*Fundamental Formation*, 81).

49. Ibid., 80.

50. Ibid., 76.

on stimulus-response dynamics is a gift of the transcendent dimension.[51] It helps us to know ultimately what to accomplish and where to go. In addition to the already identified four dimensions of the human life form, van Kaam named as transitional in regard to the transcendent dimension two additional dimensions: the functional-transcendent dimension and transcendent-functional dimension. The functional-transcendent tends to make the transcendent a servant of the functional. The transcendent-functional dimension, which usually emerges after a transcendence crisis, properly orders all subordinate dimensions as servant sources of the transcendent, and readies us for the grace of a post-transcendent life, wholly attuned to the pneumatic-ecclesial dimension.[52]

The study of human formation in general and of Christian formation in particular needs to be complementary.

> Understanding the scope of perspectives derived from the transcendent nature of distinctively human formation facilitates our understanding of the scope of the Christian formation perspective. The Christian perspective neither diminishes nor devalues, rather it complements, corrects, and expands the distinctively human formation perspective. It discloses one's participation in the life form of Christ and through this in the Mystery of the Eternal Trinitarian Formation/Interformation Event [the Holy Trinity].[53]

While all Christians share with the rest of humanity the formative dynamics modeled thus far in the field paradigm, van Kaam articulated in a complementary fashion the distinctiveness of Christian formation. Redemption does not destroy human nature but fulfills it: "Just as we have borne the image of the man of dust, we will also bear the image of the man in heaven."[54]

Pneumatic-Ecclesial Inspirations and Invitations

According to van Kaam, the dynamics of the transcendent dimension are the unique mark of all human personhood. In accordance with the revelation of the Christian faith tradition, van Kaam observed that the human spirit on its own was unable to articulate, let alone fulfill, its sense of calling and its transcendent strivings. His work expands our understanding of this distinctively

---

51. Ibid., 80.

52. These two additional dimensions will be discussed in relation to spiritual maturation in chapter 10 of this book.

53. van Kaam and Muto, "Course I," 8.

54. 1 Cor 15:49.

human characteristic of Christian formation by naming at the highest level the pneumatic-ecclesial dimension of our field of life. As he explained,

> In the Christian articulation of the science of formation, pneumatic spirituality completes and transforms the transcendent spirituality of humanity. According to the Christian form tradition, people discover that their own unaided powers are unable to attain the fulfillment of their spiritual aspirations. This tradition holds that God himself reveals to them that an original Fall of humanity led to this inability. He sends his own Son to help humanity overcome the Fall's consequences for human formation. The Son lives on in our formation history through the Holy Spirit. Insofar as our life of transcendent formation is the gift of the Holy Spirit, we call it a life of pneumatic transformation.[55]

We humans, try as we might, cannot fulfill our own longed-for ideals, due to what the Christian tradition has historically named the Fall. It obscures our self-understanding as created by God and veils the inherent inability of humans to save themselves. For complete fulfillment and transcendence to occur, the enabling grace and power of the Spirit of God through Christ and the church is essential. In the words of van Kaam,

> In moments of grace, the Spirit creates an awareness of sinfulness and impotence, of the necessity of grace to realize transcendent aspirations. Pneumatic inspirations begin to complement and elevate the natural aspirations of the human spirit. The transcendent call may be experienced as a call of the God of revelation in the Lord Jesus. The life direction is perceived as a mystery hidden in God before all ages. Final wholeness and integration is seen as an act of the Holy Spirit. The other formation dimensions are considered now both as preparatory stages for the channels of expression and as embodiments of the transforming grace of the Spirit.[56]

The dynamics of a Spirit-filled life are experienced in the inspirations of the pneumatic-ecclesial dimension and their expressions as invitations.[57] Both inspirations and invitations are attributed to the work of the Third Person of the Trinity, the Holy Spirit. Both are expressed empirically in the world through the church, the Body of Christ.[58]

---

55. van Kaam, *Fundamental Formation*, 142.

56. Ibid., 144

57. Ibid., 144; van Kaam and Muto, *Essential Elements*, s.v. "Receptivity to Transcendent Appeals."

58. van Kaam and Muto, "Course I," 9. Van Kaam also noted, "In Christian

Character Formation as Dimensional

Each of our life dimensions contributes to the formation of our character. Through the dynamics of form reception and form donation, we adopt patterns of presence and action that leave a lasting imprint on our dispositions and matching character. Such receptive and donative expressions are present in each of our life dimensions and contribute to the formation of our sociohistorical, vital, functional, and transcendent character. Consonant character formation involves an integrated flow of giving and receiving form at every phase of our life; it also guards against adoption of dissonant coercions that may deform our character.

Our sociohistorical character, as receptive, absorbs, in an absolute or relative way, the dominant attitudes, directives, and symbols surrounding us in society. The donative facet of sociohistorical character formation is what accounts for our active participation in the familial, historical, cultural, and socio-political events of the day. For example, were we raised in a family that equated worth with wealth, we may have imbibed without realizing it certain dispositions toward the poor. If we later become the owner of a company, we may translate these dispositions into decisions to give unequal pay to employees based on their social class, not on their talents. Such deformed sociohistorical character would need to be open to reformation and transformation by the Mystery.

Our vital character, as receptive, is marked by intraformative needs for emotional gratification and consolation. These needs can be expressed appropriately, or they can become so dominant that they turn mainly into strivings for a continual flood of warm, affective feelings from the people around us. Our vital character as donative can also be expressed in a wise way, or it may be disposed to overwhelm others around us by explosive expressions of romantic and charming, or angry and resentful, feelings unprocessed by any capacity for reflection.

Our functional character as receptive directs our reason and powers of observation to gather and order the information we need to manage our lives. Our functional character as donative then uses this information to develop ideas, plans, and agendas that enable us to meet the demands of our situational life effectively. Being resourceful, in terms of administration and

---

formation the Holy Spirit acts as the deepest pneumatic dimension of the human formative spirit" (*Fundamental Formation*, glossary, s.v. "Spirit Form"). Van Kaam's work clearly assumed that the Holy Spirit is not exclusively operative only through the church, but that the Christian revelation has been articulated and recorded throughout the Judeo-Christian tradition, preserved by the Spirit through the church. (See van Kaam and Muto, *Foundations of Christian Formation*, chapter 14, "God the Holy Spirit," 181–90.)

organization, is a good idea, provided we subordinate this character trait to dispositions that are more transcendent than merely functionalistic ones to enhance our performance.

Our functional-transcendent character, as receptive, attracts us to the benefits of transcendent living. This same character, as donative, prompts us to pursue ways to maximize to the fullest the gifts we have been given. However, if our functional-transcendent character sinks into functionalism, the danger is that functioning becomes the be-all and end-all of our life. The temptation inherent in functional-transcendence is that it inclines us to harness the transcendent as a means to enhance our own effectiveness. The danger escalates that the managerial side of our character becomes so dominant that we live in the illusion that we can control the Mystery while pretending to serve the Mystery.

Our transcendent character, as receptive, opens us to the graces inherent in a transcendence crisis that alone can break through the deformative grid of functional-transcendence, and ready us for a life of humble openness to, and service of, the Mystery. For example, if the owner of a company loses it to an overseas market, she may be shaken loose from any illusion that she is in control. The crisis she faces can free her to become more human, or plunge her into despair. Our transcendent character as donative prompts us to pursue the inner and outer conditions that facilitate a way of life in which all of our pretranscendent dimensions become servant sources of the transcendent. For example, sociohistorical pressures in society have less of an effect on us; using drugs or alcohol as a substitute for the transcendent ceases; projects get done, but we know when to stop working and rest.

Our transcendent-functional character, as receptive, protects us from the dominance of any one pretranscendent character trait. The light of the transcendent begins to filter into all dimensions and spheres of our formation field. Our transcendent-functional character, as donative, takes into account the limits and blessings associated with all facets of the pretranscendent. While one or the other of these character traits may still exert influence on us, the difference is that they are no longer dominant, due to the fact that they are permeated by transcendent dynamics, dispositions, and expressions.

In terms of the pneumatic-ecclesial dimension, all that we receive and all that we give is God's grace. Through the empowerment of the Holy Spirit, we are enabled to appraise ongoing directives of our Christ form. We grow more and more open to the purifying formation, illuminating reformation, and unifying transformation of the entirety of our formation field by the Holy Trinity. We learn experientially that it is Christ who chooses us to be instruments of his will in this world and to serve his church in accordance with our unique-communal life-call, vocation, and avocation.

Conclusion

There is no doubt in our minds that van Kaam believed that grace is what enables us to "know empirically and experientially about human or transcendent formation."[59] Through the "revealed and graced nature of Christian formation," one may experience and witness the ways in which grace "heals, elevates, and corrects . . . basic dynamics [of human formation]."[60] Only by grace may we be fully formed, reformed, and transformed.

Through the dimensional dynamics inherent in his formation field model, with its source and center in the Mystery, we have entered in these first two chapters into a truly holistic theory of human and Christian character formation that shows us how to give and receive form in every facet of our personal and communal life and world. We will explore an expansion of this theory in the next chapter on the integrative structures of the human life form.

Reflection Questions

1. Understanding Our Story: Reflection on Strivings during a Significant Event in Your Life

    Like the spheres of the formation field that we explored in chapter 1, its dimensions explored in this chapter further expand ways to "unpack" significant moments of formation in order to help us attend to dynamics at work that we may not have been aware of in the moment. Such awareness can help us both to appreciate the creative and varied ways God's Spirit speaks to us, and help us to become attuned to dynamics in our lives that may have resisted or nurtured a certain response to God's "still small voice."

    Call to mind a specific, and significant, event or moment in your life or the life of your faith community. (It might be the same event you explored for the exercises in chapter 1, or a different event.) Reflect in turn on each of the dimensions of your formation field at the time (sociohistorical, vital, functional, transcendent, and pneumatic-ecclesial). To the extent that you are able to do so, identify specific strivings and expressions that were active in each dimension. Looking back on the

---

59. van Kaam and Muto, "Course I," 13; van Kaam and Muto, *Foundations of Christian Formation*, 36, 59–60, 94.

60. van Kaam and Muto, *Foundations of Christian Formation*, 23-24.

situation now, how would you describe the ways the various strivings shaped you or your community during that event?

Now pause for a while to be with God and allow God to be present to you as you reflect on this important time in your life. As you do so, attend to whether the Holy Spirit has inspired you to identify any obstacles to integrating all the dimensions of your life in light of any pneumatic-ecclesial inspirations that were offered to you during this event. Can you identify any conditions that facilitated such integration of the various dimensions in your life at that time? Consider whether either the obstacles to or facilitating conditions that occurred at that time have any relevance to the way you live in openness to God now.

2. Understanding God's Story: Reflection on Dimensions of a Favorite Bible Character

Who is one of your favorite Bible characters? Why did you choose him or her?

Select a significant moment in this character's life. (It might be the same event you explored for the exercises in chapter 1, or a different event or even a different character.) Reflect in turn on each of the dimensions of the person's formation field at the time (sociohistorical, vital, functional, transcendent, pneumatic-ecclesial).

To the extent that you are able to do so, identify specific strivings that came to the person from each dimension of the person's field. How would you describe the way that these various strivings shaped the person in that moment and how each of the dimensions contributed to the person's formation?

Describe any ways that you find yourself responding to or perhaps resisting God's communications to this character in this significant moment.

Chapter 3

Integrating Structures

IN THE PRECEDING CHAPTERS, we saw that the experience of human existence includes facets of life that are in constant flux from moment to moment. Within a single hour, a person may experience different external environments, diverse encounters with other people, and varied internal reactions and responses. Life is always in a process of being formed, deformed, reformed, and transformed. In fact, in a spiritually healthy person, these changes, intentional or not, are part of the mystery of our unfolding. The van Kaamian Formation Field Model provides a way to articulate facets of our life journey open to change and in need of integration.

At the same time, the experience of human living is still felt to be more or less stable and long-lasting. Van Kaam provided a means to articulate and describe those facets of our personality that are more lasting, despite the dynamic nature of our field of life. He named them integrating structures.[1] An integrating structure is a constellation of dynamics and directives rooted in one or the other sphere of our formation field. It serves to integrate the various modes or dimensions of human presence, namely, the sociohistorical, vital, functional, and transcendent dimensions, and includes, from a Christian perspective, the pneumatic-ecclesial dimension.

---

1. van Kaam, *Fundamental Formation*, 254–55. Note that synonyms for these structures throughout van Kaam's work include: integrational structures (*Fundamental Formation*, 258), integrating forms (*Transcendent Formation*, 28), integrational forms (*Transcendent Formation*, 28-29, 58), integrational life forms (*Transcendent Formation*, 29), and integrative forming life (*Scientific Formation*, 282). In later years, van Kaam and his colleague Susan Muto settled upon the phrase integrating structures in teaching this material in their post-graduate courses at the Epiphany Academy of Formative Spirituality in Pittsburgh, Pennsylvania. In providing a means by which to describe the relatively stable facets of the ways in which we live, van Kaam was aware that there is also a certain dynamism within these integrating structures themselves. One of his favorite terms to express this dynamic facet of integrational structures was *emergent*; thus, he often referred to forms as emergent or emerging (for example, see his discussions of this in van Kaam, *Scientific Formation*, 64–65; van Kaam, *Transcendence Therapy*, 162–63).

INTEGRATING STRUCTURES OF THE HUMAN LIFE FORM

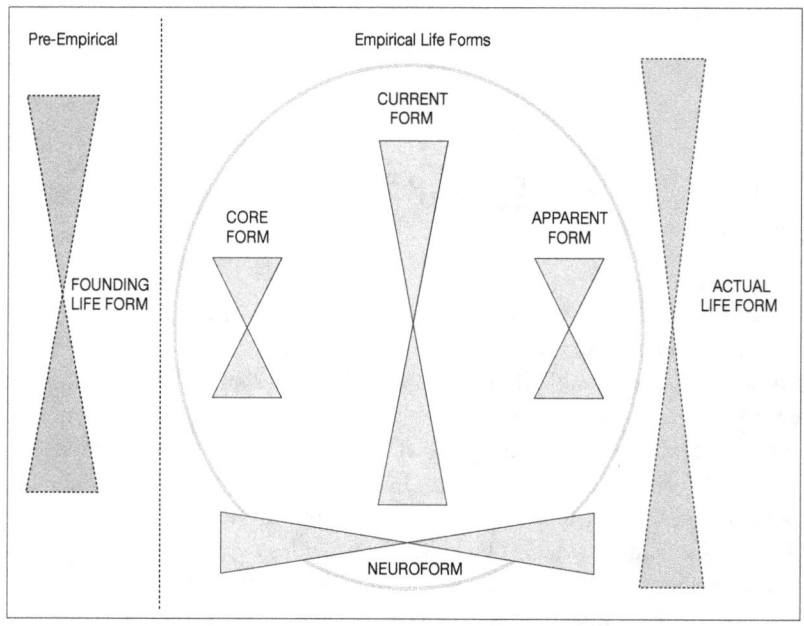

© 2016 Epiphany Association • Integrating Structures of the Human Life Form
All Rights Reserved. Not for Duplication. Used with Permission.

Paralleling the spheres of his formation field model, van Kaam identified the integrating structures of the human life form as the pre-empirical founding form, and the empirical life forms, these being, the core form, current form, apparent form, neuroform, and actual life form.[2] Both in their potency and actualization, these integrating structures articulate specific facets of our lives that are relatively long-lasting and that connect with the entirety of who we are. Integrating structures enable us to bring together "what otherwise might remain a jumble of dispersed thoughts, feelings, [and] actions."[3] Articulating them helps us to explore and understand the lived relationship between the pre-empirical and empirical facets of formation that give coherence to who we are as distinctively human.[4]

---

2. The connection between the integrating structures and the spheres of the formation field will be further explained in chapter 3.
3. van Kaam, *Transcendent Formation*, 28.
4. van Kaam, *Fundamental Formation*, 251–60.

Pre-Empirical Basis of Integrating Structures

Founding Life Form

At the basis of van Kaam's integrating structures is the founding form of life.[5] This is the preformed essence of who we most deeply are as created in the image and likeness of God.[6] It is from the founding form that we derive the preformed "genetic-vital and primordial sociohistorical context" of our existence.[7] Empirically speaking, the founding form is the basis of our unique-communal life-call, which only gradually manifests itself over a lifetime of dialogue with our formation field.[8]

The founding form is the bridge between our essence in God and our empirical existence in the world.[9] Van Kaam likened it to a road sign that provides a basic orientation to our lives:

> The unknown foundational form is gradually disclosed to us. This disclosure reveals increasingly that this unknown form is only a basic indication of the overall unique direction that the unfolding of our life should take. We could compare this to a road sign telling us that our direction is, for instance, toward the city of New York. While this sign indicates our destination, it does not explain how to dress for our journey; how to interact with fellow travelers, where to rest, where to eat, or how to drive under different weather and road conditions. How we concretely travel will depend on the dialogue we maintain with the circumstances we meet on our trip. We keep in mind our basic direction but realize that our response to such circumstances will have an influence on how we will look, feel, and express ourselves when we arrive at the end of our journey. How we give form concretely to our journey and to ourselves as travelers is not contained in our awareness of the general direction our travel should take.[10]

---

5. van Kaam, *Transcendent Formation*, 28-31. Other synonyms for this concept throughout van Kaamian writings include foundational potential form (*Fundamental Formation*, 250), and soul-form (van Kaam and Muto, *Essential Elements*, s.v. "Meaning of 'Soul'").

6. van Kaam, *Fundamental Formation*, 251.

7. van Kaam, *Traditional Formation*, 23.

8. Ibid., 23; van Kaam and Muto, *Essential Elements*, s.vv. "Actual Life Form as Integrational," "Consonance with our Founding Form."

9. van Kaam, *Traditional Formation*, 22-23; van Kaam and Muto, *Formation of the Christian Heart*, 26, 84, 226-27.

10. van Kaam, *Fundamental Formation*, 251.

The founding form links together our essence in the Mystery with our vital, sociohistorical, functional, and transcendent existence.[11] Van Kaam's formation science and formation anthropology share common ground with other human sciences insofar as they too are empirical-experiential. Yet he insisted on the necessity to differentiate his comprehensive theory of personality from both existentialism and empiricism. One of the ways he did this was to articulate as his guiding presupposition that humans have an essence (a soul-form) that is grounded in the Divine Forming and Preforming Mystery.[12] This essence precedes our embodied existence.

In contrast to Jean-Paul Sartre, who held that existence precedes essence, van Kaam posited from a theological perspective the long-held truth that human essence precedes existence.[13] This means that our essence is "preformed from all eternity in the loving mind and heart of the Trinity," such that "our deepest identity . . . is hidden in Christ."[14] There is a distinction, although not a dualism, between human essence and human existence.[15]

---

11. Van Kaam noted that the founding form is one's essence, rooted and hidden in the Divine Forming and Preforming Mystery (for Christians, the Most Holy Trinity). He said that the "ultimate criterion" of his formation science would be "the consonance of human existing with human essence as rooted in a preforming mystery that called it forth" (van Kaam, *Traditional Formation*, 22).

12. The Judeo-Christian revelation echoes this truth in such passages as Jer 1:5 (God speaking to the prophet Jeremiah), "Before I formed you in the womb, I knew you."

13. For Jean-Paul Sartre's claim that existence precedes essence, see *Existentialism and Human Emotions*, 15, as well as Sartre, *Being and Nothingness*, to which this quotation refers. For van Kaam's articulation of essence preceding existence from a formation theology perspective, see van Kaam and Muto, *Foundations of Christian Formation*, 22.

14. van Kaam and Muto, *Essential Elements*, s.v. "Essence and Existence." Note that van Kaam also differentiated the focus of formation science and anthropology on "the practical ways in which [our] essence . . . concretely expresses itself in [our] human existence," from the focus of Thomistic philosophy, metaphysics, and theology that are more concerned with "the essentials of faith traditions" (*Scientific Formation*, preface, xv–xvi). Elsewhere, he wrote, "In appreciative abandonment we may experience at moments that we are loved into uniqueness" (*Transcendent Formation*, 69).

15. Van Kaam consistently avoided any sense of such dualistic separation throughout his works; for example, see van Kaam, *Traditional Formation*, 21–23. In the first volume of their Formation Theology series, van Kaam and Muto explained, "Aquinas sees our human existence as rooted in and preceded by our essence as pre-ordained in God's eternal wisdom. Applied to the anthropology and theology of formation, this insight clarifies that 'essence' precedes 'existence,' a view that favors an 'existential,' not an 'existentialistic,' approach to the human condition. It proves that the claim made by existentialism, that existence precedes essence, is false. Any human existence that is not an expression of its preformed essence is a contradiction of terms. Our life from conception to death must be the expression of that which creates and sustains our very being and inserts who we are in a higher order of coherent truth and meaning" (*Foundations of Christian Formation*, 22).

For van Kaam, a spiritually healthy existence refers to the practical ways in which we implement our essence in relation to the direction in which the Spirit of God leads us; van Kaam and Muto wrote, "The Holy Spirit appeals to our human spirit to disclose and implement over a lifetime of existence our divinely preformed essence," an appeal to which we may respond more or less faithfully.[16] He acknowledged his fundamental presupposition of our preformed essence in the Holy Trinity as an ultimate guiding light of spiritual formation.[17] He then focused his work on observing, articulating, and describing the dynamics of spiritual existence lived in response to our fundamental essence in God.

Our founding form is the ground of our most basic makeup. It is the point of departure from whence our essence in God comes into existence. The founding form exerts a continual appeal that our spiritual formation be in consonance with its God-given ground.[18] As both "a gift and invitation" of the Mystery to us, the founding form is "who we most deeply are . . . [it is] our inmost nobility."[19] Van Kaam likened it to a "fountain of the full meaning of our personal-communal existence."[20] Delighting in the creativity of the Mystery as expressed in the uniqueness of each person's founding form, van Kaam posited that fidelity to our founding form is "the ultimate and deepest way" in which our lives can be integrated.[21]

Pride Form

While much of van Kaam's work focused on expounding the dynamics of healthy, holistic spiritual formation, he also addressed the effects of sin on personal and social world views that resist consonant unfolding and reformation. In light of the revelation of the Judeo-Christian tradition, the theological "Fall" of humankind introduced a "powerful interloper" that falsely presents itself as our founding form.[22] Van Kaam called this interloper the pride form.

16. van Kaam and Muto, *Essential Elements*, s.v. "Essence and Existence."

17. van Kaam and Muto, *Foundations of Christian Formation*, 44, 139–40. Note that van Kaam also carefully distinguished his theory from atheistic existentialism that "has no faith in the moorings of any existence in essence nor ultimately in the preforming ground of all essences and existences, namely, the radical mystery of formation [Holy Trinity]" (*Transcendence Therapy*, 29).

18. van Kaam, *Traditional Formation*, 22–23; van Kaam and Muto, *Foundations of Christian Formation*, 61.

19. van Kaam, *Transcendent Formation*, 58, 62.

20. Ibid., 28.

21. Ibid.

22. van Kaam, *Traditional Formation*, 147.

In all human beings, the pride form poses as a quasi-foundational life form, exalting itself as the ultimate source of formation.[23] This counterfeit life form obscures our true calling and produces patterns and dynamics of sin and its effects. The pride form divides the heart against itself, constantly working to distract and diminish our deepest longings for God with the danger that anything and everything becomes a substitute for the transcendent.[24] At every turn, the pride form seeks to block the formative direction that the Mystery reveals in our life.[25] The pride form seeks to deform and disintegrate our entire formation field.

The pride form causes us to resist or refuse authentic spiritual formation by "foster[ing] ignorance of the true nature of our transcendence dynamic and creating the illusion of autonomous self-formation and fulfillment."[26] It blinds us spiritually, intellectually, and emotionally. It steers us away from the recognition of our calling in God and of our potential to live a life of loving trust in relationship to ourselves and others. It seduces us instead to an autarkic existence, relying only on ourselves for self-definition and self-fulfillment. It ubiquitously suggests that we are wholly independent of anyone else.[27]

In contrast to the founding form, which van Kaam described as "basically open . . . always in search of connection, of the joy of loving consonance" with the Holy Trinity, the pride form is "isolating" and "self-absorbed, seeking relationships for its own gratification alone."[28] It resists the loving appeals of God to replace self-centeredness with other-centered care and concern.

Van Kaam used many verbs throughout his work to describe the workings of the pride form, such as: encapsulate, fixate, dominate, absolutize, idolize, exalt, isolate, idealize, refuse, push, cling, and seduce.[29] His insights

---

23. van Kaam, *Fundamental Formation*, glossary, s.v. "Pride-Form." Note that hyphenation of the term varied somewhat throughout van Kaam's work. In this book, the non-hyphenated form of the term will be used. Synonyms that van Kaam used for the pride form include the counterfeit form of life (*Fundamental Formation*, 266), quasi-founding form (*Traditional Formation*, 147), counterfeit self (*Formation of the Human Heart*, 38), and false self (*Transcendence Therapy*, 251), although note that this last example is the only case in which van Kaam connected the pride form with the more widely popularized term of false self in his seven-volume Formative Spirituality series.

24. van Kaam, *Transcendence Therapy*, 251.

25. van Kaam, *Fundamental Formation*, 266; van Kaam and Muto, *Foundations of Christian Formation*, 19–20.

26. van Kaam, *Fundamental Formation*, glossary, s.v. "Pride-Form."

27. van Kaam, *Transcendent Formation*, 61.

28. van Kaam, *Traditional Formation*, 147.

29. For but one sample of texts in which van Kaam discussed the pride form with such terms as these, see *Fundamental Formation*, 194, 266–67.

about the pride form are expressed also in descriptors such as autarkic, arrogant, and obstinate.[30] When by the grace of God we notice these illusory dynamics disrupting our lives, it is like getting a whiff of a spoiled onion in the vegetable cellar. Such dissonance signals that the pride form is at work! Astute investigation and inner purification, with the enabling power of God's grace, are steps all people need to take to address the deformative power of the pride form.

Needless to say, recognizing the power of the pride form is one thing, eradicating it is another. In one of the most well-known passages of the New Testament, the Apostle Paul writes of the struggle between the spiritual dynamics of the founding form and the pride form.

> So I find it to be a law that when I want to do what is good, evil lies close at hand. For I delight in the law of God in my inmost self, but I see in my members another law at war with the law of my mind, making me captive to the law of sin that dwells in my members. Wretched man that I am! Who will rescue me from this body of death? Thanks be to God through Jesus Christ our Lord![31]

The Christian revelation calls our attention to the redemptive work of the Trinity through the birth, life, ministry, death, resurrection, and ascension of Jesus Christ. He is our hope of rescue from the ubiquitous presence and power of the pride form in human life. Van Kaam used the construct of the Christ form to express how from the beginning of salvation history our hope for redemption would not be in vain. The grace of rescue from the treachery of the pride form is available to every Christian.

Christ Form

Grounded in the life of the Trinity, the Christ form is the redemptive structure that counters the power and effects of the pride form in the life of the Christian.[32] It brings renewal and redemption to the founding form that has been distorted by sin. Through the ongoing work of the Spirit, Christ comes among us as a gift of God to humankind, to affect the restoration of

---

30. van Kaam, *Fundamental Formation*, 54–55, 82, 204, 266, and glossary, s.v. "Pride-Form"; van Kaam, *Transcendent Formation*, 71–72; van Kaam, *Human Formation*, 79; van Kaam, *Formation of the Human Heart*, 166.

31. Rom 7:21–25.

32. van Kaam, *Formation of the Human Heart*, 268–69; van Kaam and Muto, *Foundations of Christian Formation*, 133–34.

our inmost transcendent identity. When one becomes a Christian, when the Holy Spirit enters our human spirit, our redemption is at hand.[33]

The Christ form restores our founding form to such a degree that our life-direction is "reset and imprinted" with an orientation away from self or selfish sensuality and sinful disobedience and toward the loving embrace of the Trinity.[34] In other words, when we become Christians, our pre-empirical founding form (one's "heart of hearts") returns to a right relationship with God and with our calling in God.[35] By the same token, in the promise of the body's resurrection to live eternally in the presence of God, the Christ form influences both the transcendent and pretranscendent facets of our humanity. For our redemption to be fully realized empirically, the redeemed direction and directives of the Christ form need to be both communicated and lived out in all spheres and dimensions of our formation field, which is to say that our redeemed life in Christ is meant to save the whole of who we are and how we live as human beings in the wider world.

Empirical Integrating Structures

Having explored the van Kaamian construct of the founding form as the pre-empirical essence of our existence, we turn now to the remaining empirical integrating structures, namely, the core form, current form, apparent form, neuroform, and actual form.[36]

---

33. van Kaam and Muto, *Foundations of Christian Formation*, 19–20; van Kaam, *Fundamental Formation*, glossary, s.v. "Consonant Life-Form"; van Kaam, *Formation of the Human Heart*, 267–69. Note also that for van Kaam, the integrating structure of the Christ form was synonymous with one's unique-communal life-call as a Christian (van Kaam and Muto, *Foundations of Christian Formation*, 111).

34. van Kaam and Muto, *Foundations of Christian Formation*, 40.

35. For van Kaam, as a Roman Catholic, the event of baptism marked becoming a Christian, entering into the life of Christ and the life of Christ entering the human soul. Of course, doctrinal conceptions and the languaging of this event vary among different Christian faith traditions (e.g., some describe the gift of the Christ form as being born again, receiving salvation, etc.). Van Kaam's point was that for the Christian there is a graced dynamic of spiritual formation, which he articulated through the construct of the Christ form, which comes to us as the unearned, superabundant gift of God.

36. According to van Kaam, these empirical life forms are both transcendent and incarnational. As always, he was careful to respect and represent the mystery of human life as spirit incarnated in flesh. He differentiated and yet emphasized the fundamental union of these two facets of human life. He named the transcendent source of empirical life forms to be the human spirit (which he articulated as formative transcendent mind and formative transcendent will, further differentiated incarnationally as: functional formative intelligence, memory, imagination, anticipation, and functional formative will. See van Kaam, *Fundamental Formation*, 252–53). For a thorough discussion of

Core Form

The foremost empirical integrating structure, namely our core form (or our "heart"), is grounded in the intrasphere of our formation field. It serves as the means by which we articulate the dynamics and directives of our inner life that are relatively stable and constant.[37]

The choice of the term "core" was intentional. It represents not only the centrality of this integrating structure, but also its etymological association with the more familiar symbolic term heart, which is *le coeur* in French.[38] For van Kaam, the core form functions as an existential bridge between the founding form and the other structures and dimensions of our formation field. As the central integrating structure of human life, the core form consists of our most enduring and decisive dispositions in life, as well as our deepest affections and their dynamics.[39] The core form is the interface between our continuous lasting dispositions and our matching character.[40] From a Christian perspective, the core form is the primary communicator of the Christ form to all facets of our formation field. Van Kaam called it the "guardian" of our consonance.[41] Attentive discernment of the movements of our core form, as enlightened by the Holy Spirit, is crucial to any full field appraisal of significant decisions in life.

As the primary integrator of our field dimensions and their potentials, it is the function of the core form to "nourish, sustain, and integrate" the consonance of all the dimensions of our formation field.[42] The core form does this in dialogue with the directives that emerge from its spheres of presence and action. In short, the core form serves as a holistic integrator of our field of life with its spheres, dimensions, dynamics, and integrating structures.

In contrast to this holistic integration, van Kaam reminded us that the ever-present pride form tempts us to absolutize one of the other dimensions

---

the distinction between transcendent and functional facets of the mind and will, see chapter 6 of this book.

37. van Kaam, *Fundamental Formation*, 254–55; van Kaam, *Human Formation*, 174.

38. van Kaam, *Transcendence Therapy*, 251.

39. van Kaam, *Transcendent Formation*, 28; van Kaam, *Human Formation*, 165. Van Kaam devoted an entire volume in his Formative Spirituality series (*Formation of the Human Heart*) to exploring what he identified as fundamental dispositions in spiritual formation. The role of dispositions in spiritual formation will be explored in chapter 4 of this book. Certain facets of the formative role of appraisal as a disposition will also be explored in chapter 7 of this book.

40. van Kaam, *Fundamental Formation*, 253–54.

41. Ibid., 254.

42. van Kaam, *Human Formation*, 166.

of our field as if it were primary. He gave as an example of one-sided living the possibility of absolutizing the functional dimension with its ambitions.

> The pride form . . . may suggest that functional ambition and its satisfaction is totally important, that it suffices for life's fulfillment. If we give in to this suggestion, supported as it often is by popular [sociohistorical] pulsations, our functional concerns may dominate our formation field. We become functionalistic and risk losing our distinctively human centeredness and consonance.[43]

As we have seen, the founding form (for Christians, the Christ form) is pre-empirical: it precedes our experiences. In this the founding form is more "remote" than the core form in relation to the empirical integrating structures, spheres, and dimensions of our present field of life. Our founding form (and for Christians, our Christ form) is always somewhat hidden to us. While the founding form is the deepest seat of human dignity, and while it gives meaning to our life and calling in God, it is clear from van Kaam's writing that this pre-empirical depth dimension of our existence requires translation into everyday reality. Through the human spirit, the founding form, as it is understood in part at any given time, announces itself and its general life-giving direction to the core form. The core form then translates the directing power of our founding form to the rest of the empirical structures that comprise the lived reality of our formation field as a whole.[44] The spiritually formative heart thus serves as "the empirical-dispositional core expression of our foundational life-form."[45] Van Kaam pointed out that in some sense the founding form acts as the remote core of our life. It serves, so to speak, as the nucleus of the core form, whereas the core form itself may be thought of as the more proximate center of our dispositional life. This relationship between the founding form and the core form is often heard in the common English expression, "What do you feel in your heart of hearts?"[46] Taken together, the founding form in dialogue with the core form results in the embodiment of who we are in everyday life.

This privileged link between the founding form and the core form reveals itself in what van Kaam referred to as the two complementary coformants of the core form: responsibility and sensibility. These symbolic movements "mirror in the heart the basic polarity between the transcendent and

---

43. Ibid. Van Kaam noted that none of our dimensions, including our preeminent transcendent dimension, can function as the primary integrator in our life. For a discussion of this point, see van Kaam, *Human Formation*, 165–68.

44. Ibid., 167.

45. Ibid., 173.

46. Ibid., 167.

the vital-functional dimensions of the human life-form."[47] Grounded as it is in our human spirit in dialogue with our founding form, the core form is potentially capable of responding to the Mystery as it discloses itself to us. That is, the core form has "response-ability." From the perspective of formation theology, it is through the responsibility exhibited by the core form that the redeemed human spirit is able to respond to disclosures of the Holy Spirit. Linked as it is to the gift of our vital-functional embodiment, the core form is the center of our overall affective-cognitive dispositions and our most deeply held convictions. The core form is capable of "keep[ing] the center of our formation" connected to our "incarnated, earthbound life," or to what van Kaam identified as the second feature of our core form: sensibility.[48] Through this sense-ability, we are able to sense and receive input from the various empirical spheres, dimensions, and integrating structures of our field. This sense-ability then manifests itself in our lives as our sensitivity to ourselves and our surroundings, which van Kaam described as "our central formative mood and feeling life."[49] Through the rhythms of responsibility and sensibility, we soon discover that the core form acts as the proximate, empirical bridge between our founding form and the rest of our formation field. It enables us to communicate through our entire field the most heartfelt convictions and directives of human life.

As an integrational structure, the core form has a certain constancy and permanence about it, relative to the remaining empirical structures.[50] In van Kaam's theory of personality, the integrating structures of the current form and the apparent form are "subservient to the core form" insofar as they act to enflesh in daily life "the basic inclinations of the heart."[51] They also provide information to our responsible-sensible heart for appraisal.

Current Form

The empirical integrating structure of the current form acts in dialogue with the immediate situational and world spheres of our formation field.[52] Because of its primary dependence on the changeable, exterior environment around us, the current form is less stable and long-lasting than the core form. This relative instability accounts for the fact that not all dynamics that give form

47. van Kaam, *Human Formation*, 168.
48. Ibid., 171.
49. Ibid.
50. van Kaam, *Transcendence Therapy*, 98.
51. van Kaam, *Fundamental Formation*, 255.
52. Ibid., 255–56.

currently to our immediate situation translate into the continuous, lasting dispositions of the core form and its matching character. Van Kaam gave the example that "truck drivers are dynamically influenced in the way they give form to their occupational life by the current state of their physical health, by the condition of the roads they have to use, by current speed limits, the situation of their companies, . . . and so on. All of these affect the manner in which truckers give form to their job."[53] In this example, the current form expresses the way that truck drivers give form to their work. However, such current forms do not necessarily translate into life-long dispositions of the core form (the heart). The role of the current form is to provide a means by which to describe form reception and form donation, as well as its competency, within a certain setting.[54] However, such a form ought to be seen as more provisional than permanent, which accounts for the fact that it must be differentiated from our core form.[55]

Even though the current form is provisional, formational dynamics experienced at any given moment in our field may provide rich information and insight to the core form. The dynamics of the current form may serve to deepen some basic inclinations of the heart or act as a catalyst for needed change. We may discover through the current form a directive that invites further appraisal and that casts more light on our founding form than we previously perceived. For example, in a particular place at a particular time, we might discover an activity that is profoundly consonant with who we are. Or we may notice that something in a specific time and place stirs up great dissonance for us. In this sense, attentive appraisal to the directives and dynamics of our current form often includes invitations to further formative, reformative, and transformative growth.[56] One of the ways to describe spiritual formation is the process of transitioning from one current form to another.[57]

---

53. van Kaam, *Transcendent Formation*, 65.

54. Ibid., 48.

55. van Kaam, *Fundamental Formation*, 62, 64, 251, 256.

56. Van Kaam provided many examples of the ways in which one's current form is used to inform one's life direction. For but one illustration, see his example based on potential depletion in a care-giving situation in *Formation of the Human Heart*, 302–3.

57. van Kaam, *Formation of the Human Heart*, 192; van Kaam, *Transcendence Therapy*, 252. A special type of current form was what van Kaam called a periodic form. It is related to transitions that can be correlated with or implied by biological maturation during phasic formation, for example, transitioning from childhood to puberty (van Kaam, *Transcendent Formation*, 11).

Apparent Form

The aim of the apparent form is to integrate "the many ways in which we appear in daily life to ourselves inwardly and to others outwardly . . . [including] roles that we have to take up if our life is to be compatible with the consonant demands of the society in which we are called to be effective."[58] Taking on roles is an expression of our apparent form, which is meant to be authentic, not deceptive. Apparent forms are as necessary as the clothing we wear and may more often than not be consonant with our calling.

Developing an apparent form ought not to betray who we are. When our public self is aligned with our private self, we can live socially effective lives in the settings in which we are providentially placed. That being said, van Kaam admitted that apparent forms also have the potential to become deformative, especially when "we falsely interiorize them as if they represent all that we are personally and lastingly."[59]

According to van Kaam, to align our apparent form with our core and current forms, we need to pay attention to what he termed our intra-apparent forms, our outer-apparent forms, and our inter-apparent forms. The most fundamental of the three for him is our intra-apparent form, or our self-image.[60] He noted that this form

> is not merely a mirror that passively represents who we really are. It functions also as a power of formation that helps us to generate in relative freedom a dynamic, intricately structured apparent form of life. . . . [It] co-directs the way in which we receive form in and give form to our character and personality . . . [and it also] influences the form we give to our surroundings.[61]

When consonant with our calling in life, our intra-apparent form assists us gently and firmly to say yes to who we are meant to be in relation to all facets of our formation field.[62] To the degree that our intra-apparent form is not grounded in our essential belovedness in the Mystery, it may be grounded in an image of our never being good enough to deserve love. From a Christian perspective, if we are prone to such duplicity between our Christ form and our intra-apparent form, we may at times be invited by the grace of God to "change our self-images radically," to bring them more in

---

58. van Kaam, *Transcendent Formation*, 28.
59. Ibid., 63.
60. Ibid., 59.
61. Ibid., 61.
62. Ibid., 60–61.

line with the Christ form of our soul.[63] Such invitations may come suddenly, but most often gradually, by the loving work of God as when Jesus says, "Come to me all you that are weary and are carrying heavy burdens, and I will give you rest. Take my yoke upon you, and learn from me; for I am gentle and humble in heart, and you will find rest for your souls."[64]

In addition to our intra-apparent form, we also have an outer-apparent form. Its purpose is to bring together the ways we choose to appear to others, depending on the circumstances.[65] For example, van Kaam noted,

> An undertaker on the job, no matter how jolly he may feel inwardly, must appear solemn and slightly sad when dealing with the bereaved. A bartender, on the contrary, must appear jolly on the outside even when he is somewhat cantankerous on the inside. . . . In many instances, such divergences may be necessary for effective functioning in the community. They are the expected and needed social symbols. Therefore, they are not necessarily deceptive or inwardly disintegrating as intentionally deceptive appearances would be.[66]

Consonant outer-apparent forms enable us to live at peace with others, while being true to who we are. They integrate the relationships we enjoy with the dispositions and directives of our core form as it expresses our truest self. Dissonant outer-apparent forms, used to deceive others or ourselves, are more disintegrative than integrative. The shocking fall of a political or religious leader, who is discovered to be leading a "double-life," is but one case of the fruits of a dissonant, disintegrative outer-apparent form.

Van Kaam delineated the inter-apparent form to articulate that there can be ways in which others perceive us differently from the ways in which we perceive ourselves.[67] At times, our self-perceptions are more in tune with who we most deeply are. At other times, others' perceptions of us are more insightful. Who of us has not been taken aback by the insight of a stranger who seemingly has little relationship with us, or a child, who articulates some facet of our core form to which we were blind? When outlining the ins and outs of our apparent forms, van Kaam highlighted the fact that in

---

63. Ibid., 58; van Kaam and Muto, *Formation of the Christian Heart*, 28–29. His analysis of the intra-apparent form dictated van Kaam's selection of the word "apparent" in the naming of these integrational structures. He noted in so doing the limited view any of us has as to who we truly are at any particular time (van Kaam, *Transcendent Formation*, 62).

64. Matt 11:28–30.

65. van Kaam, *Transcendent Formation*, 62–63.

66. Ibid., 63.

67. Ibid., 62–63.

the Christian spiritual tradition, it is the disposition of humility that most helps us to acknowledge the limited perceptions we have of ourselves and others.[68] Through it, we nurture a willingness for our apparent form to grow in greater consonance with our Christ form.

Neuroform

As an empirical integrating structure of our human life form, the neuroform refers to our sensate reality as enmeshed in our vital dimension. It involves our body chemistry, DNA, and autonomic nervous system. While the neuroform cannot be reduced to neurobiology, it serves as the "informer, selector, guardian, and executive neuro-hormonal agent" that affects, for example, our memory, imagination, and anticipation.[69] Deformation of the neuroform gives rise to coercive dispositions and such deformative patterns of behavior as anxiety and fear, which may become embedded in our core form and matching character.

Formational or deformational experiences, already in infancy, reveal the emergence of certain patterns that become embedded in our autonomic nervous systems and may as a result become automatically triggered.[70] The neuroform registers the patterns of our resulting vital memory; it thus becomes the "neurological referent" of the dispositions that make up our core form.[71] In other words, the neuroform refers to the ways that we neurologically embody our main character dispositions. It acknowledges how this neurological system becomes conditioned to appraise "the millions of stimuli ... that impinge every second on our inner and outer senses."[72] The physical dynamics of the neuroform are significant in our overall spiritual formation. The patterns of neurological response to stimuli may be either obvious to us or hidden. They may be "relatively available to our formation conscience and freedom or they may be coercive ... rigid and less flexible."[73]

Coercive dynamics of our neuroform not only lodge in our physicality by repetition; they may bypass our focal attentiveness altogether and become embedded deep in our infraconsciousness.[74] When this happens, such dynamics end up being resistant to reformation and transformation, though

68. Ibid., 57; van Kaam and Muto, *Formation of the Christian Heart*, 52, 55.
69. van Kaam, *Transcendent Formation*, 112.
70. van Kaam, *Transcendence Therapy*, 138–39.
71. van Kaam, *Transcendent Formation*, 112.
72. Ibid.
73. Ibid., 112.
74. Infraconsciousness will be explained in chapter 6 of this book.

not impossibly so. Our neuroform is meant to be a flexible instrument for the expression of our unique-communal life-call. If we fail to enlist its service to further our calling, we risk being at the mercy of the neuroform as it was programmed coercively earlier in life. According to van Kaam, coercive neuro-formational dispositions can be reformed with the help of God's redeeming grace. We are not liberated all at once, as if by magic, from deep-rooted deformations but, like a laser beam, the light of the transcendent can cut the link between the coercive dispositions of our neuroform and their resulting deformations.

What then constitute obstacles to reformation of the neuroform? The first obstacle is falling into the trap of believing, "that's just the way I am," and not being convinced that we are able to combat our weaknesses and submit our neuroform to reformation and transformation. The second is a lack of awareness regarding the nature of coercive dispositions, including their roots and their power. The third obstacle is not living in the light of our unique-communal life-call and remaining entrapped in activism, functionalism, consumerism, and careerism. Despite these obstacles, the Mystery wants to reconfigure the graced direction of our life, now and in the future.

What then are the conditions facilitating reformation of the neuroform that van Kaam identified? The first condition is a growing awareness of those coercive dispositions that have acquired such a power over us that it is almost as if they have become our second nature.[75] The second is a diminishment of the illusion that we can control these coercions by our own willpower alone.[76] The third condition to facilitate reformation of our neuroform is a remembrance of who we most deeply are, including the practice of restoring appreciation for our unique-communal life-call.[77] The fourth is a finer attunement to how we handle failure: are we increasingly free from feelings of false guilt and beginning to appreciate that in every obstacle there is a formation opportunity?[78] The fifth is not allowing feelings of depreciative abandonment *by* the Mystery to retard our appreciative abandonment *to* the Mystery.[79] And, finally, van Kaam highlighted the fact that we need to take moments for "inner vacation and recollection" that distance us from the reemergence of coercive dispositions and their impact upon us in the past.[80]

---

75. van Kaam, *Transcendent Formation*, 129–30, 260.
76. Ibid., 255–56.
77. Ibid., 129.
78. Ibid., 230–31, 269.
79. Ibid., 259–60.
80. Ibid., 260–61.

In relation to these reformational efforts, we must always take into account our innate temperament. Van Kaam articulated, as part of the neuroform, the importance of our inherited temperamental makeup through his construct of the temper form. He linked temperament to both our physical and our mental orientation, describing the temper form as the "genetic neuro-muscular-hormonal system" that expresses the "inherited range of our minimal and maximum rate of speed of mental and physical movement" and "the particular range and intensity of our vital emotion and passion."[81] Van Kaam noted that while we can exercise some control over the conditions and expressions of our temper form, doing so is limited, for the temper form has an enduring basic quality to it.[82]

As spirit-in-the-flesh, we exist within the boundaries of our temper form, our early conditioned neuroform, and the overall parameters of our vital human embodiment. Contrary to deterministic points of view, as we have seen, reformation of both the neuroform and temper form are possible to some degree in what van Kaam described as a post-transcendent state of life. According to his belief, the Holy Spirit works to reform and transform the entirety of who we are in the light of the Christ form. As van Kaam and Muto write in the first volume of their Formation Theology series,

> Jesus Christ in his humanity and divinity models in the fullest possible way the integration of divine form-reception and donation. He invites us to share here on earth in his pristine obedience to the Father. Through him, with him, and in him we empty ourselves of the counterfeit forms rooted in the prideform of our lapsed existence. No longer do we see our gifts as mere enhancements of our lower "I." The Holy Spirit enables us to liberate ourselves from such prideful assumptions and to find our true identity in the Christ-form of our soul.[83]

Actual Form

Finally, the actual form encompasses all the integrating structures taken together. It is the integrating principle that gathers up the dynamics of the core form, the current form, the apparent form, and the neuroform. It serves as the "present-moment integration" of our entire formation field—illuminating our consonance with the Mystery and the integration of our inner and

---

81. Ibid., 112.
82. Ibid.
83. van Kaam and Muto, *Foundations of Christian Formation*, 35.

outer life.[84] The actual form entails our basic, holistic readiness to appraise and actualize at any one moment the concrete responses we give to any situation.[85] It serves as a kind of "intermediate . . . approximation" of who we are called to be. From a Christian perspective, it refers to our living here and now in faithfulness to our calling in the Lord.[86]

Van Kaam summarized the relationship among these empirical integrating structures as follows:

> Core, current, and apparent life-forms integrate our form dimensions in an initial basic way. This integration of our dimensional *form potencies* provides us with an appropriate, general response-readiness in our typical formation field. These three integrational form structures attune us basically to the life situations we are lastingly, currently, and apparently living. In concrete everyday life, however, we are faced with events, people, and things that demand a holistic approach which integrates relevant responses contained in each one of these three integrational forms of life. Our *actual life-form* is a flexible integration of our relevant lasting core convictions, of our usual current reactions and responses to our present day situations, and of the ways we have disposed ourselves to appear to others. Hence our actual life-form not only has to select what is appropriate from the three initial integrational form structures. It must add to this its own inventive adaptations in order to deal effectively and creatively with each new emergence. Our actual life-form thus both draws upon and transcends our usual core, current, and apparent life-forms and their dispositions.[87]

Conclusion

One of the popular concepts within contemporary spiritual literature is the distinction between the true self and the false self. We have seen in this chapter that van Kaam's understanding of this distinction is more nuanced

---

84. van Kaam, *Transcendence Therapy*, 252; van Kaam and Muto, *Essential Elements*, s.v. "Actual Life Form as Integrational."

85. van Kaam, *Transcendent Formation*, 29.

86. From a van Kaamian perspective, full integration would mean that our lives were in complete consonance, or alignment, with God and with our Christ form (see van Kaam, *Fundamental Formation*, 259–60, 287; van Kaam and Muto, *Foundations of Christian Formation*, 119–20; van Kaam and Muto, *Essential Elements*, s.vv. "Outcome of Actual Life Form" and "Actual Life Form as Integrational").

87. van Kaam, *Fundamental Formation*, 260 (emphases his).

than the ways in which it is popularly discussed. He explored the fine lines of the relationship between our pre-empirical essence and the way it is incarnated in our everyday existence. He distinguished the false self more accurately as the pride form. Theologically speaking, the pride form is a pre-empirically counterfeit spiritual dynamic that results in widespread deformative consequences in all facets of our formation field.[88] Interforming with the pre-empirical pride form are the empirical integrating structures that may strengthen, weaken, or maintain the influence of the pride form throughout our life. Only with the help of grace can we be opened to the realignment of our founding form with the redeeming Christ form of our soul in us since our incorporation into the Body of Christ.

The emphasis van Kaam gave to the fact that our preformed essence, our founding form, respects both our transcendent and incarnational nature was central to his thinking as a personality theorist. It merits repeating that from the beginning, the science and anthropology of formation were designed to be conducive to and compatible with the Christian revelation. Van Kaam's essence-existence structure respects the age-old truth that grace illumines and uplifts nature and that our human anthropology is a servant source of our Judeo-Christian theology.

Reflection Questions

1. Understanding Our Story: Reflecting on an Invitation to Reformation

    In this chapter, we learned about the fact that while much of life is constantly changing, there is also a kind of relative stability to our lives and the way we give and receive form throughout our formation field. Van Kaam used the idea of integrating structures to articulate these various stabilizing dynamics of human formation. He described God's original intent for who we are made to be as our founding form, and noted that the pride form, which is part of human formation because of the presence of sin in the world, tries to exalt itself as the ultimate definer of who we are. Thankfully, because of the redemptive work of the Holy Trinity, our founding form may be transformed into newness of life, into the Christ form of our soul.

    Van Kaam also noted that much of the relative stability of our formation results from the fact that facets of our given personality and our life experiences are physically embedded in our bodies (in our neuroform). Van Kaam used all of the various integrating structures

---

88. van Kaam, *Transcendence Therapy*, 251.

to help articulate the myriad ways in which, while we are constantly experiencing the dynamism of formation, we at the same time experience a relative stability in the way we live as disciples of Jesus Christ in this world. One of the ongoing invitations of the Holy Spirit to us is for us to grow in consonance with God's will, not only in terms of what we do at any given moment, but in terms of who we are in Christ.

In this light, consider a time when you realized that your basic attitude or way of being in your life was not in tune with who God has called you to be as his beloved child. Describe what was happening: Was anyone else present at the time? If so, who? What exactly was it that brought attention to your need for reformation? When you realized that this facet of your way of living was not in tune with God's desires for you, how did you feel?

Thanks be to God, we know that as God's children, we are empowered by the Holy Spirit to be transformed "from glory to glory," into the image of our Lord Jesus Christ. For most of us, having a facet of our lives transformed into wholeness does not usually happen instantaneously (although there are instances when this may happen). Most often, habits of being are deeply embedded in our neuroform and thus they require ongoing reformation expressed in specific practices like repentance, motivated and empowered by God's Spirit, for lasting change to occur. Continue to reflect on the facet of your life that God's Spirit invited you to change by bringing it to your attention. Describe any reforming practices at the time that you felt called to begin. Has any change in this area of your life occurred since the time on which you are reflecting? If so, describe as specifically as possible what helped nurture this change in your life. If not (or if not very much), ask God now to guide your thinking to one or two new ways you can pursue to nurture needed change in your life.

Pause for a while to be with God and allow God to be present to you in these reflections. Now ask yourself how the Holy Spirit has inspired you to identify obstacles to living from your heart, as well as conditions that facilitate your openness to embodying in the whole of your life your unique-communal life-call in Christ.

2. Understanding God's Story: Reflection on the Heart of a Favorite Bible Character

   Throughout Scripture, we see many people who exemplify what van Kaam called the empirical integrating structures of the core form ("heart"), current form (expression of form reception and donation in a particular circumstance), apparent form (self-image and the image that others have of us), neuroform (expression of our physical embodiment over time), and actual form (the integration of all these empirical integrating structures in any given moment).

   Choose one of your favorite people from the Bible for whom some background and description is given (examples might include Abraham or Sarah, Moses or Jonathan, Hannah or Elizabeth, the Apostle John, or the woman with the issue of blood). Being as specific as possible, describe the person's heart (core form): what were some of the main characteristics of the person's inner life? Describe some of the ways that the person's core form was expressed in their physicality (neuroform) and in specific circumstances (current form). If you can, describe the way the person was shaped by a particular circumstance: What directives in a specific circumstance influenced the person's heart? In what ways did the person influence or give shape to a given circumstance, such that one can glimpse the person's heart expressed in actions?

   As you continue to reflect on this person, consider the influence the person had on others and the influence that others had on the person. Describe, as best as you are able, the person's self-image at any given moment in time (intra-apparent form). Describe, too, if you are able, the way the person most likely appeared to others (inter-apparent form). Were there any ways in which the person's self-image was more in tune with who God had called them to be than the way others saw them? Or were there any ways in which others saw more clearly in the person God's calling in them than the person did? Consider and, if you are able, describe any time of particular clarity and consonance in the person's life when their heart was most clearly expressed in a circumstance such that the person and others got a clear glimpse of who it was that God desired the person to be. If you are able, describe your sense of what that moment would have been like, both for the person and the other people who witnessed it.

   Describe any ways in which you find yourself responding to or perhaps resisting God's communications to this character in this moment.

Chapter 4

Dispositions

HAVE YOU EVER HEARD someone describe another person as generous, shy, bitter, or kind? In a church nursery one morning, a television monitor had been placed so that visiting parents could see and listen to what was going on in the sanctuary, where one of the regular Sunday school teachers was energetically explaining something to an adult Christian education class. Glancing at the monitor, one of the little children in the nursery asked, "Mommy, why is that man so angry?" While it had not been the teacher's intent to communicate anger during his lesson, even a toddler was able to detect what was a prominent disposition of the teacher's current, if not habitual, life form.

Dispositional Formation

While by no means describing you and me in our entirety, certain traits of ours communicate, mostly nonverbally, ways in which we approach others. These dispositions can be temporary or lasting. The term disposition points to a key dynamic of human presence and its concrete results in daily life.[1] If and when relatively long lasting, dispositions comprise and communicate a distinctive life orientation. These dispositions are identified by van Kaam as formation dispositions. He named them as such because they reveal how we tend to expend our formation energy.[2] Since they can be both formative

---

1. van Kaam, *Human Formation*, 15–17, 42–44. Van Kaam acknowledged the fact that both our human presence and our concrete interactions with our formation field interform with one another, so that there is an ongoing dialogue between actions and presence, ideally appraised as effective or ineffective.

2. Ibid., 1, 5–6. The concept of disposition is central to van Kaam's theory of formative spirituality: the word occurs more than two thousand times in all seven of the volumes of the Formative Spirituality series, and in fact one full volume of that series (*Human Formation*) is dedicated to his explication of the concept of dispositions. While related to the concept of habit, van Kaam purposefully chose the phrase "formation disposition" to distinguish this concept from what he considered rather static, functional

and deformative, they constitute powerful influences on our spiritual life that need to be appraised.

Dispositions are designed to "insure an economy of energy."[3] Rather than calling upon all of our appraisal powers to be on high alert during every waking moment, which would be exhausting, dispositions enable us to sense and respond to formation field demands in ways that minimize the amount of appraisal required to deal with them. This economy of energy allows us to reserve a more focused process for situations that do require special attention.[4] They specify and embody how we apprehend, assess, affirm, and apply what best contributes to our competency in responding to the countless situations that demand our attention day by day.[5] Some dispositions are inherent in our original makeup, while others may be learned or, in some rare cases, may be supernaturally "infused" in us by God.[6] All of our dispositions, taken together like the fibers of muscle tissue, comprise our actual form at this moment of our lives.[7]

Formation dispositions incline us to move in some directions and not in others. They help to embody our inclinations both to ongoing form reception and form donation.[8] These dual facets of dispositional formation give coherence, shape, and direction to our lives. While they are potentially open to the transcendent dimension of our human spirit, not all dispositions are, in fact, spiritually directed.

What makes a particular disposition spiritual, according to van Kaam, is its openness to the aspirations of the human spirit (and also, in the lives of Christians, to the inspirations of the Holy Spirit).[9] When these influences are acknowledged, they enable us to follow more faithfully the direction inspired by our calling in life.[10] Van Kaam named two primary characteristics of spiritual dispositions. First, they are consonant with our unique-

---

connotations of the concept of habit as it was often used in behavioral training paradigms (see ibid., 3–4, for his explanation of this choice of terminology).

3. Ibid., 6.
4. Ibid.
5. Ibid.
6. Ibid., 6–7. Van Kaam, *Formation of the Human Heart*, 122.
7. van Kaam, *Human Formation*, 1. Recall from the previous chapter that van Kaam made some distinctions as to certain dispositions being part of our heart, or core form, thus influencing our actual form. For more details regarding disposition formation, see chapter 9, "Fundamental Formation Dispositions of the Heart" in van Kaam, *Human Formation*, 165–76.
8. Ibid., 1–4, 42–44.
9. Ibid., 29; van Kaam and Muto, *Foundations of Christian Formation*, 190.
10. van Kaam, *Human Formation*, 2, 12–13.

communal life-call. Second, they are pliable, which is to say that they enable us to respond flexibly and dynamically to the directives disclosed to us in any and all formation events.[11]

The challenge we face is to align our dispositions as much as possible with our transcendent dimension and its various expressions. Dispositions that are not spiritual, for example stubborn inflexibility, may prove to be unaligned with the transcendent. Such isolated, unappraised dispositions are identified by van Kaam as merely routine or routinizing; this is what makes them dangerously deformative, especially if they have become closed off from the influence of God's Spirit.[12] Our dispositions begin to be spiritualized to the degree that we allow the light of the transcendent dimension to illumine them.[13] In Christian spirituality we go a step further and ask for the grace to place that to which we are disposed in dialogue with the pneumatic-ecclesial dimension of our life.

For example, consider a person with a pushy disposition, observable throughout her formation field, including when she is driving a car. Becoming aware of this disposition, this person may pray to spiritualize her pushiness. She may then sense that God wants to set her free from always having to be in a hurry. Her spirit becomes more receptive to this invitational inspiration from the Holy Spirit to live with more patience. She chooses to respond to this invitation by a willingness to learn new habits. She might consider leaving for work each day ten minutes earlier than usual, so that she does not feel as rushed during her drive, easing her habit of pushing by speeding and tailgating. While old habits do not disappear immediately, she can continue to ask for the grace of transformation to become more patient and gentle as she practices leaving early, driving by the speed limit, and lessening her tailgating as ways of indicating her desire to repent. As dispositions yield to influence from the transcendent and pneumatic-ecclesial dimensions, their dynamics are spiritualized.

This yielding results in dispositions that are increasingly devoid of ego-dominating coercions. Such dispositions exhibit, in turn, a rhythm of differentiation and integration. That is to say, they differentiate into dispositions

---

11. Ibid., 2–3.

12. Ibid., 31–34; van Kaam and Muto, *Formation of the Christian Heart*, 199.

13. Van Kaam noted that there are some dispositions that are, like peace and joy, by their very nature rooted in the transcendent dimension and which thus are inherently spiritual. He distinguished these from dispositions that, while not inherently rooted in the transcendent dimension, can come under the influence of the spirit. The former he noted as having a "primary affiliation" and the latter a "secondary affiliation" with the transcendent dimension (for his discussion of this distinction, see van Kaam, *Human Formation*, 29–31).

and deeds that incarnate transcendent aspirations and pneumatic-ecclesial inspirations in all facets of our formation field. At the same time, they integrate new disclosures brought to our attention the more we live in fidelity to our unique-communal life-call. We seek consonance with the Divine Forming and Preforming Mystery at the center of our field. We are grateful for the gifts of harmonious differentiation and integration as we strive to receive and give to our life consonant rather than dissonant form.

Foundational Dispositions

Formative dispositions embed and express themselves in all layers of our actual life form. According to van Kaam, those rooted in the transcendent are by far the most significant since they mirror our striving for consonance with the Mystery in awe, wonder, reverence, and adoration. Such transcendently grounded dispositions allow the expression of who we are most deeply to take precedence over dispositions embedded in the pretranscendent dimensions of our personhood, namely, the sociohistorical, vital, or functional dimensions.[14] "Christian character formation discloses a constellation of dispositions and directives that become the building blocks of our true, transcendent identity."[15] Following in the footsteps of many writers in the literature of Christian spirituality, van Kaam made note of the fact that traditional formation dispositions play a great role in character formation. Examples of such dispositions would include: faith, hope, and charity; prudence, justice, fortitude, and temperance; and humility, detachment, and surrender to God for the sake of loving and serving others. Other examples of traditional formation dispositions affirmed throughout the literature of Christian spirituality are appreciation, openness, flexibility, spontaneity, obedience, simplicity, reverence, unselfishness, non-coerciveness, courage, generosity, social presence, purity, and love.[16] Such Christian virtues permeate our faith and formation traditions while signaling the place and importance of spiritual dispositions in our overall life formation.

---

14. van Kaam and Muto, *Essential Elements*, s.v. "Hierarchy of Character Dispositions." Foundational to van Kaam's idea of consonance are the C's of consonance, discussed in chapter 7 of this book.

15. Ibid.

16. For examples, see: van Kaam and Muto, *The Power of Appreciation*; van Kaam and Muto, *Essential Elements*, s.vv. "Disposition of Transcendent Openness," "Dispositions Beneficial to Formation," and "Disposition of Detachment"; van Kaam, *Formation of the Human Heart*, 22–29, 31–52, 55–59, 90–98, 323–324; Muto, *Virtues*.

Predisposition and Disposition of Awe

The essence of the awe disposition is one of "presence in ultimate reverence and wonder to the mystery that gives form to life and world."[17] Awe is essential to our being as created in God's image. It is also a gifted expression of our existence. As such, van Kaam identified awe as the central and primordial predisposition and disposition of the spiritual life.[18]

Why is awe primordial? First of all, since it is inherently transcendent, awe extends beyond the limits of sensory perception. Its object pole is the Mystery itself, the Holy Trinity.[19] Awe "disposes us to a life of enlightened presence to the mystery of people, events, and things in their deepest being," in light of their relationship to God.[20] Van Kaam wrote that awe

> implies a minimal awareness of the epiphanic meaning that transcends immediately observable effects of cultural acts. Presence in awe becomes a listening in reverence to the deepest meaning of our formation field. It manifests itself in loving obedience and abandonment to the mystery speaking in all events, in interformative compatibility and compassion, and in respectful presence to things.[21]

Awe inspires worship. An example from a form theological perspective would be Psalm 103, which begins and ends with a swell of blessings to the Lord for the attributes (dispositions, if you will) of divine loving-kindness, holiness, mercy, and gracious sovereignty.

Welling up from the truth of who we are called to be, awe also serves as a source of consonance and unity.[22] It "endows our life with the assurance, graciousness, peace, and wholeness given to those who have discovered the Infinite in the finite, who have accepted the personal epiphany of the formation mystery in their own soul as an invitation to union with their deepest ground."[23] In this sense, it is of primordial importance in the life of the spirit.

Adrian van Kaam lived through the horrors of deprivation during the infamous Dutch Hunger Winter and witnessed its devastation in the lives of many people. Yet despite this extreme circumstance, he maintained that the predisposition for awe, while it may lie dormant due to refusal or

---

17. van Kaam, *Human Formation*, 183.
18. Ibid., 177.
19. Ibid., 177, 183.
20. Ibid., 181; van Kaam and Muto, *Formation of the Christian Heart*, 75.
21. Ibid., 215.
22. Ibid., 182.
23. Ibid., 181.

repudiation of it, never fully disappears in a person. Awe is always present and open to awakening by the Mystery due to its unbroken connection to our distinctively human transcendence dynamic.

Reflection on any experience of awe, especially what happens to us during overwhelming moments of wonder, also carries with it an awareness of the human inability to maintain consonance with the Mystery at all times.[24] The full experience of awe is a gift that inundates our total field of consciousness; it is profound and overwhelming. It involves full absorption of our form-receptive potency in a graced disclosure of the Mystery. Although we fall short of sustained awe, that experience can be diffused insofar as it runs underneath our everyday engagements in a more implicit way, as a veiled testimony to our presence to the Mystery experienced at heightened moments of full awe. Sadly, at times we can invert awe through arrogance, exalting our pride form as though it is the primordial dynamic of our life.[25] Inverted awe directs us to appraise everything in terms of self-exaltation and self-achievement. Instead of fostering appreciation of the Mystery, it increases our need for self-protection and our disrespect of others. However, when such inversion of awe happens, the dissonance one feels signals a longing to restore a sense of oneness with the Mystery in awe-filled abiding and attention.[26] Furthermore, according to van Kaam, awe can be repudiated or refused.[27] In that case, it leads to one or the other form of idolatry: certain values in the culture are idolized in isolation from the Mystery, instead of seeing them as limited manifestations of the Mystery.

The healthy, primordial disposition of awe serves as an anchoring, integrating disposition that directs us to abide "in our deepest center" in relation to the Mystery.[28] Flowing from the awe disposition are numerous other virtues that help us to become more fully expressive of our humanity, as well, for the Christian, as more Christlike.[29]

24. Van Kaam distinguished experiences of intense, overwhelming wonder, which he termed "full awe," from a life orientation toward connecting all of one's living with reverence and worship of the Mystery, which he called "diffused awe." For his discussion of this distinction, see *Human Formation*, 183–85.

25. van Kaam, *Human Formation*, 193.

26. Ibid., 205–9.

27. Ibid., 214–15; see van Kaam, *Fundamental Formation*, 161–62, for further discussion of refused awe.

28. Ibid., 182.

29. Note that when van Kaam discussed spiritual dispositions in the context of his formative theological language, he would refer to them as virtues. At times, he used the language of preexisting theological categories of virtues from his Roman Catholic tradition, such as: faith, hope, and love as infused theological virtues; prudence, justice, fortitude, and temperance as cardinal virtues; and obedience, poverty of spirit, and

Foundational Dispositional Triad

Van Kaam identified a main fruit of awe as the foundational dispositional triad of faith, hope, and consonance.[30] The connection between awe and the birth of these virtues in the Christian life is the primordial abandonment option to entrust ourselves to the source of all love, the Holy Trinity.[31] Our sense of being reborn in Christ is but one outcome of living in awe.

The groundwork of faith, hope, and consonance (love) ought to be established ideally in infancy and early childhood. Unquestionably important in this regard is the care of parents and early caregivers, who tangibly express their love for us, who hope that we have a meaningful future, and who live in the faith that we are able to move toward that goal.[32] Such faith, hope, and consonance, while potentially communicated to us through our parents or their substitutes, are ultimately graced experiences of the care of the Mystery.[33] For example, in the *Confessions* of St. Augustine, we see the way this early church father attributed the care and nurture of his infancy and childhood, given to him by his mother, Monica, to the gracious lovingkindness of God.[34] From the perspective of formation theology, when we are baptized, we are the recipients of these three foundational virtues, which are supernaturally infused in us through Christ. We receive more than the human dispositions of faith, hope, and consonance. God gradually transforms them into the theological virtues of faith, hope, and charity that exemplify the supernatural life of Christ in us.[35]

---

chaste love as the evangelical counsels (van Kaam and Muto, *Essential Elements*, s.v. "Hierarchy of Character Dispositions").

30. van Kaam, *Human Formation*, 9. Note that while van Kaam most often used the term consonance as the third disposition of this triad throughout his work, in his first volume of the Formative Spirituality series he equated his central construct of consonance ultimately with love. For examples of this correlation, among others, see van Kaam, *Fundamental Formation*, glossary, s.v. "Primordial Decision"; and van Kaam and Muto, *Dynamics of Spiritual Direction*, 85–86.

31. van Kaam, *Fundamental Formation*, glossary, s.v. "Primordial Decision"; van Kaam, *Human Formation*, 14; van Kaam and Muto, *Formation of the Christian Heart*, 197–98.

32. van Kaam, *Human Formation*, 52–54. Van Kaam identified the fact that the initial groundwork for these seminal dispositions as bodily in nature once again highlights his non-dualistic view of Christian spiritual formation. See also: van Kaam and Muto, *Essential Elements*, s.v. "Foundational Formative Triad in Childhood."

33. van Kaam and Muto, *Dynamics of Spiritual Direction*, 86.

34. Augustine, *Confessions*, 1.6.7.

35. van Kaam, *Human Formation*, 163–64; van Kaam and Muto, *Foundations of Christian Formation*, 129; van Kaam and Muto, *Christian Articulation of the Mystery*, 97–98.

Three Crucial Pairings of Spiritual Dispositions

Van Kaam identified three pairs of spiritual dispositions facilitating wholesome spiritual living and growth in consonance.[36] The first pair consists of sensibility and responsibility.[37] The term sensibility is traceable to a person's early "vital excitability."[38] Under the influence of the transcendent dimension, this affective thrust of our vital dimension contributes to our openness to every formation opportunity life offers us.[39] Its complementary disposition of responsibility refers to our cognitive capacity to respond to and act upon what we receive sensibly.[40] This disposition expresses our ability to respond to the invitations and directives that come to us from all quadrants of our formation field.[41] These two dispositions begin to emerge in childhood, but only later in life are they integrated fully with the transcendent dimension. As they come to fruition in caring hearts, they give empirical expression to our potential for form reception and form donation. Because sensibility emerges through our vital dimension, and responsibility through our functional dimension, this pair of dispositions is important in the healthy integration of our physicality and spirituality.[42]

When this integration does not occur, van Kaam and Muto caution that it may affect our quality of social presence. Following a period of exalted social aspirations and ambitions, we may detect growing dissonance between these thrusts toward egocentric activism and the inescapable reality of our situation, including how exhausted we are and how negligent our prayer life has become. We feel an inner tug-of-war between unrealistic plans and projects that, despite our best efforts, never seem to materialize, and our realistic, always limited accomplishments. To the degree that we deny this dissonance—going through the motions of ministry though our heart is not in it—we risk the erosion and possible depletion of effective social presence, shaking us to the core of our being.[43] We need to be coura-

---

36. Van Kaam devoted the third volume of his Formative Spirituality series (*Formation of the Human Heart*) to an explication of these and related dispositions.

37. These dispositions were introduced in relation to the vital dimension in chapter 2 of this book.

38. van Kaam, *Human Formation*, 58.

39. Ibid., 172.

40. Ibid., 58. For a thorough description of how we grow in the dispositions of sensibility and responsibility in relation to our life in Christ, see van Kaam and Muto, *Formation of the Christian Heart*, 68–70.

41. van Kaam, *Human Formation*, 170–72.

42. Ibid., 59, 170–73.

43. van Kaam, *Formation of the Human Heart*, 18–23.

geous enough to face these symptoms and find a solution to them, not by complaining about them or blaming others for them, but by reaffirming our willingness with the help of God to do whatever the incarnation of our duty demands within the realistic limits of our formation field. With proper repletion, we may be able to avoid depletion altogether.[44]

Another pair of formative dispositions identified by van Kaam is the complimentary set of firmness and gentleness. He wrote: "The consonant life is a blend of firm gentleness and gentle firmness. . . . Firmness without gentleness deteriorates into severity; gentleness without firmness becomes debilitating weakness."[45] Firmness calls for a gentle yet focused effort to discipline our lives. It enables us to cope with resistances in daily life, whether they arise from internal or external sources. Firmness is the key to perseverance in such issues as structural injustice and oppression. It fosters decisiveness in the face of directives that invite us to be more in tune with the Mystery's purposes for us and the world around us.[46] Firmness aids our overcoming of self-indulgences. It is formative to the degree that it is grounded in "a believing and loving presence, not . . . anger and irritation."[47] Formation in firmness is an expression of our potency for spiritual growth and Christian maturation. It is the opposite of blind stubbornness or harsh condemnation; it goes together with deep joy in the consonant incarnation of our life-call in Christ.[48] For example, Dr. Martin Luther King Jr. exhibited the dispositions of both gentleness and firmness in his leadership of the Civil Rights Movement of the 1960s in the United States. He encouraged his followers to overcome evil with love. The love he advocated was not an expression of pseudo-gentility, but love rooted in the conviction that all human persons are created in the image of God and are thus deserving of respect. And it was this kind of love that expressed itself in actions to draw attention to systemic inequities that resisted the affirmation of the equality and dignity of African-Americans.[49]

---

44. van Kaam and Muto, *Formation of the Christian Heart*, 183–87; van Kaam, *Formation of the Human Heart*, chapter 22, "Social Presence: Depletion, Repletion, Restoration," 333–59.

45. van Kaam, *Formation of the Human Heart*, 83.

46. Ibid., 6–7, 70–72.

47. Ibid., 67.

48. van Kaam and Muto, *Christian Articulation of the Mystery*, 186–87.

49. For specific examples of Dr. Martin Luther King Jr.'s sermons, exhorting people to both firmness and gentleness, see, among others, the collection of his sermons in *Strength to Love* and *I Have a Dream*.

Gentleness disposes us to be present to others in a caring way. It expresses reverence and respect for what is both "valuable and vulnerable."[50] A gentle person is better able to see the presence of the Mystery permeating their formation field. Gentleness nurtures trustful abandonment to God, patient "abiding," openness and receptivity, stillness and playfulness, all of which contribute to a healthy balance between labor and leisure.[51] Van Kaam embraced gentleness as an effective remedy to reform unhealthy anger and turn it into a healthy anger that sparks creativity.[52] He encouraged us to make a distinction between authentic gentleness and pseudo-gentility. Pseudo-gentility is a false form of gentleness. As a feat of self-mastery that entails ignoring dissonance, it can contribute to volatile forms of anger and rage.[53] Van Kaam noted that people who equate pseudo-gentility with spirituality feel as if they must act gently, no matter the reality of the dissonances they experience inwardly and outwardly. Authentic gentleness is not self-generated; it is a receptive disposition grounded in respect for and communion with the love of the Mystery for all of creation.

In contrast to the interpretation of Christian spirituality as a kind of solitary journey embedded in the intrasphere, van Kaam said, "No one can grow by private experience alone. Everyone needs feedback from the inter- and outer spheres."[54] Thus, a third pair of dispositions emphasized by him as formative for consonant living is that of privacy and communion. The disposition of privacy orients us to ponder in awe our calling in the Mystery.[55] It is a distinctively human characteristic. Privacy "inclines us to retreat periodically into . . . private life" for the purposes of "fostering consonance in our formation field as a whole."[56] The disposition of privacy "protects" the intrasphere of our formation field and disposes us to focus on the unique facets of our life-call.[57]

---

50. van Kaam, *Formation of the Human Heart*, 84–85.

51. Ibid., 85–88, 122–23.

52. Ibid., 88–90.

53. For a helpful discussion of his distinction between genuine gentleness and pseudo-gentility, see van Kaam, *Formation of the Human Heart*, 91–97, 102–14. For practical guidance in the reformation of a disposition of anger, see van Kaam, *Spirituality and the Gentle Life*.

54. van Kaam, *Formation of the Human Heart*, 151. For van Kaam's extensive discussion of formative and deformative privacy dispositions, see 125–236 (chapters 8–14 in this volume of the Formative Spirituality series).

55. Ibid., 129.

56. Ibid., 140–41.

57. Ibid., 129–31.

The complimentary disposition of communion has as its ultimate goal to help us communicate with one another, to freely form bonds of intimacy that enable us to "share convictions, dispositions, motivations, and problems in regard to specific ideals."[58] Such shared intimacy cannot and should not be forced. It is a gift that fosters balance between our awareness of being unique and yet being related in some way to everyone and everything in our formation field. In other words, while the disposition of privacy cautions us to pay attention to facets of uniqueness like congeniality and compatibility, the disposition of communion makes us more aware of our shared sense of belonging to the human family and the wider world in compassion and competence.[59] Many ancient, medieval, and modern contemplatives throughout Christian history, such as Augustine of Hippo, Teresa of Avila, and Dietrich Bonhoeffer, have witnessed to the fact that a life of prayerful solitude is never for the sake of our own fame and glory, but for the sake of loving and serving God and others in a fully called, committed, and consecrated way. For example, in her classic book on the life of prayer, *The Interior Castle*, Teresa of Avila writes: "Let us desire and be occupied in prayer not for the sake of our own enjoyment, but so as to have this strength to serve."[60]

In situations requiring appraisal, human beings have the option of withholding or exercising their privacy disposition. Even under torture, good soldiers are trained not to give information that would betray their nation. At one time, the good of the community may demand privacy. At another time, the individual may need to reveal what was kept private in order to serve the community in solidarity. Life presents situations in which people struggle to know how to exercise these two correlative dispositions with integrity. The fitting use of both privacy and communion as continuous lasting dispositions of our heart and our matching character fine tunes our spiritual sensitivity and responsibility.

Dispositional Sources and Initial Formation

When trying to ascertain the origins of formation dispositions, van Kaam concluded that they may be preformed, acquired, or infused. Preformed dispositions are those that exist in our original biogenetic givenness. They are embedded in our cells, tissues, and vital systems as part of our given physical and genetic makeup.[61] Such dispositions shape the pulsions and strivings of

---

58. Ibid., 240.
59. Ibid., 246–48.
60. Teresa of Avila, *The Interior Castle*, 192.
61. van Kaam, *Human Formation*, 6–7.

our vital dimension.[62] It is not uncommon in multigenerational families to note similarities in such preformed dispositions between children and their parents, grandparents, aunts or uncles, even when the children have had little (or no) interactions with the adults with whom they share dispositions.

Acquired dispositions are those gained by us through interformation with our field of presence and action and the events we live through, starting in earliest infancy. While our preformed dispositions exert influence on our formation field, our ability to exercise free will in choosing certain dispositions to adopt or reject is at once both free and limited. As infants, we are mainly form receptive. As such, in our earliest life we first acquire certain dispositions through "situational osmosis" and nurture.[63] As life unfolds, these acquired dispositions continue to emerge through repeated acts that form and strengthen them.[64] Van Kaam made a distinction in dispositional development between mere functional repetition and what he called formative reiteration. In contrast to functional repetition of unappraised dispositions, formative reiteration involves an intentional repeating of acts that foster "growth in insight and personal presence" with "freedom and flexibility."[65] While automatic repetition may limit our perspective and narrow our openness to change, formative reiteration fosters the development of ways of being and acting that are open to the influence and direction of spirit-filled dispositions.

A third source of disposition formation identified by van Kaam is infusion. An infused disposition is "a pure gift of the mystery, an undeserved endowment" that has "an abiding quality" that does not waver.[66] The experience of one's having been granted by grace an infused disposition has been recounted, for example, in the conversion experience of Augustine of Hippo that took place in his garden, and the sudden warming of his heart in the Aldersgate experience of John Wesley. The details of their own and others' experiences of being infused by grace are not merely personal. Such awesome gifts are traceable to Scripture itself. Consider Mary's fiat or the Apostle Paul's conversion. The consistent evidence of such infusion led van Kaam to conclude that dispositions are not merely the result of nature or nurture, genetic predisposition or environment. At times, God may choose to sovereignly endow a person with a disposition that has no other explanation than that of being a gift received by the love and empowerment of God's Spirit.

62. Ibid., 7.
63. Ibid.
64. Ibid.
65. Ibid., 7–8.
66. van Kaam, *Formation of the Human Heart*, 122.

Van Kaam wrote of infused dispositions from two distinct vantage points. First, they can be understood as an ultimate, divine fulfillment of an already existing disposition, such as elevating vocal prayer to contemplative prayer. At times, divine infusion "completes and exceeds gratuitously our acquired disposition[s]. It melts the lingering vestiges of self-will and violence" and results in a lasting formative disposition that is utterly Christlike.[67] At other times, infused dispositions may also be understood as a source that originates new dispositions not previously experienced by a person.

For Christians, baptism is a beginning point at which certain dispositions are infused in us by God, including the overall "potency and tendency to be transformed by and to serve the transformation of inspirations and aspirations of the Holy Spirit," including "the divinely infused capacity to disclose the image and revelation of God."[68] Infused in us when we become a part of the people of God are the three theological virtues of faith, hope, and love.[69] In these contexts, van Kaam described such infused dispositions as, so to speak, originating potentials we are called to actualize over a lifetime of spiritual transformation.

So how do we embody the infused potentials given to us as gifts of the Spirit? What nurtures the spiritual reformation and transformation of our character and personhood? And what about dispositions in our lives that militate against the life of the Spirit, such as greed or arrogance?

Dispositional Transformation

Because of the Fall and its effects, both our preformed and acquired dispositions are prone to dissonance.[70] Such dispositions become dissonant because they continue to resist openness to the Mystery. Coercive dispositions, like vainglory and avarice, are rooted in our neuroform and automatically trigger directives that are obstacles to consonance.[71] Examples of common dissonant dispositions include pride, anger, an excessive need to be in control, envy, gluttony, lust, sloth, and suspicion of others.

---

67. Ibid.; van Kaam and Muto, *Formation of the Christian Heart*, 64.

68. van Kaam, *Fundamental Formation*, glossary, s.v. "Pneumatic Formation Potential"; van Kaam, *Transcendence Therapy*, 260.

69. van Kaam and Muto, *Formation of the Christian Heart*, 122–23.

70. van Kaam and Muto, *Essential Elements*, s.v. "Disguises Masking Dissonant Dispositions."

71. van Kaam, *Traditional Formation*, 252; van Kaam and Muto, *Essential Elements*, s.v. "Unmasking Coercive Character Dispositions."

Dissonant dispositions drive us to harshness and rigidity. They cause us to act in ways that are resistant to our unique-communal life-call in God.[72] They are set in motion before we are focally aware of what is happening.[73] Rooted in our neuroform, dissonant dispositions are difficult, if not impossible, to change without the enabling grace of God. When we become aware of their effects, it rests upon us to bring such dissonant dispositions and their coercive directives before "the healing, transfocal light of the Spirit" through confession and repentance.[74] How do we move toward such repentance and ask for the grace of reformation?

Spiritualization of Dispositions

Growing in the desire to respond appreciatively to God's plans and purposes for our lives requires divine direction through the grace of God. We need to open our minds and hearts to dispositional change in light of the divine directives of the Holy Spirit operating in our human spirit. As van Kaam so eloquently said,

> When the spirit is illumined in its encounter with the mystery, it mirrors this light into all dimensions and articulations of our formation. The same light shines into our dispositions. Having lost their rigidity, they are not only "disposing for" but "at the disposal of" the mystery. Dispositions will always be necessary as extensions of our human form potencies into the formation field. The mystery of formation is not only to be contemplated. It intends to form the world with and through us.
>
> Hence, we see the necessity of adaptive dispositions as bridges between inspirations and the concrete formation fields we are called to cultivate. These dispositions should be available to the mystery. The disposition that is mellowed by the mystery is no longer deterministic, deformative, or dissonant. It performs its functions fluently in harmony with its deepest source.[75]

Such spiritualization of dispositions begins when we place ourselves under the influence of the transcendent dimension, as directed and moved

---

72. van Kaam, *Human Formation*, 38–39; van Kaam and Muto, *Christian Articulation of the Mystery*, 78–80.

73. van Kaam and Muto, *Essential Elements*, s.v. "Neuroform as Source of Coercive Dispositions."

74. Ibid.

75. van Kaam, *Human Formation*, 40.

ultimately by the Mystery.[76] In due time, our dispositions are reformed by the patient, persistent work of the Holy Spirit.

Van Kaam identified three sources of spiritualization. They are motivation, reiteration, and participation. Ours is a motivation "for things not immediately seen and experienced, not tangible and instantaneous."[77] It happens in response to an invitation to dispositional spiritualization by the Spirit. Being open to and nurturing such a motivation is aided by "reflection and meditation on the meaning and content of spiritual aspirations that invite us to seek the transcendent formation of life."[78] Van Kaam observed that the depth and quality of motivation is contingent on at least three factors: "the intensity of appreciation by the appraisal power"; "the decisiveness of the will and its accompanying feelings"; and "the scope of enlistment of formative imagination, memory, and anticipation."[79] It is not enough to think, "I should change." Substantive character change led by the Spirit involves and affects the whole of our formation field.

Reiteration, a second facet of dispositional spiritualization, involves a gentle yet firm repetition of acts that express an orientation of our being that supports formative decisions and actions. Reiteration in this sense is not mechanical repetition that is imposed upon us. Reiterative acts are nurtured by spiritual motivation (aspirations and inspirations) and meaning.[80] While "mere mechanistic repetition" ends up undermining the spiritual receptivity of any disposition, actions that express attentive reiteration provide a way to correct coercions and to practice ways of being and acting that are spiritually healthy.[81] Such reiteration is, in a sense, an embodied prayer of repentance and openness to the Mystery, inviting the work of the Spirit to change our "hearts of stone into hearts of flesh."[82]

A third condition van Kaam identified as facilitating formational dispositional development is wholehearted participation. It reflects the phase at which a disposition has become so deeply rooted in us that it is a consistent, defining characteristic of our character.[83] The actual movement into participation involves four facets.

---

76. Ibid., 38–39.
77. Ibid., 36.
78. Ibid.
79. Ibid., 14.
80. Ibid., 7–8.
81. Ibid., 8.
82. Ezek 11:19–20.
83. van Kaam, *Human Formation*, 36–37.

The first facet of participation is participative transformation in, with, and through the transcendent and pneumatic source of all dispositional formation, the Holy Spirit. Van Kaam was careful to point continually to the "insufficiency of our own limited form potency" and our ultimate reliance on the indwelling Spirit to empower us in any spiritualization of a disposition.[84]

Second, movement into wholehearted participation involves growing in fidelity to the Christ-form of our soul and to our life-call as we have come to understand it at this point in time. Dispositional spiritualization encourages congeniality with our founding form. The consonant dispositions we hope to foster are strengthened to the degree that a particular disposition is "interwoven . . . with dispositions we have already developed in congeniality with the unique image we are called to realize in life."[85] New disclosures of our unique-communal life-call in Christ thus strengthen and sustain dispositions congenial with them.

Third, such formative participation involves openness to and formation by all spheres and dimensions of our formation field, especially the influence of the transcendence dynamic. Dispositional transformation never occurs in isolation from, but in response to and within the context of, all the events and dynamics occurring in our formation field and in our day-to-day life in the world.

Fourth, wholehearted participation involves adherence to foundational faith and formation traditions.[86] True to his conviction that our formation is linked to these traditions, van Kaam noted that in order to initiate, maintain, and develop consonant dispositions, we need to participate in the belief systems to which we adhere in faith. They provide not only descriptions of desired dispositions, but also motivations for sustaining them. Such traditions offer supporting rituals and symbols, and "an environment and atmosphere bolstered by similarly disposed people" that facilitate the development of dispositions in full field appraisal that nurtures all the C's of consonance.[87] Through these four facets of formative participation, deformative dispositions and their coercive directives are ultimately reformed and transformed. This change is only possible through the patient, loving work of the Holy Trinity, appreciated and witnessed by us throughout our lifetimes.[88]

84. Ibid., 36.
85. Ibid., 36–37.
86. Ibid., 36.
87. Ibid., 37. We will discuss appraisal and the C's of Consonance in chapter 7.
88. van Kaam and Muto, *Essential Elements*, s.v. "Unmasking Coercive Character Dispositions." Note that van Kaam used the metaphor of water for what he called radical functional-transcendent reformation in his description of the threefold path

In his reflections on this work of the Spirit, van Kaam affirmed the necessity of our yielding to the invitations of the Spirit through a disposition of detachment. Healthy spiritual detachment frees us from the inordinate attachments rooted in our own autarkic pride form, and opens us to free and willing engagement in the leading of the Mystery.[89] In terms of formation theology, to grow in the grace of Christlikeness, we must be willing "to follow the path of suffering and joy Christ himself had to walk upon."[90] We are invited to deny ourself, take up our cross and, in his good company, to follow him.

Conclusion

Dispositional changes that shake us to the very core of our being can only be understood in relation to the initiation and empowerment of the Holy Trinity, inviting us to participate over a lifetime in the Mystery of transforming mercy and love. The process of inner and outer renewal often begins with transcendence crises that bring us face to face with the lingering coercive dispositions and directives that still cling to us like barnacles on a ship, but that until now may have escaped our awareness. Or, if we have been aware of them, we have perhaps not yet found ourselves ready to be released from their influences. Under the gentle and firm guidance of the Spirit, at the pace of grace and in the context of growing awe for the love of the Holy Trinity, through dispositional reformation and transformation, we reaffirm our choice to entrust ourselves to God in appreciative abandonment. We seek to be delivered from lifelong deformative dispositions as we choose in

---

of radical reformation, which is his way of interpreting the classic threefold path of purgation, illumination, and union found throughout much of the literature of Christian spirituality. As he developed his ideas throughout the years, he eventually chose the terminology of purifying formation, illuminating reformation, and unifying transformation. We can thus align his original metaphors of water, light, and fire with the parallel concepts of radical functional-transcendent reformation, radical transcendent formation, and radical transcendent-functional transformation. For his original parallels between these three terms and the metaphors of water, light, and fire, see van Kaam, *Transcendent Formation*, 236–37.

89. van Kaam, *Human Formation*, 164. See also Muto, *John of the Cross for Today: The Ascent* and *John of the Cross for Today: The Dark Night* for a thorough presentation of this master's insistence that "renunciation" (detachment) is the only sure road to "liberation" (free formation flow formed by union and communion with Father, Son, and Holy Spirit).

90. van Kaam and Muto, *Christian Articulation of the Mystery*, 99; van Kaam and Muto, *Foundations of Christian Formation*, 188. For further insights on this threefold path of faith deepening, see van Kaam and Muto, *Foundations of Christian Formation*, 59–60; van Kaam and Muto, *Living Our Christian Faith*, 107–9.

faith to affirm that nothing in our formation fields is beyond the purview and healing power of the Holy Spirit.

Purifying formation, illuminating reformation, and unifying transformation of our dispositions are pathways of fidelity to our unique-communal life-call and to consonance with the Trinitarian Mystery.[91] The disclosure and expression of our calling in Christ and the consonance that faithful embodiment of it throughout our formation field brings, will be detailed in the tenth and final chapter of this book.

Reflection Questions

1. Understanding Our Story: Reflecting on Awe and Other Consonant Dispositions in Our Lives

    In this chapter, we learned that van Kaam highlighted the formational significance of our basic life dispositions. He identified awe as the most primordial disposition for a healthy spiritual life, for awe both extends beyond the limits of our senses and fosters a sense of our relationship to God in reverence and worship. Van Kaam also identified as central to the Christian life the foundational dispositional triad of faith, hope, and love, and noted its foundations in early childhood development and, from a Christian perspective, in the gifts of God that come to us when we become a part of the Body of Christ. While dispositions are myriad, van Kaam also noted the need for a kind of balance and harmony in dispositions in order for us to live truly consonant lives.

    Allow God to be present to you as you reflect on the following questions:

    Gently reflect on a specific time that you experienced awe. Describe what was happening: Where were you? Was anyone else with you? What was it that inspired awe in you? As you reflect on this experience of awe, what arises in your heart now?

    Recall that van Kaam noted that faith, hope, and love are often first instilled in us from our parents or primary caregivers when we are infants. Reflect on your own infancy and childhood: Who was present to you in your earliest days? Throughout your childhood, were there tangible ways that your primary caring relationships expressed their love for you, their hope that you had a good future ahead of you, and their faith that it would be possible for you to move forward toward

---

91. van Kaam and Muto, *Christian Articulation of the Mystery*, 153–56.

that good future? If so, describe some of them and allow your heart to experience gratitude for this loving foundation in your life. If not, allow God to be present to you, for these are dispositions that God himself desires for you, as witnessed through the life of our Lord Jesus Christ as he walked on earth. Allow yourself to rest in God's love for, hope for, and faith in, you.

Three of the crucially paired dispositions that van Kaam identified were: 1) sensibility and responsibility; 2) firmness and gentleness; and 3) privacy and communion. As you reflect on these especially important formative dispositions, to which of them is your attention drawn? Why is that the case? Describe the gifts and challenges you experience in the balance between such dispositional pairs: Which of them come "naturally" to you? Which of such dispositions are more of a challenge for you in this season of life? Why do you believe this is the case? As you conclude this reflection, consider: How has the Holy Spirit inspired you to allow into your heart continuous, lasting dispositions that are more consonant with the Christ-formed character you want to be? What obstacles erode this consonance? What conditions facilitate it?

2. Understanding God's Story: Reflecting on Transformation of a Heart in a Bible Character

As van Kaam observed, while we have certain dispositional tendencies (due to genetic endowment, our life experiences, and the nurture of people around us), God invites us to dispositional transformation of any lasting dispositions in our lives that draw us away from consonance with God and who God has called us to be. For such dispositions to be changed, most often we undergo a slow process that involves motivation from God's Spirit, reiteration of practices that resist deformative dispositions and nurture formative ones, and eventually a holistic participation of all of who we are in a reformed disposition.

Choose one of the many people in the Bible who underwent a reformation of heart and life (examples include: Jacob or Leah, Judah or Esther, the Apostle Thomas or the Apostle Paul). Reflect upon the story of the person's life, and to the extent that you are able, identify the sources of their original (pre-reformed) dispositions: What made them "who they were" originally before a change of heart took place? What means did God's Spirit use in the person's life to motivate change in them? What kinds of practices did the person utilize to affirm a desire to change in the way in which God invited them? Describe, if possible, ways in which the change that you have identified was evidenced in various facets of the person's formation field: what about the person changed?

As you conclude your reflection, take time to notice what stirs in your own heart and mind as you reflect on the journey of dispositional transformation in this person's life. Describe any ways in which you find yourself responding to or perhaps resisting God's communications to this character.

Chapter 5

Faith and Formation Traditions

IN THE LIGHT OF years of research into human and Christian formation and deformation, van Kaam observed that one of the most powerful factors in the way people live is their propensity to rely on patterned, habitual ways of acting and reacting, of responding and choosing.[1]

Traditional Nature of Human Life

People form habits as a way to simplify and streamline receiving and giving form on a moment-by-moment basis.[2] These include habits of perception and of prioritizing energy, habits of assigning meaning to various daily happenings, and habits of following through on decisions.[3] Forming these habits in light of the emergence of innumerable traditions allows us to lessen the amount of time we need for routine decision-making; it saves our attention and energy for what we deem to be most important.[4]

Van Kaam termed habits and patterns of living *formation traditions*. We human beings, unlike animals, are relatively instinct-deprived. We develop formation traditions in place of instincts for everyday living, such as

---

1. van Kaam, *Traditional Formation*, 14–15.

2. Van Kaam defined a formation tradition as "a distinctive, overall pattern of receiving, expressing, and giving form in one's life and world . . . coformed by structures and elements that have attained a sufficient degree of consistency and mutual cohesiveness so that the pattern can be seen as a distinct and meaningful whole of basic dispositions, attitudes, and directives. . . . It has recognizable principles of organization" (*Traditional Formation*, 2–3). So convinced was van Kaam of the power and role of tradition in the spiritual life that he named it as one of his infrastructural principles.

3. Recall that van Kaam was sensitive to the interactions between the energy of the vital dimension and its formative dynamics with traditions; see his discussion of this, for example, in *Traditional Formation*, chapter 16, "Alignment of Vital Dimension and Form Tradition," 139–51.

4. van Kaam, *Traditional Formation*, 92.

traditions of how to dress, eat, work together, and gather in neighborhoods.[5] These traditions play a significant role in our response to or resistance of the influences on the human spirit by the Mystery.

Having lived under the Nazi occupation of Holland during World War II, van Kaam witnessed on a daily basis what happened when an ideological faith tradition like Nazism replaced a religious faith tradition like his own. Nazi beliefs, and the horrendous practices they spawned, convinced him of the need to study in detail the traditional nature of human life. Beyond people's voiced beliefs, there are patterns of perception and responses to the world around them that are embedded, as in the case of Nazism, in dehumanizing formation traditions. Van Kaam concluded that the form traditions emerging from this evil ideological faith tradition may at first not have been consciously intended or chosen by the average population but, that under the domineering voice of a tyrant like Adolf Hitler, they became powerful forces of destruction. His observations of people living through the crises of the war, as well as in those non-crises oriented circumstances in the decades that followed, left him with the conviction that what we most deeply believe (our faith traditions) and how we live and act in everyday life (our formation traditions) are inseparable. Not only does what we believe influence how we act, but how we act influences what we come to believe. Our patterns of living, our traditions, influence our openness or closure to the Spirit, whether in crisis settings or the ordinary unfolding of daily life.

Traditions require the focused attention of anyone who studies spiritual formation because they are not only powerful dynamics in the life of the spirit, but also the means by which we pass on to others, for better or worse, what we believe and how we live. Here again we see that by attending to such patterns, van Kaam resisted the tendency to equate spirituality merely with the interior life. Based on his decades of observation of the spiritually formative and deformative influences of culture and history, he conceived of two specific types of tradition that shape the practical emergence of human and Christian life.

---

5. Note that van Kaam was careful to distinguish culture from what he saw as significant communal and personal coformants of spiritual life, as it is embedded in a specific sociohistorical setting. He also distinguished the dynamics of such personalization from the individualization approaches of clinical psychology. He was interested in the ways that cultural patterns and traditions interact with the human will and spirit in processes that uniquely personalize certain facets of culture, which then become a part of a person or community's patterns of daily living. In distinction from individualization within the context of a culture, van Kaam was interested in identifying dynamic patterns of traditions being handed down from one community to another in ways that were possible to articulate and repeat. For discussions of these general concepts in relation to his theory, see van Kaam, *Traditional Formation*, 3–5, 12–13, 15–16.

Faith Traditions

We humans are drawn toward systems of meaning, or belief systems, of one kind or another.[6] A unique feature of being human is a "persistent beckoning to believe" in something beyond ourselves.[7] Implicitly or explicitly, people develop beliefs or intuitions about what brings happiness, success, meaning, and security in life. Whether one believes that life is ultimately meaningful or meaningless, has direction or is directionless, none of us can escape an innate longing to discover what the purpose of life really is. Such beliefs, be they religious or ideological, are always based on faith.[8]

By the term faith, van Kaam did not necessarily mean religious or creedal doctrines, nor did he wish to imply that faith is a belief system explicitly articulated by a person or community. First comes the unshakable conviction that our hunger for the More Than will in some way be fully satisfied. Regarding the preeminence of this confidence, van Kaam said that "the ideological conviction that [a particular] undeniable aspect of human life formation is exalted as the most basic one in the light of which all other formation aspects should be understood exclusively."[9] He spoke both of religious and nonreligious ideological systems as being thus grounded in faith. In both cases, belief is central. Religious or ideological systems require the faith that their claims can provide meaning and direction in life, and that adherents will pass them on from one generation to the next.

Around ultimate intuitions about reality cluster related sets of beliefs. For example, in the case of Christianity, believers held to the conviction that their creedal system was sourced in divine revelation; it was subsequently supported by a host of other beliefs, among them, that God initiates communication with humanity, that Jesus Christ is the epitome of God's word made flesh to dwell among us, and that the Bible is a record of God's revelation to humankind.

These underlying beliefs, as well as their related subsets, are faith traditions. They deal "primordially . . . with what one should believe about the doctrines . . . and basic rules of the moral implementation inherent in one's belief system."[10] In other words, faith traditions articulate beliefs about human meaning and its significance for generations of adherents who strive

---

6. van Kaam and Muto, *Essential Elements*, s.v. "Basic Beliefs as Self-Evident."

7. Ibid., s.v. "Commonality of Faith Traditions."

8. Adapted from van Kaam, *Traditional Formation*, 27–28. See van Kaam and Muto's *Living Our Christian Faith and Formation Traditions* for a fuller reflection on this connection from a Judeo-Christian perspective.

9. van Kaam, *Human Formation*, 208.

10. van Kaam, *Traditional Formation*, 241.

to integrate the directives their faith tradition expects them to follow. For example, adherents of the Christian belief system are expected to hold to the truth that Jesus Christ, as both divine and human, revealed what God is like to humanity and that in so doing he spoke with authority. Disciples obey what Christ directed them to do, such as "love your enemies," and "sell your possessions, and give alms."[11]

What features do faith traditions exhibit? First of all, they may be implicit or explicit, free-floating or institutionalized. When faith traditions are implicit, such as in the case when an ideology like consumerism takes precedence in a culture, it is a challenge to make this aberration explicit. For example, it was only during the housing crisis in America at the beginning of the twenty-first century that widely held beliefs about the honesty and stability of national economic institutions rose to the explicit, focal awareness of the citizenry. In contrast, some faith traditions are explicitly stated and may be institutionalized.[12] For example, the Jewish faith tradition has been codified and passed on, thanks to numerous texts and teachings, with statements of belief, prayers, rituals, doctrines, and narratives. These oral and written records are intentionally articulated by individuals and faith groupings and systematically handed down from generation to generation.

In the course of history, faith traditions may be more or less supportive of consonant human unfolding. Supportive ones foster an ongoing dialogue between the transcendent dimension and the other spheres, pretranscendent dimensions, and dynamics of our entire human formation field.[13] For example, a faith tradition that places ultimate value on human life and recognizes the equality and dignity of each person goes beyond our sociohistorical setting ("does this person belong to such-and-such a nationality or economic class?"), our human vitality ("how healthy or unhealthy is this person?"), and our functionality ("what is this person able to do or to produce?"). The ultimate focus instead is on the person as a spirit-self, made in the image and likeness of God, despite the shadows of sin.

Other faith traditions may be far less supportive of the worth and dignity of every human being. For example, an ideological faith tradition like materialism fosters beliefs that do not nurture the transcendence dynamic. In the long run, its merely functionalistic tenets are likely to become detrimental to the human condition, which is certainly more than a matter of what we possess or don't possess. By contrast, as we read in Galatians 3:26–27, "for in Christ Jesus you are all children of God through faith...."

---

11. Luke 6:27; 12:33.
12. Adapted from van Kaam, *Traditional Formation*, 27.
13. van Kaam, *Traditional Formation*, 19–20.

There is no longer Jew or Greek, there is no longer slave or free, there is no longer male or female; for all of you are one in Christ Jesus."

Another feature of faith traditions is that they may be more or less foundational. Their foundationality depends on what the legitimate authority of a faith tradition considers to be ultimate beliefs about reality. It is the nature of systems of belief to attract clusters of other beliefs compatible with them, which, taken together, would characterize them as foundational and not merely personal or special to a particular group. To the extent that any faith tradition is part of an identifiable period of history, adherents may also encounter changes in its unfolding. For example, in the Roman Catholic faith tradition, those in authority must appraise whether or not a teaching or practice follows Vatican Council II directives. Is a particular practice truly foundational now and for ages to come? Faith traditional practices need to be periodically reappraised to determine whether or not adherence to them still fits the definition of what it means to be a follower of that faith tradition.[14]

A point of tension in a pluritraditional society is that we may find ourselves immersed in a context of multiple, and at times competing, belief systems that claim to be ultimate. Various subsets of beliefs may then be spawned from faith-traditional systems already dissonant with their foundational origins.[15] It seems typical of our times that many hold to multiple, and even contradictory, faith traditions simultaneously. This confusion creates tensions throughout life that compel one to choose among competing traditions that which represents the most authentic path of fidelity to our faith and to our unique-communal life-call.

Formation Traditions

While people may hold identical or similar faith traditions, the ways in which they express them in everyday life may vary from person to person and from age to age. For example, both Francis of Assisi, an Italian Christian of the eleventh through twelfth centuries, and A. W. Tozer, an American Christian of the twentieth century, read and believed the declaration of Jesus that one could not be his disciple unless one was willing to give up all one's possessions (Luke 14:33). Francis of Assisi expressed his assent to this belief by giving away every trace of his considerable wealth, unexpectedly stripping himself naked in front of his bishop's court and establishing a rule

---

14. Ibid., 261, 263–64; van Kaam and Muto, *Living Our Christian Faith*, 92–94. Van Kaam affirmed continually that such appraisal falls within the purview of acknowledged authorities and adherents within a faith tradition, not to those outside the tradition.

15. Ibid., 17–19.

of life that forbade possessions.[16] A. W. Tozer, on the other hand, expressed his belief about the necessity of giving up all our possessions by modeling his life on the biblical character of Abraham, who although rich in material resources, lived a life of open generosity and non-possessiveness. He wrote,

> I have said that Abraham possessed nothing. Yet was not this poor man rich? Everything he had owned before was his still to enjoy: sheep, camels, herds, and goods of every sort. He had also his wife and his friends, and best of all he had his son Isaac safe by his side. He had everything, but he possessed nothing. There is the spiritual secret. There is the sweet theology of the heart which can be learned only in the school of renunciation.[17]

Both of these men held to the same Christian belief that to be a disciple of Jesus required "giving up" all your possessions. Yet the way the two expressed this foundational facet of their faith tradition took different forms.

This example shows why it is important to study the patterns by which people enflesh what they believe.[18] To this end, van Kaam developed the concept of a formation tradition as a way to identify observable patterns of living the faith as distinct from adhering to its foundational meaning. Briefly, a formation tradition is a nameable, distinctive, overall pattern of receiving, expressing, and giving form in our life and world. It includes "dispositions... formation directives, feelings, moods, and expressions."[19] In this way it gives "direction to the concrete receptive and creative formation of life and world."[20]

While faith traditions are patterns of beliefs, formation traditions represent attitudes and directives that guide "the everyday process of effective life and world formation."[21] Van Kaam took care to distinguish formation traditions from culture, while acknowledging the fact that they always influence one another. He viewed formation traditions as personalized cultural

---

16. Francis of Assisi, introduction to *The Little Flowers of St. Francis*, 14.

17. Tozer, *Pursuit of God*, 27.

18. Van Kaam was keenly aware of the hunger that people have to live out their chosen faith traditions with integrity as well as the challenge of knowing just how to do this and how to pastorally assist others in living lives of faithfulness. "Theologies and ideological philosophies, while of tremendous value for people's understanding of their faith, cannot assist them sufficiently in all details of the everyday implementation of their belief systems. Beyond helpful pastoral guidelines of a general practical and ethical nature, theologies and philosophies in themselves do not have the tools for a minute scrutiny of the practical art of dealing with daily formation dynamics, crises, conflicts, affects and images" (*Traditional Formation*, 12).

19. van Kaam, *Traditional Formation*, 2–3; van Kaam, *Human Formation*, 211.

20. van Kaam, *Fundamental Formation*, glossary, s.v. "Form Tradition."

21. van Kaam, *Traditional Formation*, 31–32.

traditions that both drew from culture and superseded it.²² For example, Francis of Assisi's decision to strip naked in front of his father and the bishop's court was influenced by his culture in the sense of it being intentionally counter-cultural, yet his action was not a typical pattern of the times. While we are influenced by our culture, being human entails the ability to transcend culturally oriented times and places by means of our human gifts of insight and freedom.²³ Thus, formation traditions are "bridges" between our culture and our faith traditions.²⁴ We live out our deeply held beliefs about human meaning and direction in the context of our culture and its sociohistorical situatedness. This being said, formation traditions are not identical with these cultural factors.

Among the identifiable features of formation traditions, van Kaam included the potential to be implicit or explicit, and to be freely chosen or merely adopted without appraisal. Formation traditions may for this reason be more or less in harmony with what we say we believe.²⁵ They may also be more or less foundational. For van Kaam, formation traditions are foundational to the extent that their practice transcends the particular situatedness of one or the other formation field. That is, foundational formation traditions go beyond specific times, places, and faith groupings, and remain open to appraisal to see if in these various contexts they are still consonant with the foundational faith traditions in which they ought to be rooted. For example, in the Christian faith tradition, prayer practices spawn foundational formation traditions, practiced across times and places, from the Carmelite nun who enters into contemplative prayer, to the Pentecostal Christian who shouts aloud a prayer of praise, to the Eastern Orthodox disciple who "prays an icon." In all of these Christian contexts, prayer is understood to be a necessary part of expressing Christian faith in everyday life.

By the same token, not all formation traditions are foundational. Van Kaam used the term accretion to differentiate non-foundational facets of traditions from those that are and have proven to be foundational.²⁶ Accretional traditions may be changed without compromising the foundations of a faith tradition. For example, the New Testament church council at Jerusalem decided that it would not require Gentile believers to follow Jewish laws

22. van Kaam, *Traditional Formation*, 27–29..

23. Ibid., 13.

24. Ibid., 27.

25. van Kaam, *Scientific Formation*, 267. Also, van Kaam explicitly noted that "Formation science looks . . . at traditional formation in two ways: from the viewpoint of form directives inherent in the tradition itself, and from the viewpoint of the personal free carriers of a tradition" (*Traditional Formation*, 36).

26. van Kaam, *Traditional Formation*, 286, 290.

in order to join the church. It determined that such formation traditions were not foundational, that is to say, not absolutely necessary, to live as faithful disciples of Jesus Christ and as baptized members of the church.[27]

In most if not all cases, it takes time to know whether or not particular formation traditions are accretional or foundational. The Jerusalem Council's decision continued to be debated for decades afterward, as is evidenced by a number of the Pauline epistles. However, given the expansion of the church throughout the Gentile world in the years that followed, the wisdom of the council's appraisal became apparent over time. It is important to be able to decide whether or not accretional traditions can be changed without undermining the underlying foundations of the faith to which they are related.[28]

The formative force, and crucial importance, of formation traditions is that they serve as a bridge between our adherence to faith traditions and our observable living circumstances, including our external actions and our internal responses. As we appraise them in the course of everyday existence, the question of whether we live what we actually profess to believe will continue to challenge us.

27. Acts 15:1–29.

28. For further information pertaining to the distinction between what is foundational and what is accretional, see van Kaam and Muto, *Living Our Christian Faith*, 233–37.

Form Tradition Pyramid

A tool to facilitate the appraisal of formation traditions and the relative intensity of their influence on us is the form traditional pyramid.[29] Van Kaam used a pyramidical structure as a means to diagram formation traditions, either of individual persons or groups, and to "[picture] a kind of lived synopsis of all our form traditions as more or less integrated into our basic [faith and formation] tradition."[30]

At the base of the form traditional pyramid, van Kaam placed our most foundational faith and formation tradition, since it exudes the most observable and describable influence on our entire life. For example, he identified his Roman Catholic tradition as being at the base of his personal formation pyramid, since it was that tradition more than any other that provided the symbols, language, rituals, dispositions, attitudes, and directives that influenced his whole life.[31]

Above the base of the pyramid, van Kaam drew a horizontal line reaching from one side to the other. This line is depicted as open-ended to represent the fact that while formation traditions are distinguishable from one another, they interform in the pyramid. This means that even though the tradition at the base of the pyramid exerts the most influence throughout our field of life, that tradition is also influenced by the other ones represented in the pyramid from bottom to top.

Listed above the base tradition are other traditions in an ascending order. The whole depiction of the pyramid shows that the traditions closest to the base exert the most pervasive influence, while those closest to the peak exert less than those listed below them.[32]

The overall purpose of constructing a formation pyramid is twofold. First, it provides a means to encourage reflection on and articulation of those traditions that most influence our lives. Second, it represents the fact that we strive to live our traditions in an integrated manner. The way we represent the order of these traditions reveals how we give more or less priority to the directives that emerge from all quadrants of our field. That being said, the pyramid model must not be seen as a reified object. Our field of life and

---

29. van Kaam, *Traditional Formation*, 34.
30. Ibid.
31. Ibid.

32. Ibid. Note that van Kaam did not strictly limit the number of formation traditions that could be distinguished within a form tradition pyramid, although experience shows that four to seven formation traditions within this construct provide plenty of substance for reflection.

its supporting constructs taken as a whole represent the dynamic nature of the processes of formation, deformation, reformation, and transformation.

When constructing a form tradition pyramid, we ought to be as honest as we can about the actual traditions that influence our way of being in the world. It can be helpful to elicit from others who know us what influences they perceive as exercising the most impact on the way we live. Are our professional commitments more important than our religious ones? Are the familial traditions in which we were raised or the national outlooks we espouse most dominant? Asking those involved in our daily lives, whether they are family members, friends, or co-workers, what they perceive as unquestionably influential on who we are and how we live, often yields excellent food for thought.[33]

An important technique to appraise the full significance of formation traditions in our lives is to construct a dual set of pyramids based on a formative event. The first pyramid ought to depict what happened before our life underwent a significant readjustment to what we considered the base of our pyramid. For example, if at one time functionalism was our basic tradition, and we were fortunate enough to undergo an awakening experience as to its deformative effects, we may now be ready to depict a second pyramid picturing the reformation we underwent. We would move functionalism higher up in the pyramid, and name it "functionality," because at the base of the pyramid we would now, for example, place love and service to our family and our church. The "before" pyramid may be called a pre-conversion pyramid, and the "after" pyramid may be called a post-conversion pyramid. In most cases, the overall ordering of a pre-conversion pyramid as compared to a post-conversion pyramid may be similar, with only a single formation tradition reordered in some way. Even so, such a reordering may represent significant formational changes in our lives, especially if the formation traditions that are reordered are closer to the base of the pyramid.

Conclusion

Through his concepts of faith and formation traditions, van Kaam sought to highlight the often unrecognized formative power of our habits of living as intimately connected with or disconnected from the beliefs to which we adhere. The relationship between what we believe and how we live these beliefs has such important implications for the study of spiritual formation as the following.

---

33. If we live with children, they may prove to be especially candid resources for assisting us in identifying our most influential formation traditions.

First, because faith traditions are grounded in ultimate beliefs about meaning and direction, their power to motivate the way we live, whether we are aware of them or not, cannot be denied. Faith traditions are not simply maxims to which people mentally assent. They represent the most deeply embedded beliefs that actually direct the actions, dispositions, thoughts, emotions, and perceptions in our day-to-day life. Faith traditions are the bedrocks of our presence and action in the world. As such, their strength results in a certain resilience that serves as a stabilizing influence in life as well as a potential resistance to change in general. For this reason our faith traditions may serve us formatively or deformatively. They may be consonant or dissonant with God's will for us. Becoming aware of our lived traditions enables us to appraise them in light of God's will as we understand it, thereby fostering the process of spiritual reformation in our lives.

Second, because faith traditions are linked to how we receive and give form in our lives day to day, formation traditions provide direct windows into how we are or are not being faithful to what we believe. As van Kaam conceived of them, formation traditions are not relegated only to the sociohistorical dimension of our formation field. They are embedded as well in our vital, functional, transcendent, and pneumatic-ecclesial dimensions. This means that the way we actually live and work in the world is an embodiment of what we believe (our faith traditions) and how we adhere to these beliefs in daily life (our formation traditions).

Reflection Questions

1. Understanding Our Story: Reflection on a Faith and Formation Tradition

    Two formative dynamics that this chapter highlighted were van Kaam's notions of faith traditions (deeply held beliefs) and formation traditions (the ways we live that embody and put into practice what we believe). Van Kaam observed both that our faith traditions shape our formation traditions and that the practice of our formation traditions shapes our faith traditions.

    For example, all Christians believe that prayer is an important Christian practice ("prayer is important" is a shared faith tradition). Yet the ways people embody this faith tradition can look very different from one another. For example, Eastern Orthodox Christians use icons extensively in their prayer practices and Roman Catholics may use rosary beads, while most Protestant Christians focus on mental prayer without any external objects as a part of their prayer practices. The shape or form of prayer looks very different in these various cases, and yet the underlying faith tradition that "prayer is important in our relationship with God" is shared by all these different Christian communities.

Allow God to be present to you as you reflect on the following questions: What is one faith tradition (deeply held belief) to which you hold? Write it down in a sentence or two. When did you first begin to hold this belief? Where were you when you first learned it? Who was involved in your learning this faith tradition? In what ways (in what form traditions) do you live out this faith tradition in daily life now? Take time to reflect on whether you embody this faith tradition in a way that it is central to your living.

Now take some time to reflect on your day so far: In what activities have you been engaged? List them as best as you are able to remember them, from the time you woke up until now. Describe any attitudes and feelings that have been a part of these activities, including transitions between activities. In addition, describe any particular thoughts that have been significant to you as you have walked through your day to this point.

Now take time to reflect on the faith traditions that anchored your actions today: What underlying beliefs do your actions and attitudes, thoughts and feelings, demonstrate? Be as honest as you can in your reflections. Write down two or three of these beliefs. Then take time to reflect on whether these beliefs are ones that are compatible with your understanding of the Gospel; that is, do these actually held beliefs that you embody in form traditions reflect the way God's redemptive love invites you to live as a child of God and follower of Jesus Christ?

Pause for a while to be with God and allow God to be present to you in these reflections. How has the Holy Spirit inspired you to identify obstacles to allowing what you believe (your faith tradition) to be embodied in how you live what you profess in daily life (your formation tradition)?

2. Understanding God's Story: Reflection on the Faith Traditions of a Favorite Bible Character

Recall that one of the constructs that van Kaam designed in order to help bring to light the way our faith and formation traditions influence us is what he called a form traditional pyramid (see Figure 3, "Exemplary Form Tradition Pyramid," in this chapter for an example).

Choose a Bible character about whom some narrative background is provided in the Scripture (for example, Abraham or Sarah, Esther or Ruth, the Apostle Paul or the Apostle Peter). Based on the actions and attitudes, feelings and thoughts (form traditions) of this character throughout the scriptural record, make a list of three to seven of the underlying faith traditions this person held. (Note that these faith traditions may not all be in harmony with one another.)

Next, select a specific moment in the person's story, and based on the formation traditions of the person in that moment, create a faith and formation tradition pyramid that shows the prioritization of their faith traditions at that time. What were the most influential beliefs that the person held at that moment, based on their actions, feelings, attitudes, and thoughts? (Recall that the most influential beliefs are at the base of van Kaam's formation pyramid construct, so your form traditional pyramid should reflect this.)

As you reflect on the form tradition pyramid you have made for this person, what insights come to you about the formative dynamics of form traditions and their underlying faith traditions, given what you know about the person's story in the Bible? Describe any ways in which you find yourself responding to or perhaps resisting God's communications to this character in this moment.

Chapter 6

Dynamics of Conscience and Consciousness

No doubt, we have all experienced at one time or another, a dilemma regarding what we ought or ought not to do. Perhaps as a child we were tempted to steal something or as a student to cheat on a test. Our conscience is that distinctively human sense of what is right or wrong in our conduct or motives. It prompts us toward right actions, whether we follow its prompting or not.

Human Conscience Development

Van Kaam reminded us that our moral conscience, and indeed our morality, is drawn from natural law, faith traditions, doctrinal beliefs, and ethical principles.[1] He further observed that even though we may know inwardly, and in the context of what we have learned, that a particular action is wrong, we may still behave immorally unless the directives of our moral conscience have seeped deeply and lastingly into what he named our formation conscience.

Our moral conscience, and our faith conscience, that is to say, what we learn from the foundations of our faith tradition, operate closely together.[2] However, day by day, we are faced with the question of why, when we know from our faith and our inner sense of what is right, we still do what is wrong. That is why van Kaam focused not so much on faith conscience, which is the province of informational theology, but on formation conscience, which is the province of formation theology. When our formation conscience is aligned with our moral, faith conscience, we at least try day by day to live what we profess to believe.

---

1. van Kaam, *Transcendent Formation*, 75.
2. van Kaam and Muto, *Essential Elements*, s.v. "Formation Conscience Strengthened by Faith Conscience."

Van Kaam identified several facets of formation conscience, each with their own gifts and challenges. He identified as the earliest type of formation conscience a facet connected to the vital dimension. Hence, he named it vital formation conscience. While it is not yet guided by mature appraisal, it works as a "seed" of "vital sympathy" from earliest childhood.[3] In other words, our vital formation conscience gives us a feeling of how we ought to respond to the pains and joys of other people with sympathy and empathy. From early life this gift helps us to lay the foundations of responsiveness to other-centered needs beyond our own. There is a significant challenge connected to the development of vital formation conscience. If it is not balanced with the later development of the functional and transcendent facets of formation conscience, it may lead to expressions of care rooted in the pride form that are not only guilt-ridden but exhausting and excessive.[4]

Of great influence on us in these early days of our lives is what van Kaam termed parental formation conscience.[5] Our parents, and the significant others who surround us, play a powerful role in the formation of our conscience. Children internalize their parents' expectations for them in such a way that they become embedded in the child's inner life and often in their neuroform.[6] For example, our parents may have attended Sunday morning worship services every week, barring illness, and may have taken all their children along with them. Whether ever spoken of explicitly, the action of attending Sunday morning worship services together as a family embedded a directive of Sunday church attendance in the children's neuroform. Parental formation conscience stays with us throughout our lifetime, whether we are conscious of it or not. The gifts of this early formation may include a rich heritage of both moral and formative directives. Though unappraised in childhood, such directives contribute to the development of our dispositions and actions.

Inevitably, there are many formation challenges bound to these parental influences. First, the directives they communicate to us may prove to be dissonant with our unique-communal life-call. In this case, the parental conscience directives we received require wise appraisal in our adult life, combined, if necessary, with gentle but firm resistance. For example, one may become an emergency room physician scheduled to work on Sunday mornings, making church attendance impossible. Still valuing going to church may prompt the doctor to explore whether or not communal

---

3. van Kaam, *Transcendent Formation*, 100.
4. Ibid., 101.
5. Ibid., 81–82.
6. Ibid., 105, 264–66.

worship services offered at different times of the week may enable him or her to participate.

A second challenge pertains less to the directives parents pass on to us and more to the way in which they were communicated. What if parents overemphasized rigid conformity to the formation traditions by which they lived more than to the faith traditions that undergirded them?[7] To the extent that such directives are isolated from the influence of the transcendent and pneumatic-ecclesial dimensions, the directives parents passed on may have developed into coercive security directives that tend to be resistant to reformation.[8] For example, parents may have established an atmosphere in which reflection on and questioning of these directives were so unacceptable that only unquestioning acceptance of and conformity to what they told us to do would be rewarded. Such an environment poses a great obstacle to the appraisal necessary for ongoing spiritual development.

A third facet of conscience formation concerns what we do with the directives we receive from friends, teachers, and peers that have been assimilated in the intrasphere of our formation field.[9] What van Kaam termed social formation conscience represents our ongoing exposure to traditions that fill the cultural and historical pluritraditional settings in which we find ourselves. These traditions may or not be expressions of the faith directives we received from our parents. For example, our parents may have reminded us how important it is to care for neighbors in need. But we may live in a culture where individualism prevails. A moral dilemma may arise when we see neighbors in need but justify the fact that we did not help them because we were too busy.

One of the challenges associated with the development of social formation conscience presents itself when we have unwittingly imbibed the directives received from the plenitude of the faith and formation traditions surrounding us, even though they may contradict one another. Such contrary directives become confusing, and perhaps at times so overwhelming that they may move us away from fidelity to our unique-communal life-call.

A fourth facet of conscience formation is what van Kaam termed functional formation conscience.[10] The gift associated with this facet of conscience is that it enables us to select directives consonant with our life-call and to implement them in respect for our own and others' well-being. The

---

7. van Kaam and Muto, *Dynamics of Spiritual Direction*, 106–8.

8. van Kaam and Muto, *Essential Elements*, s.vv. "Meaning of Mini-Obsessions," "Conformity in Childhood;" van Kaam, *Transcendent Formation*, 263–64.

9. van Kaam and Muto, *Dynamics of Spiritual Direction*, 98; van Kaam, *Transcendent Formation*, 138, 201–2.

10. van Kaam, *Transcendent Formation*, 78.

challenge associated with functional conscience is its potential to absolutize certain directives, primarily in reference to our own ambitions, in such a way that we become driven by them without sufficient attention being paid to transcendent aspirations. "We mistake a few self-centered directives for God-centered guidance and inspiration. . . . Selective functional conscience, not enlightened by openness to the transcendent, may give rise to a certain drivenness in our makeup. . . . Such pressure leads to an almost constant scrutiny of our own and others' lives, robbing us of spontaneity. . . . [The] desperate need to measure up is typical of an overwrought functional conscience."[11] The characteristic of drivenness is an indicator that unappraised directives may have been ultimized by our functional formation conscience. Such drivenness may be seen as an invitation of the Spirit to reappraise the ambitious directives associated with our functional dimension, lest they become ends in themselves and separate us from the grace of God.

Empathic formation conscience is the next facet identified by van Kaam and Muto.[12] While functional formation conscience tends to emphasize directives selected in reference to our projects, empathic formation conscience takes us "beyond ego-centricity to an awareness of the bond between us and all creatures."[13] Its directives are rooted in faith traditions. They tend to affirm the interconnectedness of all creation as an expression of God's love. We empathize but do not identify exclusively with the needs of other people. Empathic conscience pulls us outside of and beyond our own cares and "encourages us to understand all people as we hope to be understood by them."[14]

The gift of an empathic formation conscience is that it enables us to grow in openness and understanding to the needs of others, on the condition that we do not lose touch with a sense of our own personal identity. Of course, we ought not to assume that the fulfillment of directives is to be defined wholly by the felt needs and experiences of others.[15] When "not yet purified by loving obedience to the Divine Will . . . the transcendent quality of empathy may be equated mistakenly with feelings of pretranscendent

---

11. van Kaam and Muto, *Dynamics of Spiritual Direction*, 108–9.

12. Ibid., 110–11.

13. Ibid., 110. Clearly, empathic conscience is related to our earliest vital formation conscience, although empathic formation conscience differs from the vital conscience in that while directives of one's vital conscience are more innate and function before the powers of appraisal are developed, empathic conscience develops in the context of appraisal and affirmation.

14. Ibid.

15. Ibid., 110–11.

vital sympathy."[16] The challenge is that if empathic formation conscience directives are ultimized, they may lead us to try to be all things to all people.

Each of these facets of formation conscience (vital, parental, social, functional, and empathic) has its own gifts and challenges. From the perspective of formation theology, conscience directives risk becoming dissonant with our life-call in Christ if they are unappraised and isolated from the Spirit, become absolutized, or are evocative of false guilt. By contrast, if these facets of formation conscience are integrated in service to the will of God, they become servant sources of both transcendent formation conscience and transcendent Christian conscience.[17]

Transcendent formation conscience develops in dialogue with the aspirations of our human spirit and in dialogue with our life-call. Transcendent Christian conscience grows in dialogue with the inspirations of the Holy Spirit, with the Christ-form of our soul, and in obedience to our faith traditions as articulated by Christian doctrine and catechesis.[18] While van Kaam's focus of interest was primarily on the empirical facets of formation conscience development, he consistently pointed to the necessity of grounding the formation of Christian conscience in the communal faith traditions of the historic church.[19]

> Our formation conscience as dynamic is inseparable from our growth in an informed doctrinal and catechetical style of life. We need to learn firsthand the counsels and commandments of God to guide our lives from childhood onward. No "ought" precept of our formation conscience can foster our spiritual and social maturation if it contradicts the essential precepts dictated to our moral conscience by the teachings of our credal system and their continual confirmation by the legitimate ecclesiastical authority under which we choose to live and grow in our faith.[20]

16. Ibid., 110.

17. Ibid., 98–99.

18. Ibid., 106–7; and van Kaam and Muto, *Essential Elements*, s.v. "Conscience as Dynamic."

19. "The danger of creating a separation between our moral conscience and its formational 'oughts' escalates if we do not appraise the way we live in the light of our faith traditions. Unappraised directives infiltrating our conscience, especially through the media and other secular sources, may not be in tune with the pneumatic-ecclesial aspirations and inspirations flowing into our transfocal consciousness. By contrast, appraised directives compatible with our commitments inform and form our conscience under the guidance of God" (van Kaam and Muto, *Essential Elements*, s.v. "Formation Conscience Strengthened by Faith Conscience").

20. van Kaam and Muto, *Essential Elements*, s.v. "Conscience as Dynamic."

Transcendent Christian conscience, under the authority of the church's teachings on moral conscience and ethics, frees us "from [the] tyranny of rigid ego directives" and the expectations of others, "modulat[ing] these by our primary adherence to the will of God."[21] In contrast to the directives driven by our pride form, those emanating from transcendent Christian conscience are most often perceived in stillness. "Spiritual conscience saves us from engulfment in a society forgetful of the Sacred. Its source is our transcendent self and its aspirations for union with the Trinity. This facet of our conscience does not bellow loudly. It reveals itself most often in silence. It stills the busy 'managing me' and allows us to discern our divine direction."[22] As Psalm 62 reminds us, "For God alone my soul waits in silence, for my hope is from him. He alone is my rock and my salvation, my fortress; I shall not be shaken."[23]

Conscience and Guilt

According to van Kaam, we experience various types of guilt as a result of the decisions and actions processed by our formation conscience. He emphasized that an appraisal of these directives, isolated from openness to the inspirations of the Spirit, may lead us to options more influenced by the pride form than by the Christ form. This confusion sets in motion layers of guilt that may prove more unhelpful than helpful in our formation.[24]

Whereas inauthentic guilt is deformative, authentic guilt can be and is reformative. Van Kaam made every effort to identify the sources and causes of false guilt. Such guilt generally arises from directives that are dissonant with our founding form and our life-call in Christ. By contrast, authentic guilt leads to repentance and freedom of heart. Transcendent Christian conscience plays a crucial role in the disclosure of dissonant directives; it helps us to integrate the various facets of formation conscience in such a way that they begin to guide us, over a lifetime, to obedience to the will of God and fidelity to our life-call.

Ego guilt is the first of the three types of guilt pertinent to formation conscience.[25] It results from appraising the directives we receive from all

21. van Kaam and Muto, *Dynamics of Spiritual Direction*, 112.

22. Ibid., 105.

23. Ps 62:5–6.

24. See van Kaam and Muto, *Dynamics of Spiritual Direction* (chapters 8–10); van Kaam, *Formation of the Human Heart*, 287–88; van Kaam, *Transcendence Therapy*, 142–43; van Kaam, *Transcendent Formation*, 79, 88–90.

25. van Kaam and Muto, *Dynamics of Spiritual Direction*, 95–97.

quadrants of our formation field from a functionalistic standpoint only, with the aim of building up our exalted and exalting pride form. With ego guilt, conscience directives are appraised only from a pretranscendent point of view, closed to the influence of the Spirit.[26] Van Kaam and his colleague Susan Muto provide the following example:

> Ed and Rose exemplify this problem. They are proud to be among the most punctual members of their parish. They follow the letter of the law. Having been raised in strict familial circumstances they learned: "This is the way things are done by prominent Christians." Such was the unspoken slogan by which they lived, but there was little joyfulness in their prim religiosity. They could not remember ever having had a religious experience. They conformed to the comportment of the people praised as righteous in their environment. There was little or no awareness in them of a unique-communal call, of the need for inner spiritual growth, or of intimacy with the Trinity. Guilt about not listening to their deeper self as a revelation of the Divine was unknown to them. They felt bad only when their behavior deviated from that of some publicly respected, markedly judgmental, believers in their milieu. Theirs was a fastidious type of religious functionalism, reflecting precision to the letter of the law but lacking the warmth of converted hearts. People on the way to spiritual adulthood find that the opposite is true. Their pretranscendent concerns give way to the guidance of the Holy Spirit. They sense when they regress to a mere functional existence, since this turn gives rise to ego guilt alone.[27]

When ego guilt is at work, we pay attention to functional directives so much that they become our ultimate concerns.

Spiritual self-guilt is the second type of guilt pertinent to formation conscience. It results from recognizing that we have been unfaithful to the foundations of our faith tradition and our calling in Christ.[28] This form of guilt is associated with crises of identity, since it is related to directives that emanate from our unique-communal life-call that we have wittingly or unwittingly ignored. Van Kaam and Muto offer us this example of spiritual self-guilt:

> Chuck decides to become a carpenter because there are many signs that point to this profession as congenial with his call and compatible with his situation. Despite the joys and frustrations

---

26. Ibid., 95–96.
27. Ibid., 96–97.
28. Ibid., 94.

associated with an avocation that enables him to articulate his call in daily life, he still sees carpentry as being most in tune with his spiritual self-direction. He could choose another kind of manual labor yielding sufficient income for his family but offering far less scope for his initiative. His conscience tells him that accepting a carpentry position is most in keeping with who he is at this moment of his emergence. Working with his hands gives him sufficient scope to imitate Christ, to be compassionate with his customers, and to use the competence associated with his God-given gifts. If Chuck refuses to follow these inspirations, he knows he will feel guilty. This is an example of spiritual self-guilt. It is always related to our life call as a whole with its direction disclosures and the Spirit-guided decisions that enable us to implement them.[29]

Spiritual self-guilt, hijacked by erratic heroism, may prompt us to over-spiritualize where we are in life. That would explain, for example, why Chuck might be tempted to abandon his vocation as a carpenter to become a missionary or a minister. If and when Chuck's vocation is considered in the light of his entire formation field, including the sociohistorical, vital, and functional dimensions of his intrasphere, it is likely that he will avoid the dynamics of such erratic heroism, which tend to exalt inspirations and aspirations without regard to the dispositions, attitudes, and dynamics emanating from our full formation field.[30] Spiritual self-guilt ought to prompt attention to our historical situatedness; it ought to provide a corrective to pride-filled, self-directed passions that make it difficult, if not impossible, to discern how to be truly faithful to our calling in Christ, and honor the gifts we have received from God.

Ego self-guilt is the third type of guilt pertinent to formation conscience. It is most common among people actively engaged in trying to find and follow the will of God. It results from the recognition that our formation traditions are dissonant with the foundations of our faith tradition and our now recognized callings in Christ.[31] Continuing to use the case of the

---

29. Ibid.

30. Van Kaam contrasted erratic heroism with wise appraisal. He described erratic heroism as "fantastic . . . an unrealistic, fantasy-based exaltation of our appraisal of what involvement should be like. Inspirations and aspirations are blown out of proportion by exalted imagination. In the case of social visions, fantastic appraisals lead to an artificial reconstruction of our formation field that is inevitably grandiose. It is based on an exalted image of what an 'idealistic' life in service of justice, peace, and mercy *should* look like" (*Formation of the Human Heart*, 318–19).

31. van Kaam and Muto, *Dynamics of Spiritual Direction*, 94–95.

carpenter Chuck as an example, van Kaam and Muto described how ego self-guilt functions in our spiritual development.

> [Chuck] chose this profession [of carpentry] in obedience to the love-will of the Father. This response on the part of Chuck's higher self enlightens not only the commitment he made; it also strengthens the conviction that he must continue to emulate Christ in his own life as a manual laborer.
>
> If he does not live up to the standards he sets for the performance of his duty, Chuck feels guilty, first of all on the level of his organizing or "managing me," secondly and indirectly on the level of his true spiritual identity. He is aware—at least in some vague way—that if he fails on this score he may not be living up to his overall life direction. The letdown he would feel is also a sign that he may have betrayed his inmost call. Here we see an example of ego self-guilt.[32]

In summary, the arousal of ego guilt happens when pretranscendent directives are so dominant in our lives that we act with little or no reference to the transcendent. Authentic or spiritual self-guilt results when we recognize that we have been unfaithful to what we profess to believe and have allowed the divine directives beckoning us to fidelity to God to be overrun for a time by our own sinfulness. The arousal of authentic ego self-guilt happens when we in fact treat our pretranscendent directives as truly "servant sources" of our transcendent and pneumatic-ecclesial dimensions and still fail to fulfill the directives we know to be related to our deepest calling in Christ. When this happens, ego self-guilt invites us to repentance.

Human Consciousness

Based on decades of observing and researching patterns of spiritual formation, van Kaam affirmed the importance of our staying alert and attentive to the influences of the Spirit. One means by which he underlined the importance of such attentiveness was by articulating his holistic theory of consciousness. Van Kaam defined human consciousness as a "knowing that unfolds within the manifold modes of awareness of our formation field," while also being able to "transcend the formation field in a pure intuition of the spirit."[33] He maintained that consciousness can never be separated from

---

32. Ibid., 95.

33. van Kaam, *Formation of the Human Heart*, 230. Van Kaam linked his conception of human consciousness with the derivation of the term itself, noting that the word consciousness comes from the Latin *scire* ("to know") and *cum* ("with"), and so literally

the formation field with which it interacts and is immersed.[34] At the same time, the gift of human consciousness serves as a means of distancing our attention from mere drives, impulses, and instincts. We live in a way that is more than a product of our vitalistic needs and functionalistic ambitions.[35] He conceived of human consciousness multi-dimensionally as a formative awareness potential shared by all humans. He sought to articulate distinguishable, yet always interforming regions of human consciousness.

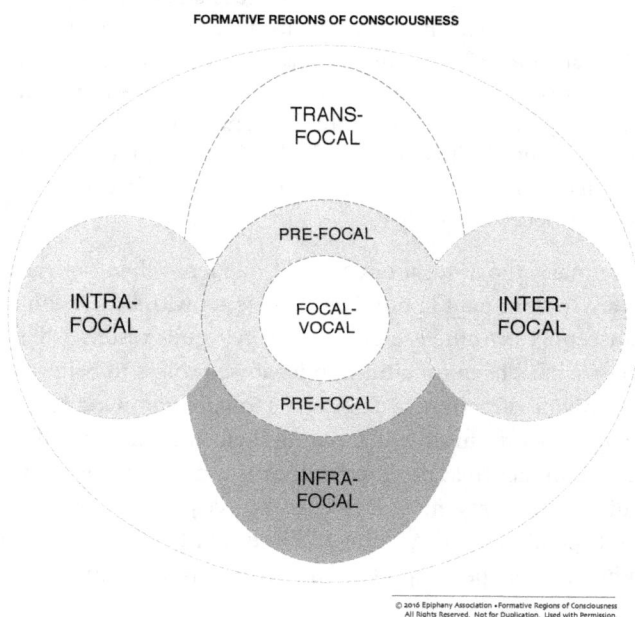

Focal consciousness points to our focused awareness of what is happening in the here-and-now moment. We can verbalize, that is to say vocalize, that to which we attend prefocally, as well as express nonverbally that about which we are aware.[36] Focal awareness is crucial in the process of our learning to pay attention to the rich treasury of insights and inspirations

---

means "to know with."

34. van Kaam, *Human Formation*, 229–31.

35. van Kaam, *Traditional Formation*, 86–87.

36. To express this relationship between explicit awareness and being able to verbalize something, van Kaam sometimes used the phrase "vocal awareness" synonymously with "focal consciousness." For further reflection on this idea, see van Kaam, *Formation of the Human Heart*, 233.

filtering through our prefocal consciousness, which can be compared to a "mighty stream that carries us continuously."[37]

Prefocal consciousness may not be verbalized yet, but it is still available to us. It consists of patterns of easily accessed "peripheral attention influences" that are closely associated with focal awareness and attention and are often directive of it.[38] The perceptions, images, apprehensions, and narratives that are part of prefocal consciousness can be lifted into focal consciousness when we least expect it. There is a continuous interplay between focal and prefocal consciousness that results from "peripheral daily perceptions and . . . residues of focal attention" that move in and out of focal consciousness with relative freedom.[39] Prefocal consciousness consists of a flood of ideas that, while not a part of our immediate verbalized or vocalized awareness at the moment, we may access with little effort. These prefocal lights and shadows contribute to our creativity. We can be giving focal attention to, let us say, how to solve an equation. We may give up, take a nap, and upon awakening, suddenly the solution is there because our prefocal consciousness has been at work.

Intraconsciousness comprises all that we have interiorized through memory, imagination, and anticipation, as well as through the feelings, emotions, and strivings that enlighten our interior life.[40] Thanks to intra-focal appropriation, we are able to personalize the traditional symbols, rituals, and directives offered to us minute by minute in our formation field.[41] Once appropriately activated, our intra-focal consciousness becomes the seedbed of making experiences, like shared ritual, meaningful to us.

Interconsciousness represents the customs, symbols, myths, form traditions, arts, and writings that we have imbibed from our culture, subculture or family.[42] The purpose of inter-focal consciousness is to call to our awareness a perception, a memory, an image, that already is significant in the context of our shared sociohistorical experiences. Van Kaam noted that inter-focal awareness may be more or less accessible to our immediate focal awareness.[43] For example, the lingual and symbolic systems we inherit from

37. van Kaam, *Traditional Formation*, 26.
38. van Kaam, *Fundamental Formation*, 262.
39. Ibid.
40. van Kaam, *Formation of the Human Heart*, 231–32.
41. Ibid., 232.
42. Ibid.; van Kaam, *Traditional Formation*, 288.
43. That is, interconsciousness may be prefocal or focal according to van Kaamian constructs. Note too that van Kaam maintained that "Tradition is . . . not constricted to clear formulations, available to the focal interconsciousness of a community. A large part of it is alive or dormant in the prefocal interconsciousness of the community of

our culture provide a network of meanings that may rise to our awareness, especially during an event like a wedding. Let's say a bride wears a red dress with sparkling sequins, instead of white or ivory. We may suddenly discover a host of meanings flooding into our inter-focal consciousness that were not thought of previously, like, "My grandmother would collapse if she saw this dress coming down the aisle." According to van Kaam, intra-focal and inter-focal consciousness mutually interact.

> Interconsciousness and intraconsciousness influence each other formatively. For instance, the actualization of the fundamental consciousness of children, with their basic human predispositions, happens through interconscious form directives. Such directives are embedded in the form traditions disclosed to them by significant people, events, and things in their formation field. During their formation journey, children appropriate and increasingly personalize such form directives in their own intraconsciousness. Such unique intraconscious appropriation enables them in turn to influence or enhance interconscious experience.
>
> For instance, people may participate as a community in the ritual of a form tradition. The participants may execute merely functionally or aesthetically the interconscious ritual directives of their traditions. Ritualism replaces the heartfelt celebration of ritual. On other occasions, however, they may spontaneously infuse their participation in the ceremony with an intraconsciously elaborated conviction of the forming value and experience of these form directives. Their heart is in it, which, of course, makes a profound difference.[44]

Infraconsciousness is that facet of human consciousness in which are embedded not-yet-accessible sociohistorical pulsations, vital impulses, and functional ambitions that, though they may or may not be traumatic, may prove to be points of departure for further, and often freeing, reflection.[45] Infra-focal consciousness holds residues of everything from childhood abuse to post-traumatic stress disorders. To the degree that these experiences remain lodged in the infra-focal consciousness, and one resists deal-

---

memory formed by a tradition. This interconsciousness, focal and prefocal, is, as it were, a consciousness that has been exteriorized in customs, images, symbols, and rituals" (*Traditional Formation*, 288). Van Kaam thus considered it a grave "social injustice to diminish or destroy violently the conditions for the survival of a faith and formation tradition of a population," citing as only one of many historical examples the case of certain tribes of American Indians (*Traditional Formation*, 289).

44. van Kaam, *Formation of the Human Heart*, 232.
45. Ibid., 169.

ing with them, they may trigger neuro-formational coercive directives. Van Kaam observed that infra-focal conscious anxiety and guilt may give rise to a rigidity that betrays itself not only verbally, but in movements and facial expressions.[46]

> A person may be able to live with these anxious attitudes and repressed conflicts for a long time. In all too many cases, however, he may have a breakdown in middle age. He may, for instance, feel strongly tempted to leave marriage, religious life, the priesthood. He may show neurotic or psychosomatic symptoms. Such infraconscious quasi-spiritual attitudes need to be worked through. As long as they are not available to consciousness, they maintain their sterile, repetitive, and non-creative influences. An attitude that, on the contrary, has been made available to consciousness can be adapted creatively to a changing situation.[47]

Van Kaam identified infraconsciousness as "the principle of stereotyping, of paralyzing the incarnational movement of the spiritual life."[48] Unlike certain Freudian conceptions of the unconscious, which deny that this level of awareness is available to human consciousness, van Kaam insisted that the symbols, images, and experiences previously locked into infra-focal consciousness may, with good formation and the grace of God, filter into pre-focal consciousness and become vocal, thus aiding the healing process.[49]

Transfocal consciousness is a manifestation of our distinctively human transcendence dynamic.[50] It serves as the receptor of the inspirations and aspirations that, so to speak, flood into our consciousness "from on high." In the van Kaamian theory of consciousness, transfocal consciousness holds primacy in the realm of spiritual formation.

> Of these . . . regions [dimensions of human consciousness] and their accessible operations, our transconsciousness [transfocal consciousness] plays a special role in faith deepening due to the infiltration of our human spirit by the Holy Spirit. These Spirit-guided, inspiring call-disclosures may appear at times to go beyond the bounds of human reason, but they are not incompatible with either the reasons of our heart or the foundations of our

---

46. van Kaam, *In Search of Spiritual Identity*, 113.
47. Ibid., 124–25.
48. Ibid., 121–22.
49. That said, van Kaam acknowledged that access to infrafocal consciousness may require "extraordinary means, such as, for instance, psychoanalytic treatment or formation counseling in depth" (*Formation of the Human Heart*, 167).
50. van Kaam and Muto, *Essential Elements*, s.v. "Regions of Consciousness."

faith. The truth of both transcendent aspirations and pneumatic inspirations protects us from false piety or narrow devotionalism that may lead to irrational explosions of spiritualistic feelings capable of contaminating all regions of our consciousness.[51]

From this perspective, it is possible to say that the Spirit calls us beyond the narrow confines of our pride form and at the same time constrains the extremes to which this counterfeit form of life tempts us. Through the inspirations flowing from our transfocal consciousness, we can witness at privileged moments the transformation of our whole life.

Transcendent Mind and Will

In expanding upon his theory of consciousness, van Kaam identified two additional formative constituents: transcendent mind and transcendent will.[52] The transcendent mind points to the reality that we have a way of knowing that orients us to what is more than we are. It includes, but also goes beyond, rational analysis.[53] The transcendent mind intuits the presence of the Mystery, making us more open to aspirations and inspirations.[54] The transcendent will points to the reality that we can either assent to or resist divinely guided directives received by our transcendent mind.[55]

Our transcendent mind is also receptive to wisdom and insight flowing into our transfocal consciousness from the Spirit. It helps us to apprehend dispositions that lead to the formation of our Christian character and personhood. When our transcendent mind is illumined by the Spirit, our dispositions of openness to the Mystery and appreciation of God's goodness to us become embedded in our hearts. Our transcendent will gives us the freedom to be receptive or resistant to these divinely guided directives.[56] Transcendent willing enables us to pursue the consonant goals of formation that have been apprehended by our transcendent mind. Our transcendent will prompts us to assent to formative acts and dispositions that are in tune with God's will for our lives.

To the extent that our transcendent will is receptive to the leading of the Spirit, we may experience authentic willing. Our transcendent will

51. Ibid.
52. van Kaam, *Transcendent Formation*, 125..
53. van Kaam, *Fundamental Formation*, 252; van Kaam, *Human Formation*, 71-72.
54. van Kaam, *Transcendent Formation*, 125; van Kaam, *Human Formation*, 102.
55. van Kaam, *Human Formation*, 101-2.
56. Ibid.; for discussion of this from a Judeo-Christian formation theology viewpoint, see van Kaam and Muto, *Divine Guidance*.

orients us to love God and others with our whole mind and our whole heart, and to be humbly responsive to the signs of God's love for us. Van Kaam identified this Mystery-oriented way of life as the "love-will."[57] Insofar as we continue to grow in consonance with the will of God, our transcendent will leads us to a more loving life liberated by grace.

Functional Mind and Will

Corresponding to transcendent mind and will is functional mind and will. Functional mind prompts us to implement the directives received in our formative mind as transcendent.[58] Functional mind heightens our awareness of the concrete conditions within our formation field that need to be taken into account if we are to execute the directives calling for incarnation and action in our everyday world. Functional will enables us to embody these directives in a gentle and firm way, always conscious of the obstinate remnants of the pride form that may affect our decisions and actions.[59] If transcendent will orients us to love, then functional will orients us to serve. Taken together, transcendent mind and will, complemented by functional mind and will, prevent us from sinking into will-lessness, as if there is really nothing we can do about anything. Functional mind, complemented by functional will, prevents us from falling into the opposite extreme of willfullness, which makes us think that we have the power to control life and do whatever we want to do without reference to the Mystery. This aberration deceives us into thinking that we can master the Mystery rather than allowing the Mystery to master us.

---

57. Note that throughout his writings van Kaam also referred to the transcendent will as the love-will (van Kaam, *Transcendent Formation*, 20–21; van Kaam and Muto, *Essential Elements*, s.v. "Function of Formation Acts"); the primary will (van Kaam and Muto, "Course I," 96); and the orientation will (van Kaam and Muto, *Essential Elements* s.vv. "Directives Conducive to Consonance," "Functional Dimension," and "Will-to-Formation as Affirmative"). For the term functional will, van Kaam used the synonyms executive will (van Kaam and Muto, *Essential Elements*, s.v. "Functional Dimension"; van Kaam, *Human Formation*, 101); managing willing (van Kaam, *Human Formation*, 101); implementation will (van Kaam and Muto, *Essential Elements*, s.v. "Directives Conducive to Consonance," and "Functional Dimension"); and the pretranscendent will (van Kaam, *Traditional Formation*, 148).

58. A synonym for functional mind is functional formative intelligence (van Kaam, *Fundamental Formation*, 252).

59. van Kaam, *Transcendent Formation*, 21.

Formative Memory, Imagination, and Anticipation

In further expanding upon his theory of consciousness, van Kaam identified three transcendent and functional incarnational sources of our human life form: formative memory, formative imagination, and formative anticipation. We remember past experiences, we imagine how our life may change, and we anticipate the fruits of this transformation. In the infra-focal region of our consciousness, residues of unarticulated memory, imagination, and anticipation may affect us deformatively until we bring them into the light of transfocal consciousness.

Formative memory makes available "past transcendent . . . truths and events."[60] It probes their meaning by enabling us to remember them in the context of faith. We realize that these instances not only formed us then, but still exert power over us in the present.[61] Formative memory enables us, not by means of rote memorization, but by means of formative reiteration and the human ability to tell stories, to reflect on past events in a way that unifies them with our awareness of how the Mystery has shown us so far who we are called to be.[62] Through the distinctively human capacity of storytelling, as an expression of the mind as formative, significant events in our lives may be reflected upon for lessons still to be learned.[63] In other words, memory as both a transcendent and a functional source of formation points to a remembered range of persons, things, and events that have given form to our lives in the past, and that in some way continue to form us in the present.

Formative memory is operative in all the dimensions of our life form. Sociohistorical memory refers to past pulsations that we never quite forget. For example, the way our family celebrated Thanksgiving rituals years ago may be continued in our gatherings today. Vital memory refers to past impulses and compulsions that continue to influence us physically. As much as we would like to remove chocolate-chip cookies out of our diet, we still find it hard to resist them. Functional memory refers to past ambitions that enable us to function with more ease in the present. When we want to build a backyard swing for our child, suddenly all that our father taught us about

---

60. van Kaam, *Fundamental Formation*, glossary, s.v. "Transcendent Memory."

61. Ibid.

62. van Kaam and Muto, *Essential Elements*, s.v. "Attention in Relation to Memory, Imagination, and Anticipation; van Kaam, *Human Formation*, chapter 8, "Formative Memory and Anticipation in Relation to Disposition Formation," 139–64.

63. The formative power of memory is one reason why the loss of memory, for example, through a disease such as Alzheimer's, is so devastating. Such memory loss kills the capacity to relate formative events, and rightly prompts state-of-the-art research to prevent destruction of this vitally important gift.

carpentry is ready to hand. Transcendent memory refers to past aspirations and inspirations that have proven to be congenial with the kind of person we are. Such a memory may foster a union of likeness between us and the Mystery that inspires our way of functioning today and for the rest of our lives.[64] For example, when Teresa of Avila read the *Confessions* of Augustine, in which he tells how his life was changed when he "put on the Lord Jesus Christ," the impact his conversion had on her drew her again and again to seek intimate communion with the Trinity.

Formative memory as functional helps us to implement current plans and projects more effectively by assisting us in the appraisal of the directives we receive in relation to our past experiences.[65] We consider how we have implemented transcendent directives with relative success, and how that experience might inform the way we apply them in the present. This is the way we benefit from our experience, learning from our mistakes in the past and improving how we decide and act now and in the future.

For example, we may be inspired by the Mystery to nurture a new habit of practicing regular rest. Our functional memory supports this aspiration, reminding us that in the past, taking a short nap in the afternoon while recovering from an illness gave us strength through the remainder of the day. While not experiencing illness now, our functional memory enables us to recall that because we have a regular Wednesday evening commitment, we feel extra tired on Thursdays. Perhaps we could plan a regular nap Thursday afternoon, as a concrete way to listen to formative directives that inspire us to rest.

In biblical terms, formative memory is evidenced frequently in the Psalms. Various psalmists recall God's care for them in the past, and their reliance on it in the present: "Answer me when I call, O God of my right! You gave me room when I was in distress. Be gracious to me, and hear my prayer"; or "O Lord my God, I cried to you for help, and you have healed me. O Lord, you brought up my soul from Sheol, restored me to life from among those gone down to the Pit."[66] Our Lord Jesus himself prompted his disciples, who had forgotten to bring bread on a journey, to use their transcendent memory to recall God's past provision of food, saying: "You of little faith, why are you talking about having no bread? . . . Do you not remember the five loaves for

---

64. van Kaam, *Fundamental Formation*, glossary, s.v. "Transcendent Memory"; van Kaam, *Human Formation*, 150.

65. van Kaam, *Fundamental Formation*, glossary, s.v. "Functional Memory." A synonym for functional memory is functional formative memory (see van Kaam, *Fundamental Formation*, 253).

66. Ps 4:1; 30:2–3.

the five thousand and how many baskets you gathered? Or the seven loaves for the four thousand, and how many baskets you gathered?"[67]

Formative imagination as functional enables our human mind to create symbols and images that point us toward the Mystery.[68] It helps us to incarnate both the aspirations of the human spirit and the inspirations of the Holy Spirit.[69] Van Kaam emphasized the formative power of images in the mind, when they are connected to transcendent truths, as well as the deformative power such images can exert when they are disconnected from transcendent truths.[70]

Formative imagination also interfaces with all dimensions of our human life form. Consider, for example, sociohistorical images that carry cultural trends influencing, for example, what we buy through the pressures of the world of advertising. Vital symbols appeal to our senses, both formatively as, for example, color combinations on a hand-stitched tablecloth, and deformatively, such as pornographic images on the internet. Functional symbols, as elegant as the Golden Gate Bridge in San Francisco or as pedestrian as a stop sign, appeal to our functioning in everyday life. Transcendent symbols, such as the quest for the Holy Grail or the spire of a gothic cathedral, may evoke images that we associate with something sacred. In short, most of our life is guided by focal, prefocal, intra-focal, inter-focal, infra-focal, and transfocal imagery, which can exert either a consonant or dissonant influence on us. In particular, dissonant imagery can dissipate formation energy, and evoke the endless ruminations of a fantasy life. That explains why a change in life direction requires a change in imagination that enables the images we ponder to become more consonant with our life-call. Lacking this attention to imagery, our life may be swamped with a collection of paralyzing, depreciative images that cause us to lose contact with the everyday demands of life. Van Kaam gives the following example of how we can reform deformed images:

> Consider the task of having to write a paper. We should prepare for this task by appreciative imagination. We should imagine ourselves in advance sitting before the [computer], appreciating what we may do. We highlight imaginatively the advantages. It is much more pleasant to sit here than it would be to dig a ditch,

---

67. Matt 16:8–10.

68. van Kaam, *Fundamental Formation*, glossary, s.v. "Transcendent Formative Imagination."

69. van Kaam, *Human Formation*, chapter 7, "Formative Imagination and Disposition Formation," 108–38.

70. van Kaam, *Fundamental Formation*, glossary, s.v. "Functional Formative Imagination"; van Kaam, *Formation of the Human Heart*, 204.

to sit in a dark foxhole during a war, to lie chronically ill in bed. Instead, we have the privilege of working with ideas. While we are typing, we will be growing in reflection, self-expression, and dexterity. We do not allow negative images to creep in, such as "the miserable paper that I doubt I can do." Such depreciative images kill the vital flow we need to accomplish the task. Instead, we should relax and imagine being pleasantly seated. We have only to worry about a line or two. Once we have accomplished that, imagine how interesting it will be to extend these slowly to a paragraph, then perhaps to a page. Writer's block often comes from the neglect of appreciative imaginary preparation *before* we sit down to write our paper.[71]

Formative imagination presents to us for reflection images and symbols involved in the process of realizing our ambitions and aspirations here and now. In our former example of wanting to practice regular rest, we imagine that putting a pillow out on the couch Thursday mornings would serve as a symbol reminding us of our commitment to develop this new habit.

In biblical terms, have we not at times relied on the beautiful formative imagery of Psalm 23 to comfort us in times of sorrow or weariness: "The Lord is my Shepherd. . . . He makes me lie down in green pastures; he leads me beside still waters; he restores my soul"? Or perhaps we have pictured the bounteous provision of God for us in times of great stress. "You prepare a table before me in the presence of my enemies; you anoint my head with oil; my cup overflows."[72] Symbols offered to us through our formative imagination supply us strong sustenance for growing in our trust in God.

Formative anticipation as functional is the incarnational source by which we try to forecast what we hope lies ahead in the future. Van Kaam distinguished it from expectations of outcomes based on our own desire to control the future. He said that anticipation is Mystery-centered and open-ended, whereas expectations are more connected with the functional dimension and tend to close us off from the unexpected.

Formative anticipation organizes itself in anticipatory configurations in dialogue with formative memory and formative imagination. What makes formative anticipation so important is that it helps us to apprehend potential life-situations and projects to some degree, before they emerge. For example:

> Future parents may anticipate the arrival of their first baby. What do they foresee as the best environment for the baby?

---

71. van Kaam, *Human Formation*, 121 (emphasis his).
72. Ps 23:1–3a, 23:5.

> What effect will this birth have on the relationship between the parents? How will they make space for a new life while remaining faithful to their congenial and compatible marital commitments? These and many other anticipations may lead to a modulation of the dispositional life of both parents.[73]

Formative anticipation presents for our consideration concrete directives that aim to increase the efficacy of our actions in the future.[74] Following through on our former example, writing "nap" on our calendar every Thursday for the next month is the way formative functional anticipation helps to support our transcendent aspiration to rest. The reminder on our calendar, and using the symbol of the pillow by placing it on the couch Thursday mornings, exemplify how these three incarnational sources work together to support the transcendent inspiration to practice regular rest.

Van Kaam described what happened to him in this regard in his memoirs, where he reflected on "Return to Normalcy." His experience shows us the importance of both transcendent and functional anticipation, even when life does not unfold as we pray it will.

> Once Holland was liberated and I could return to the seminary, my longing for a more normal life began to be fulfilled. Due to the study time I lost during the Hunger Winter, my ordination to the priesthood had to be delayed by one year. It would be almost another year before I received my first official appointment as a priest—not to the mission field but to teach courses at Gemert that would include philosophical anthropology, educational psychology, and the philosophy of science. In fidelity to the Thomistic tradition, I taught philosophy in its pre-theological context as the "handmaiden" of doctrinal theology. I tried to structure my courses in such a way that the students received in a complementary fashion both informational theology about the Revelation and its application to everyday life as formational. The experiential approach I formulated during the Hunger Winter came to fruition in the seminary. As much as I had wanted to be assigned to the missions as most of my classmates were, I was blessed in retrospect by the fact that my health in those days, aggravated by a severe bout of psoriasis, precluded travel to tropical climates. This condition meant that I had to befriend books while my confreres

---

73. van Kaam, *Human Formation*, 159.

74. van Kaam, *Fundamental Formation*, 253, and glossary, s.v. "Functional Formative Imagination," "Functional Anticipation"; van Kaam, *Human Formation*, 159–62.

secured the official documents they needed to do first evangelization in foreign lands.[75]

Introspection and Transcendent Self-Presence

In expanding still further upon his theology of consciousness van Kaam distinguished between two forms of reflection, "one being introspective, the other transcendent."[76] Introspective reflection means looking anxiously into ourselves in "an aggressive attempt to figure everything out, to dig up the roots of my failure, to trace it back to the past, to analyze piecemeal, my thoughts, feelings, deeds, and expressions."[77] Transcendent reflection may deal with the same experience that gave rise to such food for thought, only now with dispositions of peaceful surrender and a quiet acceptance, creating more room in us to be filled with the Eternal Presence. As believers, this kind of reflection may renew our faith in the redemptive love of the Lord. We put ourselves in his hands, trusting in his redemptive mercy and forgiveness. In short, "introspective reflection tends to be analytical and aggressive; transcendent reflection tends to be integrated and gentle."[78]

Van Kaam saw the danger of our falling into mere introspectionism rather than maintaining attentiveness to transcendent self-presence. He elucidated ten characteristics of what can occur when we make self-enclosed introspection rather than open-ended transcendent self-presence a lasting disposition.[79]

---

75. van Kaam, *Life Journey*, 61.
76. van Kaam, *In Search of Identity*, 172.
77. Ibid., 173.
78. Ibid., 174.
79. This chart is adapted from van Kaam and Muto's previously unpublished material as presented in terms of formation anthropology and formation theology. See "Introspection versus Transcendence," a chart in van Kaam and Muto, "Course VI," 47, which was itself based on van Kaam, *In Search of Spiritual Identity*, 172–96. For further discussion of the distinction between introspection and transcendent self-presence, see van Kaam and Muto, *Dynamics of Spiritual Direction*, 324–28.

Introspection	vs. Transcendent Self-Presence
1. Looking anxiously into myself in a coercive attempt to figure everything out	Putting myself totally before the Divine Forming and Preforming Mystery with my sadness, guilt, shame, anger, and failure
2. A disintegrative, analytical emphasis on aggressive intellectual knowledge cut off from heart knowledge	An integrative, assimilative, receptive openness to head and heart
3. Inordinate focusing on the past	Contemplative presence to past, present, and future
4. Divisive and hurtful	Unitive and healing
5. Efficiency-minded, unrealistic ideal of individualistic self-perfection	Mindful of the Mystery from whence each unique being emerges uniquely and communally
6. Fixated on self-centered, privatized needs	Concerned for other-centered integration and interformation
7. Results in isolated interiority and psychological self-actualization	Leads to intimacy with the Holy Trinity
8. Sees oneself as determined by childhood history	Has faith in the providential plan of God, embracing us continually
9. Hungers for the extraordinary	Stays in tune with daily life and the richness of the ordinary
10. Deformative and depreciative	Formative and appreciative

The side of the chart representing introspection exemplifies the deformative traits that are characteristic of self-centeredness, isolated from openness to the Mystery. By contrast, transcendent self-presence fosters a balanced, integrative life that is Mystery-centered rather than self-centered.

Conclusion

To become more consonant with the will of God, it is imperative that we align all levels of conscience formation with the highest ideals expressed by our faith and formation traditions. The guilt that we feel when dissonance overtakes us needs to be examined. Is it false or true? Is it plunging us into anxious feelings about ourselves and our lack of perfection, or is it drawing us to repentance and a new start aided by grace?

We have found in our reflections thus far that the more we can bring Mystery-centered and Spirit-inspired inspirations to focal attentiveness, the more likely it is that we will enjoy the fruits of fidelity to our unique-communal life-call. Through wise and prudent openness to the movements of our memory, imagination, and anticipation, we discover the meaning of what has transpired in our lives so far. We imagine with joy and courage how to submit our lives more fully to God's plan for us. We anticipate, with all believers and sincere seekers, inspired by Scripture and the spiritual writers, how to encounter the Mystery in love for the rest of our lives. We learn, as a consequence, that the Mystery draws us to live in trust of what has been, and in hope of what is to come.

Reflection Questions

1. Understanding Our Story: Reflection on a Coercive Security Directive

    In this chapter, we learned that van Kaam gratefully acknowledged the myriad gifts and complexities of the human mind. His faith-filled perspective led him to affirm that all facets of our human consciousness (whether focal, pre-focal, intra-focal, inter-focal, infra-focal, or transfocal) are open to the transforming work of God's Spirit. While focal consciousness seems most obvious in our everyday thinking, it is often dynamics of more remote regions of consciousness that power coercive thinking and actions in us. Van Kaam's hopeful message was that all of who we are is potentially open to transformation. But for such transformation to occur, coercive dynamics in the deeper regions of our minds and hearts need to be brought into the light of God's presence, love, and transformative power.

    One means that van Kaam offered for opening ourselves to such transformation is to attend to coercive security directives and their dynamics when they arise in us. When we notice (or someone else notices in us and names for us) actions or habits that are dissonant, reactive, and full of intensity, this is often a signal of a coercive security directive at work. Often such reflexive actions are cloaked in anger, frustration, and irritability, and carry with them an intensity that can actually be startling to the people around us. Rather than arising from focal awareness and free choice, coercive directives are embedded deeply in our neuroform and are prefocal. As such, they are highly resistant to reformation. But, van Kaam reminded us, nothing is too difficult for God. When we experience an event that triggers such intense reflexive actions on our part, van Kaam invited us to reflect on such actions not with mere introspection, but with transcendent self-presence that is gently and receptively open to God, trusting that God wants to transform our deepest neuroform and regions of consciousness from rigid captivity by the freeing dynamics of God's loving Spirit.

Allow God to be present to you as you consider the following questions: Gently reflect on your life over the past week or so, inviting God to bring to mind any moments that you may have experienced the deformative dynamics of coercive security directives at work. Examples might include road rage, intense defensiveness or fear, shouting at people, or acting in ways that are not in consonance with who God has called you to be and that carry with them a relatively high level of intensity. There may be several such moments that come to mind, but for now, choose just one.

Aware that you are in the presence of God during this time of reflection, first describe what happened. What were the circumstances? Was anyone else involved? What seemed to trigger your reflexive response? Articulate as best as you can your internal state as the event unfolded: What were you feeling? What were you thinking? How did you feel immediately afterward?

Now that you have brought the event to your focal attention, ask God to be present to you and to lead you in your further formation with this event. To the extent you are able, place yourself wholly before God with any guilt, shame, anger, or failure that you may be recalling, remembering that in spite of these powerful dynamics, God's acceptance of you and God's delight in you as his child remain unchanged. Allow yourself to rest with all that you are in God's presence.

Next, gently acknowledge your desire for God's truth, forgiveness, and freedom in this coercive facet of your life. Humbly ask for insight into the roots of this coercion, committing yourself to remain open now and in the days ahead for God's work in this area. Imagine how differently you will live when you are released from this coercion. What would such consonance look like in your daily living? Who else would be affected by your freedom?

Allow gratitude to arise in you, for it is also God's desire that you be freed in this area of your life. The pain you may be undergoing in the moment, leading you to the alignment of your will and God's will, is well worth the effort.

In awareness of the love of God that surrounds you now and always, allow yourself to anticipate with expectancy any ways that God will work on this coercion in the coming days as you prayerfully wait for God's healing in your life. Remember God's creative Spirit knows you better than you know yourself, and thus knows how to bring you insights in ways that you can notice and respond to them. Commit to God your willingness to engage your mind and will in responding to God's leading in practical, everyday ways that will express your desire for wholeness in the days ahead.

As this reflection draws to a close, how has the Holy Spirit inspired you to be more open to all the regions of your consciousness rather than blocking their entrance to your focal awareness? What hinders your mindfulness in this regard? What helps its unfolding in every phase of your formation?

2. Understanding God's Story: Reflecting on Guilt Dynamics in a Bible Character

Van Kaam and Muto identified three types of guilt as most often operative in relation to the appraisal of directives that arise from our various types of conscience. The first is what they called ego guilt, which only appraises such directives from a functional perspective (e.g. "I failed to do what was expected of me and so I feel ashamed"). The second is what van Kaam and Muto termed spiritual self-guilt, which recognizes that in some way we have been unfaithful to our most basic faith traditions and calling (e.g. "I failed to live up to who God calls me to be and to my most deeply held beliefs"). Lastly, and most common among people seeking to follow God, is what van Kaam and Muto identified as ego self-guilt, which recognizes that a regular habit or form tradition is not in tune with what one most deeply believes or who one is called to be. Each of these types of guilt is evidenced throughout the stories of Scripture.

Choose from Scripture a person who experienced some form of guilt (examples include Adam, Eve, Cain, David, Naomi, and the Apostle Peter). Which of van Kaam and Muto's three types of guilt was present in this particular situation for this person?

Describe the situation from which the person's guilt arose. Consider the formational dynamics of the spheres and dimensions of the person's formation field: What influenced them to behave in ways for which they experienced guilt? Were there any coercive security directives involved, or does the incident seem fairly isolated? Who brought their guilt to their attention: did someone else name it for them, or did they experience it directly without anyone's involvement? What, if anything, did the person do in response to their guilt? Did the person's response bring them to greater or lesser consonance with God's will for their life?

As you reflect on the formative event and its associated guilt as you have articulated for this person, describe any insights that come to you about the formative dynamics of guilt revealed by this person's story in Scripture. Are there any facets of it to which you can personally relate?

Describe any ways in which you find yourself responding to or perhaps resisting God's communications to this character in this moment.

Chapter 7

The Appraisal Process

WHEN I (REBECCA) WALKED into the kitchen this morning, in a single moment my eyes took in the scene along with an onslaught of directives, all crying for my attention: dinner dishes that had dried overnight were waiting to be put back in the cupboards; the dog greeted me expectantly hoping to be taken outside; the tea kettle waited to be filled and heated to whistling; and the reminder note by the telephone to call the mechanic seemed to say, "Don't forget to take care of me today, too!" On the kitchen table was an Easter centerpiece with a little lamb nestled among purple and gold material, along with symbols from the Passion story. And in my memory, having now seen the table, there was yesterday's conversation with my daughter at breakfast about whether or not she would enjoy some oatmeal before school today—if I would be willing to make it for her. Upon entering the same room, my husband would probably notice some of these things and ignore others. At the same time, he would notice things I had overlooked, such as windows that needed to be washed or a scrape on the door in want of retouching. Each person's formation has attuned them to attend to some and to ignore others of the myriad of possible directives that confront us in any given moment. Every day, during every minute, every sphere, dimension, dynamic, and integrating structure of our formation field presents us with sets of directives to which we may or may not be attentive.

Full Field Appraisal

To live in presence to the Divine Presence in our here-and-now situation is an invitation worth pursuing. But how is one to decide what merits attention and what to ignore? What does such presence to the Divine look like in daily living? And what about those times of special significance at those crucial junctures of life when one is faced with choices of great importance to oneself and others: Do I stay in this job or move to another one? Should I fulfill the longing in my heart to go to seminary, or do I need to wait until my children are through college themselves? Is it time to look for institutional housing for our aging parents, or is it possible to have them live with us in our home?

Van Kaam evolved the theoretical-practical construct of full field appraisal to help us apprehend the meaning of directives emerging day-in and day-out from our formation field.[1] This appraisal makes us attentive to whether or not a directive is consonant or dissonant with our unique-communal life-call as we currently understand it. Full field appraisal moves us from mere reactions toward mature responses that honor the way the Mystery is guiding our field of presence and action.[2] Van Kaam understood appraisal as a uniquely human potential rooted in our preformed transcendence dynamic. As spiritually formed and forming persons, we are challenged not only to be decision-makers, but also to become appraising persons.

Appraisal as a Disposition and a Process

Van Kaam emphasized that appraisal must be understood as both a prefocal disposition and a focal process. We need to be disposed to the regular practice of bringing our entire field of meaning into dialogue with the invitations of the Mystery to form, reform, and transform our lives, and to recognize deformative events that despoil this process. However, there are also events and seasons in life that call us to engage in appraisal as a focal process that requires additional time and attention beyond the regular rhythms of our life.[3] Such events may be so conflicted that they often demand that we move from one current form of living to a new form that is significantly different from what we had become accustomed to. In such crises, focused, sustained appraisal is called for.

Day after day our senses are bombarded by sights, sounds, smells, tastes, and touches. Our minds are full of past, present, and future

---

1. van Kaam and Muto, *Essential Elements*, s.vv. "Affirmation in Relation to Appraisal," "Appraisal as Provisional," "Appraisal of Vital Formation," "Elaboration of a Global System of Appraisal," and "Transempirical Methods of Appraisal." Note that van Kaam, as always, chose his terminology purposefully. He chose the term appraisal, as distinguished from the traditional word discernment, to emphasize that finding and following God's will involves not only attention to one's interior life, but to one's entire formation field.

2. For an overall articulation of appraisal as process, see van Kaam, *Traditional Formation*, 296–97. For van Kaam's description of the appraisal process from the perspective of appraisal dispositions, see van Kaam, *Transcendence Therapy*, 253–55.

3. Note that van Kaam argued that transcendent symbols of one's faith and formation tradition can evoke and sustain spiritual attention (van Kaam, *Traditional Formation*, 242–43, 260–63).

happenings, our hearts with emotions that often feel overwhelming. The expectations and judgments of other people confront us continually. We are immersed in formative events we would like to process on the spot but that are occurring beyond the bounds of our focal consciousness. In the midst of this constant stimulation, we are aided by our neuroform to the degree that it guides our attention to what we choose as most in need of appraisal. However, often the directives, habits, and dispositions to which we ought to attend are overlooked or ignored altogether precisely because we have not sufficiently developed a prefocal disposition of appraisal that prompts us to attend to what might otherwise go unnoticed until it becomes a demand we cannot overlook.[4]

The A's of Appraisal

Now is the time for entering into a sustained process of focal appraisal that takes into account not merely our interior life, but all spheres and dimensions of our field.

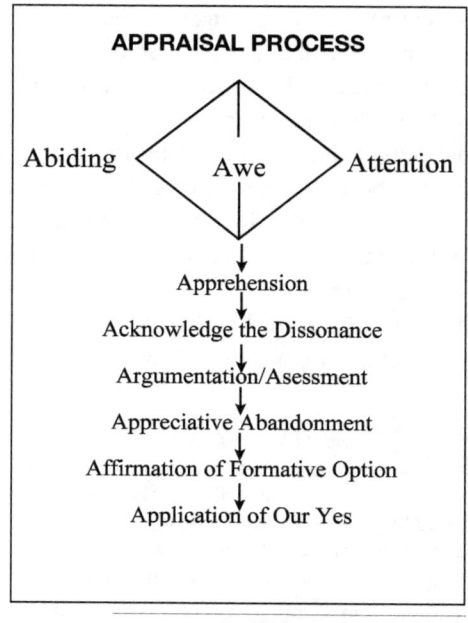

© 2016 Epiphany Association • Appraisal Process
All Rights Reserved. Not for Duplication. Used with Permission.

---

4. van Kaam, *Transcendence Therapy*, 237–38; van Kaam, introduction to *Scientific Formation*, xxvii.

Abiding in Awe-Filled Attention

The predisposition that enables us to proceed with the appraisal process is abiding in awe-filled attention. Awe means orienting ourselves in worshipful reverence to the Mystery. It establishes an environment in which we are able to reflect on the spiritual meaning embedded in any situation. Abiding means neither rushing through nor past what is happening, nor stumbling ahead of the pace of grace and clamoring for solutions. Instead, we linger in a stance of humble, receptive listening.[5] We try to link abiding with gentleness, which "stills the greediness and aggressiveness of a merely functional life."[6] Attention means becoming aware of directives and dynamics of formation relevant to pending appraisal, as they emerge from prefocal to focal consciousness. Taken together, abiding in awe-filled attention allows us to slow down and remain with the disclosures of the Mystery. Unless we take the time to abide in awe-filled attention, we may miss the opportunity to understand to the full the formative meaning of crises and conflicts. In this worshipful atmosphere, our entire formation field manifests a transcendent dimensionality. People, events, and things are beheld in their relatedness to the More Than.

Apprehension

Our attention to what needs to be appraised in our life may remain prefocal unless we move to the second dynamic of the appraisal process: apprehension. Van Kaam described it as a "movement of sensate and rational cognitive presence to the object . . . selected for attention."[7] In today's language, when we feel apprehensive, it is as if we fear the unknown. That is to say, apprehending what requires appraisal often entails a mixture of both a fascination, evoked by the possible discovery of a deeper meaning, and a fear, associated with the risks of attending to that which is likely to require significant change in us.[8] But another meaning of the word is implied here. Namely, we grasp with our mind, that is, we apprehend, certain disclosures of our call and the demands it may subsequently make upon us. Apprehension reminds us of the vastness of God's plan for us and why we need to

---

5. van Kaam, *Transcendence Therapy*, 253–54; van Kaam, *Formation of the Human Heart*, 86.

6. van Kaam, *Formation of the Human Heart*, 86. Van Kaam wrote beautifully in this passage of gentleness as something that "nurse[s] distinctively human dispositions" of the heart.

7. van Kaam, *Scientific Formation*, xxvii, 53; van Kaam, *Transcendence Therapy*, 254.

8. van Kaam, *Transcendence Therapy*, 254.

appraise how the Mystery is at work in our lives at the moment. Recognizing that this or that directive requires further appraisal may pose a challenge to us. After all, it is an invitation from the Mystery that can be accepted or resisted. Early in the appraisal process, apprehending what we believe God invites us to appraise may be rather vague and centered on secondary matters. Therefore, it is crucial that we move from apprehension to the remainder of the appraisal process.

Acknowledge the Dissonance

No sooner have we apprehended some incoming directives that must be appraised than dissonance arises. We stand on the threshold of a fuller appraisal of what is happening to us, but we feel pulled away from that appraisal by the tendency to ignore or deny it. We must acknowledge this "pull" if we are to see the dissonance as a call to deeper consonance. Van Kaam highlighted the need to acknowledge dissonance with candor and courage, especially prior to making a commitment to a particular course of action. Such acknowledgement requires humility and prevents the pride form from ultimizing (and inevitably isolating) a new directive as though it were the final, foundational source of meaning in our lives. It also serves to limit any isolating or exalting tendencies the pride form might exhibit in pressing dissonant dynamics into our infra-focal region of consciousness, thus bringing us further away from the light of transfocal inspirations of the Holy Spirit. Gently acknowledging dissonance as a servant source of deeper consonance is a healthy way to keep us on the path of sound, humble, and realistic formation.

Especially helpful at this juncture of the appraisal process is van Kaam and Muto's articulation of how consonance must be assessed in relation to dissonance. Their C's of consonance are congeniality, compatibility, compassion, and competence.[9] In terms of the intrasphere of our formation field, consonance means that our inner life is congenial with our founding form as redeemed in our Christ form.[10] Directives that are consonant with our intrasphere elicit and express the truth of our being and becoming the persons we are created to be. Van Kaam and Muto chose the term congenial to describe this facet of consonance in respect for its etymological relationship to the Latin *cum* or *con* "with" and *genesis* "origin."[11]

9. van Kaam and Muto, *Foundations of Christian Formation*, 265–66.

10. van Kaam and Muto, *Essential Elements*, s.v. "Consonance Coformed by Our Intrasphere."

11. van Kaam and Muto, *Commitment*, 118.

In relation to our immediate situational sphere, consonance expresses itself as patient compatibility with the "frame of reference in which one finds oneself by virtue of one's calling," and one's attunement to formative events.[12] Consonant directives, when compatible with our here-and-now situation, take into account our human situatedness in this world. The word compatible was chosen for its etymological relationship to the Latin *cum* and *pati*, meaning "to undergo . . . the limits of a situation; to be subjected . . . to the prevalent styles and customs of a locality or position."[13]

In relation to our intersphere, van Kaam and Muto connected consonance with compassion for and empathy with others. Compassion is evoked by "the consequences of the fallen state of formation and the vulnerability it entails for human life."[14] Consonance that directs us to be more compassionate considers not only the expression of our life-call in its uniqueness but also in its connectedness with others in community. The term compassion was chosen for its etymological relationship to the Latin *cum*, "with," and *passio*, "to suffer," meaning "to suffer empathetically with our own and others' vulnerability."[15]

Finally, van Kaam and Muto associated consonance in relation to the world sphere with the concept of competence, in the sense of contributing our giftedness to the pursuit of excellence in a sensible and responsible way in this world, and thereby impacting the entire cosmos with right and proper decisions and actions.[16] Human life elicits and expresses consonant directives through competence when we are faithful to our God-given gifts, and are willing to share them with others for the sake of serving the world at large, albeit most often in barely noticed, anonymous ways.[17] The term

---

12. Ibid., 119; van Kaam, *Fundamental Formation*, glossary, s.v. "Consonant Life-Form." We have somewhat simplified his idea here for clarity of presentation. Van Kaam also referred to compatibility in relation to undergoing the limits of situations with others, which is related to the intersphere.

13. van Kaam and Muto, *Commitment*, 119.

14. van Kaam, *Fundamental Formation*, glossary, s.v. "Consonant Life-Form."

15. van Kaam and Muto, *Commitment*, 120.

16. van Kaam, *Fundamental Formation*, glossary, s.v. "Consonant Life-Form." Here, van Kaam used the term "effective" for what in later works he referred to as "competence."

17. Note that the theme of consonance as expressed through congeniality, compatibility, compassion, and competence is ubiquitous throughout the van Kaamian corpus, to which van Kaam often added candor and courage (for example, see van Kaam, *Traditional Formation*, 167, 251; and van Kaam, *Transcendent Formation*, 32, 60–61, 124, 211). For the application of consonance in these categories as applied to intra-apparent forms ("self-image"), see van Kaam, *Transcendent Formation*, 60–61. For van Kaam's comments as to the animosity of the pride form to consonance in these categories, see van Kaam, *Human Formation*, 219. For his comments regarding the application

competence was chosen for its etymological relationship to the Latin *cum*, "with," and *petere*, "to seek, to aim at," in the sense of having the capacity and ability to function or develop in a particular way.

Only when we test our life in the light of the C's of consonance can we acknowledge the dissonance and begin to see it as a servant source of renewed consonance. Now we are ready to move candidly and courageously to the next stage of the appraisal process, which is the inevitable push and pull between argumentation and assessment: Should we go in this direction or not? Of what value is it to us?

Argumentation/Assessment

At this point in the appraisal process, we need to gather as much information about what to do and where to go as possible. We have no choice but to take a sober look at our entire formation field, including the thoughts and feelings this phase of appraisal evokes.[18] Argumentation deals with the pros and cons of our options for change. It calls for us to use the gifts of our rational mind to effect a certain distance that enables critical and creative reasoning.[19] Distancing moves us from impulsive reactivity toward responsive consonance with what is happening in our life at the moment.

Assessment, combined with honest and open argumentation, aids appraisal by making room for the in-breaking of the transcendent mind and will in the midst of the use of functional mind and will. Assessment points to the possible outcomes of what we feel guided to do. It ought to move us toward humble openness with disclosures granted to us by God's grace. It ought not to end up in aggressive, divisive battles driving us to forfeit our dependence on God and others.[20] Only when the dissonance around argumentation and assessment settles may it signal that we are ready to move toward the next A of Appraisal: appreciative abandonment.

---

of these categories of consonance in relation to a transcendence crisis, see van Kaam, *Fundamental Formation*, 264–65. There are dozens of such examples throughout all of van Kaam's Formative Spirituality series and van Kaam and Muto's Formation Theology series.

18. van Kaam, *Transcendence Therapy*, 254; van Kaam, *Scientific Formation*, 195–96, 221–22; van Kaam and Muto, *Formation of the Christian Heart*, 209–10.

19. van Kaam, *Scientific Formation*, 139–40. Note that in regard to appraisal proper, van Kaam said that "argumentation is decisive . . . [because it] takes into account, critically and creatively, not only . . . affinity and affective appraisals but also other significant coformants of the field" (*Scientific Formation*, 196).

20. van Kaam, *Human Formation*, 96.

Appreciative Abandonment

In the midst of "seeming inconsistency, emptiness, deformation, cruel fate, and death," appreciative abandonment to the Mystery allows us to dare to believe and hope that from the shadowland of dissonance, the Mystery may offer some means of spiritual renewal "for ourselves and for others, now or in the future."[21] Despite feelings of despondency and fear of the unknown, appreciative abandonment is ultimately a choice we can make. When all is said and done, have we been abandoned by the Mystery, or can we, in total trust, abandon ourselves to the Mystery? Appreciative abandonment becomes not merely a choice we make, but a lived disposition that deepens over a lifetime.[22]

Living from a stance of appreciative abandonment facilitates our perception of the invitations, challenges, and appeals offered to us by the Mystery. It aids us in avoiding fixation on one facet of our calling as if were the whole of who we are. Appreciative abandonment nurtures us in the art and discipline of listening to the leading of God more than to the dissonant stirrings of our individualistic ego.[23]

Appreciative living in abandonment to the Mystery is also transformative in observable ways. It changes the basis of our life from fear to love, lessening our anxiety and increasing our sense of "a listening presence to the Mystery in everyday living."[24] It fosters a disposition of gentleness, modulating an otherwise anxious life-style to one of benign yielding as we learn to trust in God's care for us.[25] It enhances our ability to persevere in serving and caring for others, even in the face of seeming ingratitude.[26] By intentionally practicing "instant appreciative abandonment," by choosing to affirm our decision to trust God's care for us despite "a flood of depreciative information to our powers of attention," even coercive dispositions of our tenacious neuroform may be modulated and reformed.[27]

---

21. van Kaam, *Fundamental Formation*, 237.
22. Ibid., 240–41.
23. van Kaam, *Transcendent Formation*, 229.
24. van Kaam, *Formation of the Human Heart*, 32.
25. Ibid., 86.
26. Ibid., 299–302.
27. van Kaam, *Transcendent Formation*, 259–60.

Affirmation of Formative Option

Affirmation is the act of engaging our human will in saying "yes" to consonant directives and "no" to those that are dissonant. In relation to reaching the culmination of the appraisal process, affirmation must emerge from, and be embedded in, the intrasphere of our personhood. We must freely affirm the divine directives we have appraised as consonant with our life-call, and worth pursuing for a lifetime.

Now is the time in the appraisal process that we say a deep and sincere "yes" to what the Mystery is asking of us. Resistance and refusal are put to rest. We now understand that dissonance was in service of our being led by the Mystery to consonance. This affirmation evokes a new sense of peace and joy, and activates these dispositions of our heart to such a degree that they become lasting. When we affirm the abandonment option and the direction in which it leads us, we move from fear to faith, from doubt to hope, and from coercive dispositions to formative liberation. We find ourselves on the threshold of the final A of Appraisal.

Application of Our Yes

Having abided in awe-filled attention, apprehended directives for appraisal, acknowledged any residual dissonance, engaged in argumentation and assessment, and finally affirmed to the best of our ability directives we believe to be in consonance with the will of God in appreciative abandonment, we come to the actual enfleshing of these invitations in our everyday life. We reach the A of Appraisal van Kaam identified as application. Now we are in a position to give actual form to received directives and to put them to the test of reality in everyday life.[28]

Application is neither a static goal nor an endpoint of appraisal, because this process is always open ended and "provisional."[29] It happens again and again in our human existence. Appraisal, as both a disposition and a process, is always dynamic. It is always open to the forming, reforming, and transforming work of the Spirit. Any directive needs "reality testing" by reiterated implementation in our lives. Within the context of appraisal, application readies us to receive new disclosures. Once a directive has been tested

---

28. van Kaam, *Scientific Formation*, 140–41.

29. van Kaam and Muto, *Essential Elements*, s.v. "Appraisal as Provisional." Van Kaam actually proposed at least three distinct facets to application, in view of its provisional nature, which he termed intraspheric proformation, tentative application, and definite implementation. See van Kaam, *Scientific Formation*, 141, for a discussion of these facets of application, as well as van Kaam, *Transcendence Therapy*, 255.

over time and confirmed as consonant, its application "can sink back in the realm of our prefocal consciousness. There the dynamic regains or acquires for the first time spontaneity," a hallmark of a healthy, mature spirituality.[30]

Conclusion

Van Kaam invited us to make a shift from considering appraisal only as a process to also recognizing it as an ongoing disposition of our heart and its matching character. We are not to live haphazardly from moment to moment. We are invited gently but firmly to seek the meaning of all that happens to us and in us. We bring to focal awareness signs of dissonance and consonance and appraise them accordingly. We are invited to utilize the tools of formative spirituality provided in the preceding chapters and to sharpen them through practice in service of resisting our pride form and growing in fidelity to our calling in Christ. The aim of so doing is to instill in our awareness the need to remain consonant with the Mystery at the center of our life and world. Thus every decision we make, every action we take, is to become more congenial, compatible, compassionate, and competent with our life-call in God. Through candid and courageous appraisal, our entire formation field mirrors and manifests increasing consonance with the Trinitarian Mystery at the center of our field of presence and action.

Reflection Questions

1. Understanding Our Story: Reflection Using the C's of Consonance in Appraisal

    One of the basic invitations of the Christian life is to appraise God's purpose in any given circumstance, and to seek to live in consonance with it. In this chapter, we learned that van Kaam and Muto offered one means to such appraisal through what they called the C's of consonance: congeniality, compatibility, compassion, and competence. Each of these provides a way to reflect on the various spheres of our formation field, in an effort to perceive any directives coming to us from those spheres and to discern whether or not such directives are consonant or dissonant with who God has called us to be and God's purposes in any given moment.

---

30. van Kaam, *Scientific Formation*, 141.

Call to mind a season or event from your past during which you were called upon to discern specific direction from God. Allow yourself to be present to God, and God to be present to you, in this time of reflection.

First, consider the C's of consonance. For the specific event you have in mind, describe which (if any) of the four C's of consonance was particularly formative in your appraisal process and take time to reflect on why you think that was the case.

As you look back on this time of appraisal in the context of other times of appraisal in your life, is there any particular one of the C's of consonance that generally tends to exert more influence on your appraisal process? Why do you think this might be so?

Are there any of the C's of consonance which has tended to be minimally influential in your habits of appraisal? If so, take some time to reflect as to why this may be the case. How has the Holy Spirit inspired you to identify what is dissonant in your life? Describe what for you are the main obstacles to consonance with God in all spheres, dimensions, dynamics, and expressions of your field of life. What conditions facilitate for you this kind of full field appraisal?

2. Understanding God's Story: Reflection on Appraisal in Favorite Bible Characters

   Recall that van Kaam understood appraisal as both an important disposition of the Christian life and, at times, as an intentional process.

   a. Appraisal as a Disposition: What are some of your favorite scriptural texts that encourage one to nurture an openness to God's leading in everyday life? Consider these Scriptures in relation to your understanding of van Kaam's concept of appraisal. In what ways do these Scriptures (and perhaps others that come to mind as you reflect) assist you in appraising consonance in your life? In what ways do these Scriptures (and perhaps others that come to mind as you reflect) assist you in appraising dissonance in your life?

   b. Appraisal as a Process: Consider the various facets of van Kaam's A's of appraisal: abiding in awe-filled attention; apprehension; acknowledge the dissonance; argumentation/assessment; appreciative abandonment; affirmation of formative option; and application of our yes.

      Reflect on Bible characters in relation to their needing to discern God's direction in their lives—or, if they did not know

God, in relation to their needing to make an important decision affecting their own and others' lives. Name at least two Bible characters who either engaged with—or ignored—each of the A's of appraisal.

Describe what you notice about the ways that appraisal, open to God or not so open to God, affected these people's lives and the consonance or dissonance of their formation field. Then take a few minutes to reflect on the ways in which these various facets of appraisal were formative in each of these person's situations. As you conclude your reflection, take time to notice what stirs in your own heart and mind as you reflect on the importance of appraisal. Describe any ways in which you find yourself responding to or perhaps resisting God's communications to the various characters on whose lives you have reflected.

Chapter 8

Modes of Direction

WHEN WE HEAR THE term spiritual direction, we often think immediately of an encounter between two believers, one who serves as the director, and the other as the directee. However, this mode of direction is only one of a three-pronged experience that must be placed in its proper context. The main mode of direction, according Adrian van Kaam and his colleague Susan Muto, is spiritual self-direction. This means that over a lifetime, we open ourselves to God primarily through the reading of Scripture and the spiritual writers, and through the guiding power of the Holy Spirit in the light of our adhered-to faith and formation traditions.

The second, and indeed the most important mode of direction, the one modeled most of the time by our Lord Jesus Christ, is what van Kaam and Muto identify as spiritual direction-in-common. They provide a model that must be understood as more than Bible study or shared spiritual reading. It entails a definite technique that can be of great help in a seminary, a congregation, or an institute of higher learning, where students and participants want to join together to appraise the divine directives that best emerge "where two or three are gathered" in the name of the Lord.[1]

Less common in practice, and indeed not to be equated with the meaning of spiritual direction as such, is one-on-one, or private, direction. This is a privileged encounter that requires the presence of a wise, learned, and experienced director who can help people in intense moments of formation, such as in religious life, during a novitiate, or in a seminary where one may be in pursuit of ordination, to more deeply appraise one's call, one's vocation, and one's avocation. In the general population, the need for one-on-one direction is short-term; it most often occurs at what is an emergent life moment when persons may feel conflicted about what God wants of them and need to consult with someone who will guide their listening in the light of the ultimate guidance of the Holy Spirit, the Divine Artisan at the center of all three modes of direction. In both one-on-one direction

---

1. Matt 18:20.

and direction-in-common, it is essential to redirect the person or group to always ongoing spiritual self-direction.²

These three modes of direction foster our openness in humility to the directives disclosed to us by our growing and graced intimacy with the Mystery of the Most Holy Trinity at the center of our formation field. They foster the discovery and unfolding of our life-call in Christ, in consonance with the will of the Father as revealed by the Spirit. As van Kaam and Muto write,

> To move in the direction ordained by the Spirit in our Christian heart changes our perspective on our previously taken-for-granted life of faith and its sad loss. It takes time and patience to let go of coercive security directives. The initial consolations associated with spiritual awakening tempt us to stay within the safe confines of a "feel good" spirituality. We would rather not opt for the self-stripping asked of us by adherence to the cross of Christ. Frightened as we may be of the risk of faith, our Divine Artisan nudges us onward, readying us to move from midnight moments of fear and trembling to the dawn of mature discipleship.
>
> The art and discipline of spiritual direction may hold the key that unlocks the secrets of God's design for our lives. Every time we approach a new threshold of choice, the Spirit prods us to let go of previous attachments, real or imagined, that prevented full abandonment. This appreciative advancement is not only true for us personally; it also characterizes the ongoing story of Christianity over the millennia. Christ sent us the Paraclete to set in motion the ongoing process of disclosing the legacy of faith we have been given. Sinful though we may be, however unworthy we may feel, the Father asks us to participate in his Son's mission of salvation.³

Spiritual Self-Direction

Spiritual self-direction is a life-long commitment to open our spirit, heart, mind, and will, under all circumstances, to the directing power of the Holy Spirit. It counters our tendency to place ourselves at the center of our formation field, and fosters our appreciation for the way the Mystery calls us over a lifetime to love and serve others. Such attention to the whole and Holy lifts us beyond the limits of our pretranscendent individuality. Spiritual

---

2. For an in-depth explanation of these three modes of spiritual direction and their dynamics, see van Kaam and Muto, *Dynamics of Spiritual Direction*.

3. van Kaam and Muto, *Formation of the Christian Heart*, 199.

self-direction offers us, so to speak, daily oases amidst the stresses of frantic functionalism. It helps us to put relationships before selfish emphases on me, my, and mine. It teaches us to be attentive to how the deepest self that we are is always under the direction of the Spirit.

Obstacles

The main obstacle to this mode of direction is the functionalistic achievement disposition. Once it becomes dominant in our life, and therefore resistant to spiritual self-direction, it breeds what van Kaam and Muto identify as the fallacy of perfectionism, the monolithic fallacy, and the fallacy of self-sufficiency.

Perfectionism prevents our flowing with God's mysterious way of revealing something of who we are in the very imperfections with which we must cope.[4] This fallacy seeks to make self and others faultless carbon copies of preconceived molds, rather than unique-communal epiphanies of the Christ form.[5]

The monolithic fallacy forces as many people as possible into the same apostolic effort, whether or not it is in tune with their own life call.[6] It renders one oblivious to the plight of abandoned souls at all levels of society, among rich and poor, powerful and powerless, urban dweller and rural farmer. It is a reductionistic fallacy that concludes, in effect, that "one size fits all."

The fallacy of self-sufficiency fosters the illusion that we can independently carve out or invent our direction, oblivious to the mysterious life-direction intended for us by God.[7] It tempts us to operate independently of the foundational wisdom of our faith and formation traditions.

These pretranscendent orientations fuel our drives for self-actualization and individuation. They push us to seek meaning not in the divine directives we receive from God, but from the sociohistorical pulsations, the vital pulsions, and the functional ambitions that continually threaten to override our transcendent aspirations and pneumatic-ecclesial inspirations. Rather than living a life of consonance, we begin to experience dissonance in ourselves and divisiveness with others. This is why the self who we are is always in need of spiritual direction by the Divine Artisan of the Trinity.

---

4. van Kaam and Muto, *Dynamics of Spiritual Direction*, chapter 13, "Fallacy of Perfectionism," 141–46.

5. Ibid., 142.

6. Ibid., chapter 14, "Monolithic Fallacy," 147–55.

7. Ibid., chapter 15, "Fallacy of Self-Sufficiency," 157–64.

Facilitating Conditions

The main condition for spiritual self-direction is to foster a transcendent achievement disposition. It points to the fact that all of our pretranscendent dispositions are now servants of the transcendent. They enable us to do what we have to do to fulfill God's will, in the light of our unique-communal life-call and the moment-by-moment graces we receive to remember that the Mystery is the center of our field of presence and action. In the light of the transcendent, we see individual skills, aptitudes, and talents as gifts of the Mystery that help us to put into practice what inspires us in the give-and-take of daily life.

Another condition that facilitates spiritual self-direction is to make focally aware as soon as possible any signs of dissonance in our core form. We need to attend to ways in which the Spirit may be directing us to see such dissonance as an invitation to deeper consonance with the Mystery. We might want to ask ourselves such self-directive questions as: what would Jesus do in this situation? Can we try to let his attitudes and actions become our own in the light of what we appraise as further disclosures of our call?

Three dispositions at the heart of spiritual self-direction facilitate its life-long unfolding. They are: openness, which tempers our fear of the unknown and assures ongoing appraisal of our call; detachment, which nourishes the trust that each situation the Lord allows contains a rich bounty of divine directives; and patience, which enables us to approach both simple and complex situations in a relaxed way that lets us see more of what could be done, if we step out of the way and let God be God in our lives.

Essential Disciplines

These following six disciplines facilitate the life-long practice of spiritual self-direction.[8] The first discipline is to cultivate silence as an interior disposition as well as to seek exterior silence insofar as possible. Christian spiritual writers agree that silence is a fertile ground for intimacy with God, self, and others. It is a condition for the very possibility of remaining present to the Mystery. "Be still and know that I am God."[9]

The second discipline is formative reading, which must be distinguished from the kind of informational reading we do to prepare a class or write a paper. It means listening to the text at hand, especially Holy

---

8. See Muto, *Pathways of Spiritual Living*, for a fuller presentation of these six disciplines.
9. Ps 46:10.

Scripture, with inner ears of faith, and allowing it to address us in our here-and-now situation.

The third discipline is meditative reflection. It teaches us to adopt a respectful and receptive stance toward the divine directives we have received. We move, with the help of grace, from head to heart, and abide lovingly with the Mystery as we seek to allow God's word to us to become God's word for us.

The fourth discipline is prayer, understood as offering our whole selves to God, and living a life of worshipful presence to the Trinity in the world. Now we are ready to move, with God's help, from merely saying prayers to practicing the prayer of presence.

The fifth discipline is contemplation, which means that we sense, we believe, and we experience that we truly are temples of God. We abide with the Mystery in contemplative stillness, and ready ourselves to receive the ineffable gift of peace. We grow in the virtues of humility, detachment, and charity. We wait upon the Lord in our interior and exterior lives. We live serenely yet fully committed to Christ in the situations in which Divine Providence places us.

The sixth discipline, action, means that we are on the way to becoming contemplatives in action. Because our lives are increasingly grounded in God, we live in a gracious rhythm of worship and work, presence and participation, leisure and labor.

Direction-in-Common

This model of spiritual direction unfolds in a group setting of approximately seven to twelve participants, with a trained facilitator, all of whom are respectfully aware of the Holy Spirit at the center of this gathering.[10] Direction-in-common brings people, rather quickly, from get-acquainted exchanges of information or mere problem-solving, to sharing on a deeper level of faith formation. It utilizes texts from Scripture and Christian spiritual writers as centerpieces for reflection. It operates in accordance with distinct components that, once experienced, can also be applied to various ministerial and pastoral situations, including, for example, delivering a sermon or participating in worship services or spiritual conferences.

Direction-in-common is oriented toward both what we humans have in common and the disclosure of directives that facilitate human and

---

10. See van Kaam and Muto, *Epiphany Manual*, for an extensive review not only of the structure of such a formation-in-common group, but for an exploration of common dynamics in such groups, both in leaders and participants. Reading the manual is an essential first step to understand, prepare for, and practice, direction-in-common.

Christian formation, reformation, and transformation. The focus here is not on one author or one school of spirituality or one facet of a tradition, but on what is foundational in our quest for a deeper spiritual life in the world. The practice emphasizes what is experiential rather than merely speculative, for the purpose of evoking how God's guiding love resonates in an intentional gathering, the aim of which is to receive spiritual directives for everyday life in family, church, and society.

In direction-in-common sessions, facilitators are not lecturers, but "master listeners" to the Holy Spirit present in each person and in the group as a whole. Their role is not to critique participants based on their own experience, but to offer steady encouragement. Participants address one another gently and firmly for the purpose of detecting common directives that will be disclosed as the session unfolds over the hour or hour-and-a-half when people are together. Direction-in-common does require a certain continuity of sharing, for example, over a three-to-six month period. In summary, this mode of direction offers an excellent way to rise above individualistic argumentation and facilitate respectful interformation in compassion for self and others in honor of the Mystery that sustains and embraces us all.

Obstacles

What hinders the flow of a direction-in-common experience is any posturing of intellectual superiority that draws participants into issue-oriented debates, pop spirituality, or pretentious spiritual practices. Crassly competitive and impatient communications that show arrogance or condescension, and lead to disruptive mood-breaking, also hinder the process.

To be avoided are subtle entrapments in functional ambitions that spark envious comparisons and one-upmanship. Worst of all are forced efforts to hasten divine direction disclosures and to push against the pace of grace. To be avoided at all costs is the establishment of a "personality cult" around a popular facilitator or participant, or to use this process for proselytizing or other persuasive tactics.[11]

Facilitating Conditions

Trusting exchanges between believers and sincere seekers in a small group setting like that of direction-in-common is the first condition that facilitates

---

11. van Kaam and Muto, *Epiphany Manual*, 43–48; see also van Kaam and Muto, *Dynamics of Spiritual Direction*, chapter 25, "Obstacles Hindering Direction-in-Common," 281–89.

this practice. It presupposes strict confidentiality outside of the session. Related to trust is the condition of being receptive and responsive to the leading of the Holy Spirit throughout the course of the group's time together. This means listening to the appeal of the Spirit heard within the heart of each person in the group, thus illuminating the path to redeemed living sought by all.

This practice is also facilitated when we disclose together common themes of faith deepening, embedded in what we believe and how we live these beliefs in daily life. What follows is the facilitating condition of being patiently open to the inspirations emerging from written and spoken words, and to the respectful processing of resistances to, and resonances with, the centering text. Last but not least, all participants pray that the seeds of self-direction already implanted in them by the Spirit may come to fruition in direction-in-common.[12]

Six Components of a Direction-in-Common Session

1. Contemplation
2. Conference
3. Conversation
4. Communion
5. Closure
6. Commitment

Essential Components

Contemplation is first component of a direction-in-common session. It fosters a gentle shift in consciousness through invitations to silence and prayerful presence to the Divine Presence.[13] It is when the members of the group intentionally place themselves in an orientation of awe-filled abiding with the Holy Spirit, who is the Director of all directors. Examples of contemplative practices may include, among others, a brief opening prayer of gathering followed by a few minutes of silence, the soft playing of a melody of praise, or an invitation by facilitators to still our hearts before the Mystery.

The second component of a direction-in-common session is conference.[14] This is when facilitators introduce, in an experiential way, the text

---

12. van Kaam and Muto, *Epiphany Manual*, 35–38; van Kaam and Muto, *Dynamics of Spiritual Direction*, 265–80.

13. van Kaam and Muto, *Epiphany Manual*, 19–20.

14. Ibid., 20–21.

chosen for reflection, and when participants gain a sense of commonality about the text through a shared story or anecdote.[15] For example, facilitators may share a happening in their lives that resonates with the centering reading. Participants may read through the text either aloud or silently, followed by the facilitator's lifting up experientially a sentence, an image, or an idea for further reflection.

The third component of direction-in-common is conversation.[16] During this, the longest period of the session, the members of the group share both what they resonate with and what they resist in the text. Also important is the recognition of emerging themes that have common implications for all, as opposed to theoretical discussion or going off on a thousand tangents. If and when such distractions should happen, the role of the facilitator is to draw the attention of the group back to the centering text. To be avoided is the urge to talk all the time. Silent pauses facilitate the emergence of common directives. Experienced facilitators allow direction-in-common to happen; they temper the need to steer the group in a preconceived direction.[17] Here, as in all these modes of spiritual direction, members of the group must be open to the often surprising disclosures of the Spirit.

The fourth component is communion.[18] This is the time when the facilitator lifts into the light and summarizes common themes heard in the sharing, emphasizing the directives all have received. The facilitator may then invite the participants to name what they recognize as common themes.

The fifth component is closure.[19] Now is the time to identify the common directives elicited in the session and to celebrate the ways in which all have benefited from this time together. A way of doing so may be to encourage participants to offer a thank-you prayer.

The sixth and final component is commitment.[20] Briefly, the facilitator affirms again the divine directives disclosed in this session, forecasts upcoming sessions, and encourages everyone to renew the commitment to live these directives more intentionally between sessions. This is when facilitators and the group go forth with a blessing for what they have shared in trust and confidentiality. Everyone cordially departs, perhaps after a closing prayer.

---

15. Selecting a text for focused attention in advance of the direction-in-common session is one of the responsibilities of the group facilitator. For helpful criteria in selection of such texts, see *Epiphany Manual*, 73.

16. van Kaam and Muto, *Epiphany Manual*, 21–22.

17. Ibid., 22.

18. Ibid.

19. Ibid., 22–23.

20. Ibid., 23.

One-on-One Direction

The mode of one-on-one direction, in response to the Spirit's leading, is especially important in emergent life situations.[21] In van Kaam and Muto's view, one-on-one spiritual direction is of relatively brief duration, requiring usually no more than three sessions of fifty minutes each, and must never be seen as a substitute for needed pastoral or psycho-therapeutic counseling.[22] A director must know where the dynamics of ego-functional psychology leave off, and where the dynamics of a transcendent and transcendent-functional, pneumatic-ecclesial life-call begin.[23]

In one-on-one direction, seekers in need of spiritual guidance at threshold periods of life, or amid genuine transcendence crises, enter into an intentional relationship with a wise, learned, and experienced director to ascertain if their appraisal of significant call disclosures is in tune with God's will. This appraisal, as distinct from general formation counseling in a care-giving setting, takes place in keeping with the teachings of the church and in fidelity to both the director and the directee's shared formation traditions. Once the Spirit's leading becomes clear, it is the responsibility of directees to embody these disclosures in humble, faith-filled obedience within the authoritative directives of the ecclesial traditions which they and their director share. Full, ongoing attentiveness to directives received from the Spirit in the context of the directee's entire formation field is essential.

Thanks to the art and discipline of full field appraisal, both the director and directee begin the process of spiritual direction in awe-filled abiding, attentive to the movements of the Spirit both transfocally and focally, and ready to apprehend divine direction disclosures in everyday life.[24] Since the appeal of the Holy Spirit is the central point of spiritual direction, the director has to find the right balance between speaking and listening, distance and nearness. To answer the summons of the Spirit, the director has to suspend concentration on anything but the directee's response during this

---

21. van Kaam and Muto, *Dynamics of Spiritual Direction*, 372–73.

22. Ibid., 319–21. While most one-on-one direction is understood to be short-term, there are some exceptions, as in the case of initial formation in religious life (a novitiate) or in preparation for the priesthood or other ordained ministry. In all cases, one must be redirected always to ongoing spiritual self-direction to shed further light on disclosures received either in direction-in-common or one-on-one direction.

23. For a fine explanation of the requisite preparation for serving as a director in one-on-one spiritual formation, including an extensive set of obstacles and facilitating conditions for such ministry, see van Kaam and Muto, *Dynamics of Spiritual Direction*, "Part III: One-on-One Spiritual Direction," 319–439.

24. van Kaam and Muto, *Dynamics of Spiritual Direction*, chapter 32, "Place of Appraisal in Private Direction," 351–60.

hour of graced guidance.[25] Never central in this relationship are the physical, emotional, or cultural assets or deficits of the directee. Always central is the movement of the Spirit, urging the directee to go against his or her lacks and attainments to deeper fidelity to his or her life-call. Now is the time for the director and the directee to discern together what blocks the flow of grace and to foster growth in the Lord, regardless of one's past experiences.

Obstacles

What despoils the art and discipline of one-on-one direction is an unprepared director who creates an atmosphere of sentimental indulgence, irresponsible leniency, or indiscriminate compliance. It is always a mistake to show an interest in a person's spiritual life only when it appears to be an extension of one's own. An atmosphere of spiritual excitation, promoting one current of spirituality above another, or posturing it as "the way" for all, is a danger.[26]

A related obstacle is to focus on a director's personal devotions to the exclusion of a consideration of the foundations of a directee's faith tradition. In the same vein, it is problematic to point so much to the side benefits of prayer and meditation that one neglects to consider the meaning of the cross. Were directors to put their subjective interests or issue-orientations before the objective truth of the revelation, one might hinder the Spirit's work during this privileged encounter.

To be avoided always is playing on the needs of vulnerable directees who want a quick and easy solution to their quest for direction. As a result, what one risks is the danger of arousing in them false guilt feelings if they do not follow to the letter a formula for perfection.

In the end, all of these obstacles point to the overall problem of dissonant directorial domination or its opposite, a morally relativistic, nondirective posture, by which we listen more to our directees than to the Holy Spirit's direction for them.

Facilitating Conditions

Mindful of one of the few one-on-one encounters of spiritual direction in Scripture, that of Jesus with the Samaritan woman in John 4:1–42, directors try

---

25. Ibid., chapter 33, "Dynamics of Giving and Receiving One-on-One Direction," 361–74.

26. Ibid., chapter 34, "Currents of Spirituality Affecting Private Direction," 375–84.

their best to be prayerfully responsive to the Spirit in this person-to-person, heart-to-heart contact. Directors try to create during this time together an atmosphere of unconditional faith, hope, and love, of trust and confidentiality.[27]

A director remains aware of the life of a directee in the light of the Spirit's presence between them, exuding a disposition of relaxed acceptance, rooted in the love and forgiveness of God, embodied in voice and posture that communicates listening deeply to verbal and non-verbal exchanges. Directors ought never to underestimate the importance of silent pauses, or feel obliged to fill them in with chatter. They know that silence gives the Spirit room to work.[28]

The director shows the right balance of interest and detachment, of silence and speaking, thus giving directees a chance to assess what is on their heart without reacting to them emotionally in a favorable or unfavorable manner. That is why their encounter remains sincere, straight-forward, honest and truthful, firm yet flexible, and always aimed at full field appraisal.

One-on-one direction is facilitated in a particular way by five dispositions. Receptivity communicates how open directors are to the often private and delicate disclosures of directees, to say nothing of the subtle directives communicated by the Spirit.[29] The disposition of detection suggests that directors are able to help directees find and follow the divine direction disclosures in their life. Inquiry means that directors have a special knack to know when to ask a question that will evoke more self-discovery on the part of directees, and when to answer questions directees may pose without feeling obliged to answer with a long oration.[30] The disposition of expression points to the fact that directors avoid communicating abstract information, and instead draw directees towards experiential, formative disclosures of where they are, and of where they believe God may be leading them. And finally, embodiment points to the importance of a director's voice, gesture, and comportment, and whether or not one embodies prayerful acceptance, gentleness, and sincerity throughout the encounter.[31] There is no fidgeting allowed, no roaming eyes, or looking at one's watch. In short, one must do all that one can to create a welcoming atmosphere that encourages honest exploration of God's will and the courage to follow it in everyday life.

---

27. Ibid., chapter 35, "Practice of Private Direction," 385–97.

28. Ibid., 394–95.

29. Ibid., 341–42 (where the authors describe this disposition under the topic of "Acceptance"), and 352.

30. Ibid., 385–87.

31. Ibid., 344 (where the authors describe this disposition under the topic of "Gentle Encouragement").

Essential Skills

The first skill anyone offering one-on-one direction needs is description, by which fully mature spiritual directors know how to help directees identify and describe the formative event that brought them to this encounter.[32] This skill encourages factual description, not quick interpretation or evaluation. Initially one needs mutual listening in the Spirit, not preconceived analysis. One must, so to speak, step out of the way, so that the guidance of the Holy Spirit takes primacy.

The second skill, articulation, enables directors to name for consideration from whence directees have come, what they may be going through, and, with the help of grace, to what they may be drawn by the Holy Spirit.[33] Thanks to this skill, directors guide people beyond mere introspection toward dialogue with their whole formation field, fostering a transcendent, pneumatic-ecclesial vision of their life, rather than one that is merely functional or vital. This skill helps directors, when the time is right, to disclose obstacles to and facilitating conditions for better attunement to God's will.

The third skill, elucidation, is that by which directors help directees to bring into the light the dynamics and motivations behind the event or crisis with which they are struggling.[34] Elucidation happens in an atmosphere of trust, where one listens not only to oral language, but also to body language. At appropriate moments, directors may reiterate key phrases, or ask questions, to prompt reflections on obstacles to and facilitating conditions for consonance with the Mystery. Elucidation is especially effective when directors have a lively prefocal consciousness, which enables them to draw appropriately upon narratives, symbols, images, and metaphors to shed more light on what God may be asking of directees.

The skill of consultation means that the directors have ready-to-hand books and articles, Scripture passages and spiritual writings, that are relevant to what is occurring in this encounter.[35] Consultation helps directees move beyond the "this-could-only-happen-to-me" syndrome to a sense of common bonding with other seekers at the present moment and in past.

---

32. The skill of description here is related to van Kaam's methods of formation science, articulation and selection (*Scientific Formation*, 104–5). The essential skills discussed here are based on applications of van Kaam's analysis of these methods, outlined in *Scientific Formation*, 89–96.

33. van Kaam, *Scientific Formation*, 94. For a form theological perspective on articulation in the Christian life, see van Kaam and Muto's *Christian Articulation of the Mystery*.

34. van Kaam, *Scientific Formation*, 94–95.

35. Ibid., 95. For examples of the use of classic Christian resources in formative consultation, see van Kaam and Muto, *Living Our Christian Faith and Formation Traditions*.

The fifth skill, translation, means that directors can literally translate the insights gained in these confidential encounters into a person's own language and symbol system.[36] Insights thus translated show the connection between what is happening now and the rich contributions of our faith and formation traditions.

Finally, the skill of reflection encourages directees to meditate daily in the context of spiritual self-direction, on the lights and insights they have received, and to apply the lessons they have learned as fully as possible. Such reflection avoids anxious introspectionism with the self at the center, and turns toward transcendent self-presence with God at the center. As van Kaam and Muto write,

> Formative, reformative, and transformative direction could be compared to a widening spiral. Starting out humbly, directors and directees experience how grace opens them little by little to the aspirations and inspirations of the Holy Spirit. Their prayerful presence to one another and to God during these private sessions frees them to relinquish any directive at odds with obedience to their destiny.[37]

Conclusion

Especially in times of crisis, when we find ourselves at the threshold of crucial options that may affect the rest of our lives, some form of direction would be advisable. Formative self-direction, direction-in-common, and one-on-one direction may prevent us from succumbing to the dictates of our self-centered pride form. Popular pulsations, vitalistic pulsions, and functionalistic ambitions may stifle the transcendent orientation of our spirit unless we find the help we need to see beyond the obstacles blocking our path to inner freedom and phasic maturity, the conditions that shed light on what is congenial, or uncongenial, with our calling in Christ.

In this chapter, we have seen the importance of appraising everyday situations as sources of life directives. We have confirmed the importance of living in fidelity to our call in every sphere of our formation field. Our emphasis on holistic appraisal has facilitated our emergence in and with the Mystery of formation.

---

36. Ibid., 96.

37. van Kaam and Muto, *Dynamics of Spiritual Direction*, 368. For specific guidance as to how the skill of reflection may be experienced, review Figure 2 ("Introspection vs Transcendent Self-Presence") in chapter 6.

To be called, committed, and consecrated as an adopted child of God is to ponder God's plan for our life, however mysterious and hidden it may be. We know that every experience may be a pointer to self-emergence in the future. The effort and courage to let go of our old current self is painful, but, as we hope to reveal in the next chapter, only when we do let go can we be led by the Mystery to new disclosures of our life-call with all the blessings this discovery grants.

Reflection Questions

1. Understanding Our Story: Reflecting on Dispositions and Practices of Spiritual Self-Direction

    As we have learned in this chapter, spiritual self-direction, through which we express our life-long commitment to remain open to the Holy Spirit's guidance in everyday life, is the most common of the three modes of spiritual direction outlined by van Kaam and Muto. They identified common obstacles to and facilitating conditions for spiritual self-direction, as well as noting six essential disciplines for maturing in our receptivity to the direction of the Spirit.

    Allow God to be present to you as you reflect on the following: Describe some of your own current dispositions and practices of spiritual self-direction. What would you identify as the key dispositions in your life that nurture your openness to divine directives? What practices most help you to be aware of the gentle promptings of God's Spirit in your everyday living? What practices better enable you to respond in obedience?

    Take some time to prayerfully reflect on the common obstacles that van Kaam and Muto said may block our awareness of directives and invitations of God's Spirit to us (a functionalistic achievement disposition, perfectionism, a monolithic fallacy that purports that "one size fits all" in regard to what living a mature Christian life looks like, and autarkic self-sufficiency). In what ways have you noticed these or other obstacles in your life posing as resistances to your commitment to follow Christ?

    Van Kaam and Muto noted six disciplines that have helped many committed Christians in their spiritual self-direction throughout the ages: cultivating silence, formative reading of Scripture and Christian spiritual writers, meditative reflection, living in prayerful presence to God moment-by-moment, contemplation, and actively living rhythms of worship and work, presence and participation, leisure and labor. To which of these disciplines do you find yourself drawn? Why do you believe that is the case? Describe ways in which the practices to which you are drawn might facilitate a response to the obstacles that you noted previously.

2. Understanding God's Story: Spiritual Self-Direction in a Bible Character

The Bible is filled with accounts of women and men, boys and girls, apprehending, appraising, and obeying invitations and directives from God (examples include Noah and Samuel, Esther and Ruth, Mary and Joseph, the women at the tomb Easter morning, and the disciples in Jerusalem after Jesus' resurrection).

Choose one of your favorite people in the Bible for whom some background and description is available, who heard and responded in obedience to directives from God. Describe the ways in which the person perceived divine directives: was it through their intrasphere, or perhaps through another person, or through the circumstances of their life (consider all the spheres of the person's formation field)? Describe the ways in which the dimensions of the person's formation field (sociohistorical, vital, functional, and transcendent) influenced their response to God's directives to them. Describe, too, the ways in which the person's obedience to God in turn gave form to their formation field.

Describe any ways in which you find yourself responding to or perhaps resisting God's communications to this character. As you conclude your reflection, take time to notice what stirs in your own heart and mind as you consider the ways in which the full field context of people's lives shapes their openness and obedience to God's direction.

Chapter 9

Transcendence Crisis

OUR FUNDAMENTAL THRUST TOWARD transcendence can emerge at any time from infancy to adulthood, although it makes itself known most often in late childhood or adolescence; it then continues to unfold throughout adult life.[1] The transcendence dynamic is the highest and the deepest ground of human life. Thanks to this dynamic, we can integrate all the spheres and dimensions of our lives in the light of the radical formation Mystery.[2]

Transcendence Dynamic

The transcendence dynamic is preformed in us by the Mystery. It is as much a given of our formation as is our biological makeup.[3] It is that distinctively human dynamic that disrupts any tendency in us to wait until after a crisis to seek liberation from coercive security directives.[4] This dynamic creates a restlessness in our souls that draws us beyond our current life form, through a crisis, to a new current life form. At crucial points on our journey, this

---

1. van Kaam, *Transcendence Therapy*, 9; van Kaam, *Transcendent Formation*, 223.

2. van Kaam, *Traditional Formation*, 79, 186. Note that van Kaam recognized that this human potential to go beyond an immediate vitalistic or functionalistic purpose, the potential to transcend, can be realized in more or less harmful or helpful ways. (See van Kaam, *Traditional Formation*, 29–30, for further discussion of varying realizations of the transcendence dynamic potential that he observed.) Van Kaam was intentional about integrating this dynamic in his formation field so as to avoid any dualistic tendencies that might suggest that our spirit unfolds in isolation from the entirety of who we are. He posited this integration via the concept of the transcendent dimension of his formation field model. He viewed the transcendence dynamic as giving rise to the transcendent dimension, the dimension that is comprised of both responses to this dynamic and the influence of this dynamic throughout the other dimensions of the formation field (see van Kaam, *Traditional Formation*, 79–80, for discussion of the relationship between the transcendence dynamic and the transcendent dimension).

3. van Kaam, *Transcendent Formation*, 3; van Kaam and Muto, *Essential Elements*, s.v. "Awakening of the Transcendence Dynamic."

4. Ibid., 62; van Kaam, *Transcendent Formation*, 263–64.

restlessness "can increase to such a degree that it becomes a crisis" of our overall sense of meaning and direction.[5] When such a time of disruption occurs, we are invited by the grace of God to a greater depth of reflection and action. We are challenged to leave behind our current life form and to follow the new directives emerging from our life-call.[6]

Formative Events

Having been trained as both a priest and a psychologist, van Kaam respected the role of narrative in the articulation of our progress through life. He delighted in listening to others share memorable events, whether around a dinner table, during a walk, or in a formal therapy or spiritual direction setting. He saw all of life as formative. He noted that while all events are potentially more-or-less formative, some are especially so because they shake us to the foundations. We have to redirect our course whether we want to or not.[7]

Van Kaam chose the modifier *formative* to distinguish such occurrences from the unexamined experiences that make up the normal course of our sociohistorical, vital, and functional lives.[8] As he reflected on the significance of formative events, especially those involving transcendence crises, he noticed a descriptive pattern emerging. He named it the formative action pattern, or the from-through-to movement. It facilitates the description of what actually happened in a formative event under consideration.[9] The movement we detect is *from* one set of dynamics at play in our current form, *through* the layers of choices and decisions that must be made if we are to move forward, *to* an observable change that initiates a new current life form. A formative event is a "special expression of our formation field

---

5. van Kaam, *Transcendence Therapy*, 111.

6. van Kaam, *Transcendent Formation*, 69, 110, 216; van Kaam and Muto, *Essential Elements*, s.v. "Transcendence Dynamic and Crises of Disclosure."

7. van Kaam, *Formation of the Human Heart*, 361–62.

8. van Kaam, *Scientific Formation*, 107. Van Kaam honored such experiences by requiring his graduate students to begin their studies in formative spirituality by the narration of such events, but encouraged his students to then reexamine such experiences through a specific theoretically grounded methodology in order to "[wean] students away from an exclusive preoccupation with their subjective spiritual experiences" and help them to disclose "subjectivistic limitations and possible self-deceptions inherent in private or group experiences" (*Scientific Formation*, 109).

9. van Kaam and Muto, *Essential Elements*, s.v. "Focus of Anthropology and Theology of Formation."

as a whole."[10] Van Kaam noted that not only individuals, but entire social groups, may experience formative events, as happened to the Dutch during the Hunger Winter.[11] As he wrote in his memoirs,

> During the hours we had to spend in black-out periods, I had time to think about the nature of a transcendence crisis. Long talks with a Jewish banker hiding in the same place as I led me to the disclosure of what I would identify in later writings as a "formative action pattern." In his case, he had moved from a life of relative luxury to living in a barn. How was he to find his way through this radical change? Would the memory of his past life paralyze him to such a degree that he dared not look ahead? Was there a future to which he could go as he moved from one current life form, through this crisis, to a new current life form? All we knew at the moment was that we stood on the verge of a gruesome winter that would wrench us from any hope of quick liberation, that would take us through the ravages caused by occupation, and that would bring us to a new time of recovery that for now was only like the dimmest light on an otherwise dark horizon.[12]

Crisis of Transcendence

If there is any event worthy of full field appraisal, it is a transcendence crisis. Throughout the course of our lifetime, when we find ourselves overwhelmed with a sense that our way of living is no longer adequate, a crisis may occur that it is impossible to ignore. Perhaps we experience a loss—a beloved friend or family member dies, we are out of work, we discover that we have a terminal illness, a treasured relationship has deteriorated—or we find our zest for living waning and we don't know why.[13] Daily life becomes

---

10. van Kaam, *Human Formation*, 22.

11. For an exploration of the communal influence of shared formative events, see van Kaam, *Formation of the Human Heart*, 269–70.

12. van Kaam, *Life Journey*, 50.

13. van Kaam, *Human Formation*, 195. In *Transcendent Self*, van Kaam identified and explored nine basic types of transcendence crises: crises of confinement (related to human limitations); crises of contingency (related to our dependence on people and circumstances); crises of appearance (related to the effect of our appearance on others); crises of expectation (related to who and what we take for granted); crises of idealized life directions (related to aspirations we have that are not aligned with our life-call in Christ); crises of continuity (related to how past life forms relate to current and future life forms); crises of direction (related to new ways of being that are more in tune with

more of a chore than a joy. A certain weariness of spirit may overtake us. We may feel confused about what to do next. We find ourselves asking such questions as: What does life mean? Where am I going? Where have I been? Why has my life been so disrupted?[14]

When such disruption does occur in the normal course of our lives, the dissonance it creates signals that the way we were accustomed to being and doing may be breaking apart or collapsing altogether. Lacking answers for what is happening, we experience a crisis, though, at the moment, we do not yet understand where it might take us. All we know is that life has taken an unexpected turn. We have lost our way. We are unsure of ourselves.

Such moments of crisis represent a tense interplay of dissonance and consonance. A transcendence crisis always unfolds on the razor's edge between growth or stagnation. The English word *crisis* comes from the Greek *krineo* meaning "a parting of the ways," one side being danger, the other opportunity.[15] On the side of danger, one might deny the dissonance by, for example, pretending to oneself that nothing really important is happening here, so why pay attention to it? On the side of opportunity we may intuit that this event will further disclose some facets of our unique-communal life-call, and that one may grow beyond dissonance to greater consonance.[16]

The nature of a transcendence crisis is such that, if we opt to remain on the side of danger and deny the dissonance we feel, such denial will lead to a deformative appraisal, resulting in the conclusion that we have been abandoned by the Mystery. The end result will be further disintegration. Subtle or overt feelings of discouragement, depletion, and despair may invade our prefocal consciousness.

To turn to the side of opportunity means that we affirm the dissonance we feel. Almost at the moment we do so, formative appraisal begins. Having chosen to abandon ourselves to the Mystery, our life begins to be reintegrated in some way. We try to see meaning in what we may have previously interpreted as meaningless. We accept that our limits do not represent the whole of who we are. Rather, they are challenges to open ourselves candidly and courageously to the Mystery. Affirming the dissonance means that we are no longer imprisoned by it. We begin to feel more encouragement, accompanied by a sense of hope and inner repletion.

---

our life's direction); crises of de-activation (related to reevaluating past involvements crucial to our self-identity); and crises of ultimate meaning (related to questions of whether or not our life has lasting meaning for ourselves or others) (van Kaam, *Transcendent Self*, 44–45, 63–64, 71, 74–76, 81, 88–91, 95, 101, 105–8).

14. van Kaam, *Transcendence Therapy*, 114.

15. Ibid., 113–14.

16. Ibid.

Rather than being able to make a clear-cut choice between depreciative and appreciative abandonment, we often experience great ambiguity in the midst of a transcendence crisis. It is as if we move back and forth between these two paths. At times, our heart feels like a veritable battlefield between dissonance and consonance. Crucially important at this point is that we do not deny the dissonance evoked by such ambiguity and uncertainty. We accept it as part of the appraisal process that must accompany a transcendence crisis. In time, we begin to feel more hopeful and willing to wait upon the Mystery, rather than to seek a quick solution to our difficulty. Now we see dissonance as a call to deeper consonance. We accept the fact that transcendence crises will happen many times over in our lives. What matters is that we name what is happening to us for what it is, and welcome it as part of our faith and formation journey.

Abandonment Option

As we have seen, in the human condition, the abandonment option is primordial and unavoidable. It is tied directly to our always situated freedom of choice.[17] As van Kaam explained,

> Our foundational human life-form distinguishes itself from other known forms in the universe by its relative freedom. This freedom makes the primordial formation decision unavoidable. It becomes impossible for us to keep hovering indefinitely over a decision between meaningfulness and meaninglessness. We may try to escape this decision for a lifetime by simply not choosing at all. However, the decision not to choose, if final in intention, is itself a choice. For we actually say no to the mystery of formation. In fact, we deny its beneficial meaning. In this decision for no choice at all, we even refuse to leave open the possibility that we may grow to an appreciative abandonment. We cut out of our life even the possible meaningfulness of formation. Factually, we choose an agnostic formation indifference. In reality we do not abandon ourselves to the mystery of formation as ultimately meaningful and beneficial in seminal faith, hope, and consonance.[18]

---

17. For van Kaam's arguments as to the situated versus unsituated nature of human freedom, see *Fundamental Formation*, 221–23, 229. For his arguments as to the primordial nature of the abandonment option, see *Fundamental Formation*, 240–41. For his observations linking the primordial nature of the abandonment option with early childhood experiences, see van Kaam, *Human Formation*, 53–54.

18. van Kaam, *Fundamental Formation*, 229.

All of our life decisions are traceable to this primordial option. The decision regarding our being abandoned by or to God, made in faith, is not one of simple mental assent. It is instead a choice resonating in our entire personhood, whether we have raised it to the level of consciousness or not.[19] Since the very nature of the abandonment option is one of faith, it is an issue that seldom, if ever, results in complete clarity. At times, we may forget that we have chosen to abandon ourselves to the Mystery. We may become entangled in the distractions of enhancing functionalistic success only. The way we live may suggest that we believe that there was no one else to trust but ourselves, let alone God. That is why the abandonment option offers two alternatives that merit further explanation.

Appreciative abandonment is a "basic inclination to strive for consonance with" the Mystery, which is fostered by (and in turn fosters) a conviction that ultimately one is cared for by the Mystery.[20] We live in awe-filled appreciation of the faithful love and care of God in which we are immersed at all times and under all circumstances. As a person who was part of the Dutch resistance to the Nazis during WWII, van Kaam was no naive optimist. He insisted that neither was appreciative abandonment a childish choice. "We acknowledge the deformation of people and societies, of form traditions, formation segments, and communities. We see it starkly in all its horror and darkness."[21]

The depreciative abandonment option is the choice to believe that we have been cast into a meaningless series of events, and forced to find our own way in situations where we feel helpless and hopeless. This option, once embedded in our core form, shows up in a tendency to dismiss or explain away any sign of meaningfulness in life. We are quick to notice and attach our thoughts to an indicator of seeming meaninglessness. Depreciative abandonment "disposes us to skepticism and despair," "implies the collapse of hope," and results in dissonance and a certain paralysis of life.[22]

Van Kaam was deeply concerned about the unfortunate outcomes of depreciative abandonment. Whereas its appreciative counterpart fosters increased sensitivity to the meaningful presence of the Mystery in our lives, depreciative abandonment decreases sensitivity to life's meaningfulness and gradually closes us to life as worth living.[23] It takes the courage of candor to

---

19. Ibid., 225–30.

20. Ibid., 235; van Kaam and Muto, *Essential Elements*, s.v. "Abandonment by or Abandonment to."

21. van Kaam, *Fundamental Formation*, 236.236.

22. Ibid., 230, 228, 232–33.

23. Ibid., 232.

face how such depreciative dynamics erode our relationships with God and others. We must try our best, with the help of grace and good counseling and spiritual direction, not to let this happen.

Fidelity to Our Call

The advantage of working through a transcendence crisis is that we are forced to reassess whether human life has an overall purpose or direction or not. Is our life seen as a fragmented set of discrete occurrences that are merely coincidental or as a beautiful tapestry in which every thread has a meaning? At the end of his memoirs van Kaam wrote,

> I have lived long enough to know that we do not know what awaits us. All we can do day by day is to live in faith and to open ourselves to the purification (*the crucifying epiphany*) that readies us for paradise (*the resurrection epiphany*). As long as we listen to the shy whispers of the Holy Spirit in our heart and continue to say *yes* to them in the always changing climates that characterize our life, all will be well. When the time comes for us to say with Jesus, "It is finished," we will pass over to eternity with the peace he gives. For now our duty is simply to carry on in fidelity to our unique-communal call and the divine destiny that is ours from the beginning of our life to its benign end.[24]

Though the Mystery of our call beckons us from birth to death, we may not always heed its invitation. At times we act as if we were the masters of our fate, bound with ball and chain, to make our existence meaningful. What we are invited to experience instead is the emergence of our unique-communal life-call. Our call orders and transcends what seem to be disconnected and jarring events over the course of our lives.[25] Our call goes beyond our projects and ideals. It expresses our love relationship with the God who loves us.[26] In their book *Foundations of Christian Formation*, van Kaam and Muto described the Spirit's gift of joyful gratitude.

> The joy that overflows our hearts in moments of enlightenment is a gift of the Spirit, bestowed upon us after we walk, perhaps for years, along the thorny path of purification. Many of us have to struggle against the temptation to lose joy. We withdraw into

---

24. van Kaam, *Life Journey*, 310.
25. van Kaam, *Traditional Formation*, 248–51.
26. van Kaam, *Traditional Formation*, 196–98; van Kaam and Muto, *Christian Articulation of the Mystery*, 107.

the dusty corners of fear or despair. We run away from God, but to what avail? It is better to beg the Spirit to raise us beyond prejudice, envy, distrust, and insecurity, beyond the self-enclosed imperatives that silence his freeing inspirations. Thoughts and feelings, words and gestures, decisions and actions, when transformed by the Spirit, enhance our openness to divine invitations, challenges, and appeals emanating from every sphere and dimension of our solitary and shared fields of life.

The Spirit's gift of joyful gratitude also changes the way we treat others. Through the pristine pane of the Paschal Mystery of Christ's death and resurrection, we see people, events, and things not as closed in upon themselves but as open to becoming epiphanic expressions of the splendor the Spirit lets shine forth in the magnificence of created forms. In them the Trinity unveils little by little what a life of everyday holiness means for our personal and communal existence. New lights radiate through the lenses of our faith-illumined field of inner vision. The Spirit attunes our listening heart to the music of the spheres. In due course we begin to behold his subtle movements in every joyful stirring of our core form and its matching character.[27]

Our unique-communal life-call reveals itself not only in the tensions experienced during a transcendence crisis; it emerges in the ups and downs of everyday living. The formative potential of our life-call is powerful. It not only provides specific disclosures and directives; it also exudes continuous, lasting dispositions of our heart that in turn become matching traits of our character and personhood.

Van Kaam used the term "call efficacy" to describe how we embody dispositions, attitudes, and directives in daily life.[28] One way to strengthen call efficacy is by call affirmation, which is an act of freely affirming a directive that we have appraised as consonant with our call.[29] Van Kaam distinguished affirmation from confirmation. Confirmation is the way in which others express their support of the call disclosures that characterize our life.[30] Just as affirmation is a part of the unique facet of our life call, so confirmation is part of its communal nature. Healthy confirmation of life-call disclosures in childhood lays the groundwork for later self-affirmation. When others confirm and nurture directives that are consonant with our

---

27. van Kaam and Muto, *Foundations of Christian Formation*, 186–87.

28. van Kaam, *Traditional Formation*, 216.

29. van Kaam, *Formation of the Human Heart*, 21; van Kaam and Muto, *Christian Articulation of the Mystery*, 75–76.

30. van Kaam, *Formation of the Human Heart*, 21.

call, we are better able to affirm ourselves.[31] While confirmation by others is helpful, we must exercise caution when it comes to relying too much on what others say about us. According to van Kaam, healthy affirmation is

> based on our faith and hope that this mystery affirms us lovingly in our self-appreciative intra-appearance. The mystery appreciates our striving for consonance as well as our repentance about dissonance. Such faith and hope make us grow in appreciative abandonment to the mystery. We hear much today about finding, asserting, and expressing our real self. These words often refer exclusively to our apparent form as falsely mistaken for the mystery of our true self. But this deepest self can never be seen and appraised in its fullness this side of the grave.[32]

As we mature in call affirmation and call efficacy, we experience an increase in our potential for intimacy with others. We grow in our skills of appraising life-call disclosures, all the while finding that it gives us joy to confirm the unfolding Christ form in others.[33]

Fidelity to our call is greatly aided by the disposition of transcendent commitment. In contrast to ways of living based on autarkic self-centeredness, commitment of this higher sort is a purposeful placing of ourselves at the disposal of God's call in the core of our being.[34] What we give up is not our "own judgment, insight, freedom, and responsibility, but our pretranscendent self-centeredness."[35]

Transcendent commitment implies self-respect grounded in respect for God's call to us and our firm and gentle honoring of it. We then enjoy relative independence from pressures and dissonant dynamics erupting in our outer spheres.[36] Far from causing greater reliance on our isolated self, transcendent commitment flows from a wellspring of "free and relaxed confidence [that] is rooted in the experience of one's integration in life, culture and society, in nature, in the world of a supra-personal tradition, in one's

---

31. van Kaam, *Transcendence Therapy*, 205–6. For insights into the affirmation and confirmation of our calling in Christ, see van Kaam and Muto, *Foundations of Christian Formation*, 174–76.

32. van Kaam, *Transcendent Formation*, 63–64.

33. van Kaam, *Transcendence Therapy*, 242; van Kaam and Muto, *Foundations of Christian Formation*, 246–48.

34. van Kaam, *Transcendence Therapy*, 152; van Kaam and Muto, *Foundations of Christian Formation*, 266.

35. van Kaam, *Transcendence Therapy*, 152.

36. Ibid., 156.

founding life call and its mysterious ground . . . [in] joyful surrender" to our life-call and to the Holy Trinity who is its source.[37]

Call affirmation and commitment lead to a life of consecration, meaning that we understand our formation field as centered in the Mystery.[38] We also experience that, despite our best intentions, as a result of the Fall, our efforts to witness to called, committed, and consecrated living in light of our calling in the Lord will be vulnerable to interference by our pride form.

> Our isolating pride-form exercises a powerful urge to usurp the role of this self-disclosure. It wants to disclose to us how successful and fulfilled we can be merely by doing what we will, exclusively on the basis of either personal or shared power. Our pride-form urges us to appraise our formation field as the ultimate measure of life, to deny its transcendent horizon. We live no longer in the disposition of gratitude for what the mystery allows into our life.[39]

Such a state requires a renewal of transcendent commitment rooted not in the counterfeit life form but in the Christ form. We are both ready and willing to embody our consecration to Christ in our vocations and avocations. The dispositions of sanctity and service manifest themselves in all that we are called to be and do.

Conclusion

As we have seen in this chapter, van Kaam's treatment of transcendence crises is inseparable from the reality of dissonance and consonance in life. He claimed that our distinctively human transcendence dynamic urges us to foster the heart-felt conviction that when all is said and done, life is more meaningful than meaningless.

Story after story in classic and contemporary narratives of God's saving actions demonstrate the efficacy of formative action patterns lived in appreciative abandonment to the goodness, truth, and beauty of the Mystery. In his memoirs, *The Life Journey of a Joyful Man of God*, van Kaam described this pattern in the life of his friend Mat, who from his personal confrontation of the depths of human suffering during the Hunger Winter, gained wisdom as a writer committed to share the worst and the best of his experiences with others. Van Kaam said that a letter he received from Mat

---

37. Ibid., 152; van Kaam and Muto, *Foundations of Christian Formation*, 139–40.
38. van Kaam, *Formation of the Human Heart*, 225.
39. Ibid.

confirmed the formative action pattern he had frequently pondered "the from (*van*), through (*door*), to (*naar*) event no one in dire straits can avoid. Mat had to cope with being wrenched *from* his familiar surroundings in Gemert; with going *through* the hell of the bombardments; and with trying *to* put his own and others' lives together again. Though he would never be the same, these changes would have far reaching consequences."[40]

Van Kaam's realistic description of the painful dynamics of transcendence crises affirmed his faith conviction of the Paschal Mystery: in every dying there is a rising. There is no lamentation for the Christian without a celebration of the ultimate mercy and forgiveness of God. Because life crises are inevitable, the best course of action is not to deny or reject them, but to perceive them as messengers of the Mystery, signaling the next step in our lifelong process of moving from purifying formation, through illuminating reformation, to unifying transformation.

Reflection Questions

1. Understanding Our Story: Reflecting on a Transcendence Crisis

    In this chapter, we learned that van Kaam named as central and distinctive to our human makeup the fact that we are gifted with a human spirit, that is to say, our transcendence dynamic. This transcendence dynamic both disturbs our status quo and fosters the integration of our entire formation field. That is, it both makes us long for more and also urges us to seek points of connection and meaning among every facet of our lives. It is our transcendence dynamic, our human spirit, which is the receptor in our lives to the inspirations, invitations, and beckonings of God's Spirit that occur throughout our formation field.

    Often, we witness the work of our transcendence dynamic most dramatically during what van Kaam called a transcendence crisis: a point in our lives when we are thrust into facing the reality that the way we used to live simply does not work for us any longer. Such times are often extremely painful, confusing, and even frightening. Often, fundamental beliefs that we hold about God, the world, and ourselves are deeply shaken. (Sometimes, we even experience questioning whether we have been abandoned by God, or whether it is still possible to abandon ourselves to God. This is what van Kaam called the primordial abandonment option.) In such times, there is real danger

---

40. van Kaam, *Life Journey*, 148.

that we may lose our way. At the same time, van Kaam maintained that transcendence crises offer us significant opportunities for us to discern fresh inspirations from God's Spirit that open us to learning deeper ways to trust in God and greater realizations of God's redemptive work throughout our formation field.

Allow God to be present to you as you gently reflect on the following questions: Have you ever experienced a transcendence crisis? (If not, there are many examples of transcendence crises in Scripture you might reflect on if you yourself have not had such an experience, such as the Apostle Peter denying Christ, or the rich young man's encounter with Jesus.) If so, describe what was happening in your life from the perspective of the formation field: What were the circumstances? Who was involved? What did this crisis stir in your heart and mind? What cultural and familial pressures, if any, were at work? What physical factors came into play? Which of your functional skills were involved, or were challenged? What desires of your human spirit became evident? Were there any ways in which God's people or communal worship contributed to what was happening? As you recall this experience, what stirs in you now? Have you had enough time since the crisis occurred to be able to perceive what inspirations from the Spirit of God were involved with your crisis?

Pause for a while to be with God and allow God to be present to you in these reflections. How has the Holy Spirit inspired you to identify obstacles that caused you to deny the dissonances pointing to this transcendence crisis? How has the Holy Spirit inspired you to identify facilitating conditions for entry into this from-through-to experience of living more fully in appreciative abandonment to God?

2. Understanding God's Story: Reflection on a Formative Event of a Bible Character

    Recall from this chapter van Kaam's concept of the formative event: something that happens in our lives that changes us, that moves us from one way of living in the world to a different way of living. Formative events need not be particularly dramatic, although they can be. With reflection, we can identify in them a formative action pattern: a movement *from* one way of living, *through* something that happens, *to* another way of living. For example, on the night of his denial of Jesus, the Apostle Peter proudly asserted that even if all the other disciples would fall away from following Jesus, he would always stand with him. Through his experience of denying Jesus, Peter moved "from" living in pride, "through" the experience of betraying Jesus, "to" a more realistic awareness of his limitations (as well as God's unconditional forgiveness for the repentant).

Choose one of your favorite Bible characters who experienced a formative event and about whom some narrative background is provided in the Scripture (for example: Abraham or Sarah, Ruth or Esther, Zacchaeus or the Apostle Paul). Often, people in Scripture are described as having numerous formative events, but for this exercise, select just one. Describe what happened in this character's life. Then describe what changed in this person's life: what made this event formative? Finally, in a single sentence, summarize the formative action pattern by naming specifically what the person moved "from," "through," and "to" during their formative event.

As you reflect on the formative event that you have articulated for this person, describe any insights that come to you about the formative dynamics of God's Spirit on the human spirit, given what you know about the person's story in the Bible. Describe any way that you find yourself responding to or perhaps resisting God's communications to this character in this moment.

Chapter 10

Phases of Human and Christian Formation

As our life unfolds, all of its dimensions contribute to the maturation phase in which we find ourselves. This dimensional focus often (though not always) correlates with the physical and chronological life-stage in which we find ourselves.[1] Van Kaam used the construct of phasic formation to identify the connection between life form dimensions and the transitions we experience from one phase of life to another.

To live more effectively in light of who the Mystery calls us to be and become does not happen all at once, but phase by phase over the course of a lifetime. As long as we live, we witness periods of slow or sudden emergence. The moment any periodic form, or phase, has achieved its mission, a transition occurs that upsets us to be sure, but that turns out to be a necessary bridge to a new phase and form of maturation. Our life could be described as a chain of such temporal transitions that unveil the providential meanings hidden in each passing episode of our divinely emerging existence.

Sociohistorical Phase

The sociohistorical phase of formation begins while a child is still in the womb.[2] It relates to the ways in which our coming into the world falls under the influence of familial, cultural, economic, and religious traditions into which we are born. This first phase of formation expresses the fact that each person's emergent self is embedded historically in powerful givens that shape our deepest beliefs. These sociohistorical, cultural, and familial givens

---

1. van Kaam, *Fundamental Formation*, 263–64; van Kaam, *Transcendent Formation*, 10–11, 184. Van Kaam also articulated phasic formation as "character formation" related to human biological changes (for this articulation of phasic formation, see *Transcendent Formation*, 119–20).

2. van Kaam, *Transcendent Formation*, 119–20.

influence, for better or for worse, the empirical ways in which we express ourselves.[3] Their effect on us cannot be underestimated.

All of us have to come to terms with the sociohistorical phase of our existence. It constitutes the first challenge to the form we eventually want to give to our life. So significant is the sociohistorical phase that we have to take it into account in all successive phases of our life. What we learn in our family of origin will always be with us in some way. So, too, will be the ideas and ideals received from extended family members, neighbors, teachers, and friends. This is the phase when we are first inserted into language uses and cultural customs over which we have no control. That is why we can never underestimate the role parents play in helping us from our earliest years to express and maintain our incipient form potency.

This phase of formation, if confirming of who we are, motivates us to affirm and maintain what we find to be best in us throughout life. Lacking a lived experience of such unconditional regard in childhood may cripple, to a degree, our ability to accept ourselves in adulthood.

One dangerous aberration of the sociohistorical phase is what van Kaam identified as socio-historicism.[4] This occurs when the sociohistorical dimension of our life form becomes the exclusive explanation and determinant of all subsequent formation, rather than a phase of life guided by the transcendent. By contrast, the more consonant our life becomes, the more our social experiences mirror our unique-communal life-call.

The sociohistorical phase is not, therefore, an end in itself, but a lifelong challenge, calling for ongoing appraisal, especially of prejudices we were too young to critique. That being said, this phase can breed an atmosphere of separation from others, or an openness to our own gifts and theirs. The first way leads to deformation, the second to reformation and transformation.

Vital Phase

The vital phase of formation points to what van Kaam described as a kind of "primitive slumbering" in the maternal ambiance.[5] At this stage, there is no distinction between a wet diaper and the entire universe. All infants feel is that they are soaking in something and they need to be dry. They have no capacity to think to themselves, "It's three in the morning and my parents are tired; I'll go to sleep soaking wet and wait until they get up."

---

3. Ibid., 127.
4. Ibid., 160.
5. Ibid., 170.

Provided the infant is not in an abusive setting, this is generally a blissful phase. It is one of vital embeddedness in one's body, and total dependency on caring others. Dominant now are such vital instincts as hunger, and such emotional effusions as crying. Another way of describing this non-differentiated, global phase of prepersonal vitality is to speak of it as the phase of "vital-oral reception and donation."[6] Nothing is as yet experienced in any individual way. While infants may experience the seeding of their intrasphere, theirs is not yet an enduring awareness of an inner life. This is the phase when infants experience the "sweet slumber of prepersonal existence."[7]

As the infant grows, there may be a shift, however slight, to a kind of prefunctional vital phase.[8] Children show signs of their own attraction to color and images, for example, on the mobile above the bed. There is an emergent sense of time awareness: time to sleep, time to be fed, time to be changed. Sensory-motor dynamics relevant to the emergence of their neuroform reveal themselves. Van Kaam also observed that the vital phase reveals some preverbal differentiation, exemplified by dynamics of pleasure and displeasure. Infants have a "pulsion prevalence": an explosive instantaneous unloading of whatever doesn't belong in their ambiance.[9]

Marking the beginning of typically human formation is the fact that, at this phase, imagination, affection, and cognition play a preliminary role, along with the structuring of the neuroform, contributing to the infant's growing ability to fashion some sort of time awareness. Though dynamics of restraint and discipline may be incipient, they are not strong or effective enough to prevent an instantaneous explosion of compressed formation energy.[10] As the vital phase of formation unfolds, a just-awakening potency for freedom begins to reveal itself, though, in this phase, it is still tenuous, intermittent, and often erratic.

The most decisive event of childhood formation is the unfolding of our vital-lingual form potency.[11] First utterances, like "Dada" or "Mama," point to rudimentary forms of interfocal consciousness. It is mainly through lingual formation that children become aware of themselves as part of a community of people whose attention and care they require. At this stage, the child's mind is not yet capable of functional, linear thought. Nonetheless, there is evidence, in the normal course of growth, of further dynamics of

---

6. Ibid., 172.
7. Ibid.
8. Ibid., 174.
9. Ibid., 182.
10. Ibid., 171–77.
11. Ibid., 186–87.

lingual formation. A child may be able to understand, for the first time, the past, as well as something that promises to happen in the future. This apprehension expands the awakening of intraspheric consciousness and opens the child to directives that are more than merely vitalistic.

The gifts of the vital phase are obvious; its challenges, as identified by van Kaam, are fourfold.[12] The first is a "struggle against dominance by vital dynamics" that tend to pull the child back into the maternal ambiance and safety of vital embeddedness, rather than risking the adventure of a more independent intrasphere.[13] That is why parents and significant others must beware of both over-direction and over-protection. The second challenge entails following "the call to give form to some rudimentary childlike originality despite the pressure of absolute conformity carried by certain lingual communications," such as a "no" that is so strident and threatening that children are afraid to do anything on their own.[14] This second challenge relates to the third, which has to do with lack of confidence in our ability to exercise some originality, albeit in a "prefocal, elementary, and childlike way."[15] There is, finally, "a struggle to bear, without discouragement, embarrassment and debasement," the "failure, ridicule, or depreciation, real or imagined," which may accompany bold or timid attempts to foster our lingual expressions and functional choices.[16] At this point, lack of confirmation may make self-affirmation in the future extremely difficult.[17]

As one matures, a lingering danger of this phase is that vital pulsions and impulses become ultimized substitutes for transcendent aspirations and pneumatic-ecclesial inspirations. When this happens, the "less than" of such things as addictive drugs and pornography may be imbibed as substitutes for the "More Than," since they feel so vitally fulfilling. The deformation that results may entrap one in coercive security directives that become deeply embedded in one's neuroform, entrapping one in an unending cycle of vital compulsions.

Functional Phase

The functional phase is marked by a process of growing beyond the vitalistic dominance of the preceding phase. Under the influence of both transcendent

---

12. Ibid., 193–94.
13. Ibid., 193.
14. Ibid., 194.
15. Ibid.
16. Ibid., 194.
17. Ibid., 82–83; van Kaam, *Transcendence Therapy*, 70, 134–39.

and pretranscendent dynamics, our intrasphere keeps on differentiating itself. Interestingly enough, this differentiation often shows up in what child psychologists call the "no phase." Such newly emerging functional dynamics as practical apprehensions and appraisal, functional language usage, and increasing degrees of effectiveness emerge in a noticeably stronger way.[18]

Between the ages of four and seven, one experiences especially the emergence of the "managing me."[19] Children begin to exercise increasing control over the vital, biophysical facets of life, symbols of which are toilet training and eating with a spoon or chopsticks. To boost these initial experiences of appropriate control, children begin to learn what they ought to do and how they ought to act. Around the age of seven, concrete practical thinking reveals increasing degrees of effectiveness and management of the child's surroundings. They may have a keen awareness of their room, or their books, or their favorite shirt. Moreover, in this phase, the child's language usage becomes increasingly proficient, together with skills like reading and drawing. There also occurs further differentiation within the instrasphere, marked by a more lingual functionality.[20] The gift of this phase is that children no longer see themselves only as vitalistic objects of attention; rather, they begin to sense that they can exercise their own choice of likes and dislikes. They increase their vocabulary and use language to demarcate their own sense of being able to function more independently, saying, for example, "Don't worry, I can do that."

The functional phase facilitates the emergence of formation conscience as an expression of moral conscience.[21] Such formation consists of a lingual, cognitive, and effective cluster of intraspheric directives that point to appreciable or depreciable ways of functioning within our family, school, or neighborhood. Whereas dynamics of parental appreciation lead to a growing child's sense of self-appreciation, the depreciations they receive or observe may give rise to thoughts and feelings of guilt and questions of self-worth.[22] Gradually, effective and properly praised functionality readies us for the emergence of the next phase of formation: functional-transcendence.

---

18. van Kaam, *Transcendent Formation*, 214.

19. Ibid.

20. Ibid., 198–204.

21. Ibid., 199–200. For a review of formation conscience and its various regions, see chapter 6.

22. Ibid., 200–201.

Functional-Transcendent Phase

The functional-transcendent phase marks the stage of life during which transcendence dynamics begin to announce themselves. Functionality may be subordinated to an evolving deeper sensitivity to the More Than. We may long to discover our true transcendent identity beyond its pretranscendent dimensions, dynamics, and expressions. Moments of experiencing our intrasphere in depth, beyond mere vital-functional strivings, may emerge. There is a desire to actualize our form potency in alignment with our unique-communal life-call, but, despite this attraction to the transcendent, the emphasis at this stage is still on pragmatic effectiveness. Because this tension between the functional and the transcendent has to be worked through, van Kaam identified it as the crossover phase from functional-transcendent living to transcendent-functional living.[23] Much is at stake, and this crossover is not always achieved.

Central to the functional-transcendent phase from a crossover perspective are the dynamics of detachment. They entail a process of disidentifying with our functional appearances to create room for a new functional-transcendent awareness. This means that we are no longer inclined to identify ourselves uncritically with the functional-apparent forms that made us effective and acceptable to ourselves and others. We feel the urge to modulate, subordinate, and integrate these forms under the watch of our emergent life-call and commitment.

The challenge of this phase is not to close it off prematurely. What we need to understand is that it is readying us for an even higher form of disidentifying detachment, that is to say, a detachment from the functional-transcendent dimension itself. The danger is that we may mistakenly appraise this functional-transcendent phase as the peak of distinctively human character and personality formation, rather than only as a crossover.[24]

The gift of this phase is that the transcendent dimension continues to announce itself. It disrupts our complacency; it makes us feel inwardly restless. The problem is that we may try to control this transcendent potency, rather than letting it guide us. If we feel overly self-sufficient and begin to be dominated by our exalted and exalting pride form, we may end up encapsulated in this crossover phase of "pretranscendent, managerial transcendence."[25] Harnessing the transcendent becomes a way to make us more functional, more successful, more in control of our lives. One can see this dynamic, among

---

23. Ibid., 215–16.
24. Ibid., 216–17.
25. van Kaam and Muto, *Christian Articulation of the Mystery*, 79.

other things, in the recent interest practitioners have in harnessing people's "spiritual life" for healing purposes. Classes in meditation and stress reduction techniques have as their goal increased physical stamina and mental acumen, more than increased intimacy with the Mystery.

The subtle temptation of functional-transcendence is to think we can manage the Mystery, rather than abandoning ourselves in abiding attentiveness to it.[26] We can appraise the functional-transcendent phase either as an endpoint in itself, or as the most important crossover in our formation journey. To make of it an endpoint is to miss the fact that it was only meant to free us from domination by managerial transcendence and open us to the joys and freedoms of transcendent-functional existence. Now is the time for a shift, from self-actualization to self-abandonment, in alignment with our transcendent life-call.[27] Now is the time not to exalt our own spiritual self-sufficiency, but to detach ourselves from functional appearances. Now is the time to open ourselves to the grace of spiritual maturity that enables us to follow the guidance of God and not the directives of our own clever calculations for how to be more in control.

Transition to Transcendence

The movement to a state of life in which transcendence is dominant is now upon us, but before entering the transcendent-functional phase, there are preliminary steps that aid this transition. Van Kaam identified four steps in this passage.[28] Step one entails submission. It means that when we feel inspired by the Mystery to go beyond the previous phase of functional-transcendence, we have to recognize that challenges still face us. Although we are more sensitive to transcendent aspirations, there are remnants of functional striving that still remain dominant.

This first step of submission means that we must submit this pattern of dominance to a process of inner purification. This very decision triggers a "crisis of transition."[29] At first, the previous phase of our journey threatens to encapsulate us in the illusion that we can enter the next phase of life by our own autarkic powers. Humble appraisal of these temptations at this point discloses how much we still rely on human efforts and pretranscendent techniques to move us where we long to be.[30] It goes without saying

26. Ibid., 78–80.
27. van Kaam, *Transcendent Formation*, 216.
28. Ibid., 225–26.
29. Ibid., 118.
30. Ibid., 226.

that the more we allow the functional dimension to remain dominant, the more we risk being alienated from the transcendent.

Step two could be characterized as an awakening experience.[31] Van Kaam said that we awaken to the ways in which inner purification, or purgation, with the help of grace, may free us from residues of autarkic strivings. Events of awakening that accompany this step evoke awe. It is as if the Mystery is disclosing the deeper meaning of our unique-communal call. This awakening generates renewed attraction to the hidden treasures of classic faith and formation traditions.[32] From them we may gain fresh insights into what is occurring in the core of our being. We continue to question if we are on the right track, and yet we long to free our interiority from its secret self-centeredness.

On more than one occasion, we are reminded by grace that our functional dimension is the servant, not the master, of transcendent transformation. We have been awakened to the truth that if we make these self-actualizing strivings absolute, they will fail to grant us peace. This step in the process reminds us that consonance with the Mystery cannot be attained unless we are willing to face the remaining residues of domination of clever, pragmatic controls, resulting in ambitious pseudo-spiritual projects.

It is at this point in the process that we enter into full field appraisal, seeking what it is that the Mystery asks of us. In this third step, awakened people apprehend appreciatively the nearness of the Mystery. We know now that our transcendent identity cannot be reduced to its pretranscendent sources. We admit, in humility, that the basis of our true character and personality formation is not any achievement attained by us, but by our openness, day-by-day, to the call of the Mystery.[33] We welcome the divine initiative that invites us to give up our attempts to live a spiritual life in great measure by our own powers of formation. The experience of such nearness sustains us in this process of transition, because we believe in the promise that it will purify and reform us as never before. Each new showing of the love of the Mystery for us evokes growing intimacy with the More Than in the ordinary circumstances of daily life.

We begin to appreciate in a new way the people, things, and events that appear in our everyday existence. Van Kaam said that they form a mysterious ambiance inviting us to pursue a life where the functional serves the transcendent, and not the other way around. Treasures once hidden in the transfocal region of our consciousness begin to flow into our prefocal

---

31. Ibid., 225, 227–28.

32. Ibid., 225, 229–30. Van Kaam and Muto's work regularly draws upon the resources of classic Christian faith and formation traditions, as evident, for example, throughout *Living Our Faith and Formation Traditions*.

33. Ibid., 225, 230–31.

and focal consciousness. They make us aware that this transitional experience is a gift we can no longer deny or dismiss. We want to take the time to understand and pursue it. Such moments of intimacy with the Mystery may be prolonged as we become more attentive to directives emerging from the inner and outer spheres of our field of formation. We discover in them epiphanic showings of the Mystery. When transcendent intraformation prevails, our field as a whole seems to be illumined by our presence to the Divine Presence. A deeper sense of awe begins to diminish the pride-filled taken-for-grantedness of functional-transcendent self-actualization.

The fourth step is marked by what van Kaam identified as a "second transcendent childhood."[34] We cannot return to the first innocence in which we once lived. Too many sins, too many experiences, have become part of our journey. But the grace of this step means that new formation dynamics emerge in which "true childlike transcendence prevails" as we are moved by the Mystery toward the transcendent phase of our formation journey.[35]

This phase facilitates the emergence of childlike forms of presence to the Mystery that complement and transform with childlike wonder our sociohistorical, vital, functional, and functional-transcendent dimensions of life. There begins to occur a change in our self-apprehension, which leads to a reformation of our inmost identity. We find ourselves becoming more Mystery-oriented than self-centered. Our "first childhood," with its remnants of pretranscendent childishness, begins to be replaced by a second transcendent childhood.

As the phase of transition to transcendence draws to a close, the Mystery may gift us with an anticipation of the transcendent and post-transcendent ways of living that await us. "No disposition is more desirable," as a fruit of our detachment from functionalistic self-centeredness, than the gift of formative anticipation.[36] It gives us a new sense of hope arising from the summons to "give up control of our life by mastery alone."[37] No longer are we duped by a search for spirituality that represents the "happy ending" of our own projects of self-actualization. We know that for which we search is a gift that cannot be compelled by our endeavors only. We "cannot expect it, but we can hope for it" when we "toss the anchor of our life into the bottomless harbor of peace in a turbulent world."[38] We may now be ready to be led

---

34. Ibid., 192, 221.
35. Ibid., 220.
36. Ibid., 231.
37. Ibid.
38. Ibid.

by the Mystery beyond the phase of functional-transcendence to the next phase of transcendent-functional formation.

Transcendent-Functional Phase

As the Mystery readies us to go beyond the functional-transcendent phase of life and enter the realm of transcendent-functional formation, van Kaam chose a powerful and original metaphor, the cave trial, to explain what happens to us.[39] He said that the experience of the cave trial does not mean the eradication of our passions, diminishments of our innate needs and gifts, or denial of our biophysical makeup. What the cave trial means is a radical reformation of our pretranscendent life, including functional-transcendence, making it a source of our transcendent dimension and its life-giving dynamics. Diminished but never destroyed are functional mind, memory, will, imagination, and anticipation.

The cave trial illumines who the Mystery has intended us to be all along. At the "shadowy entrance of the cave," we experience, understandably with fear and trembling, the beginning of functional-transcendent reformation.[40] Van Kaam used the symbol of rushing water to characterize the erosion of rocky deformations associated with still lingering attachments to functionalistic power, status, self-perfection, possessions, and mere vitalistic pleasures.[41] Entering the cave is the first challenge of the threefold process of in-depth reformation of our vital dimension, together with reforming our pretranscendent strivings for fulfillment and exertion forgetful of the Mystery.[42]

The second challenge of the threefold path draws us deeper into the darkness of the cave. There may be glimmers of faint light as transcendent formation focuses like a laser beam radically and painfully on the inadequacy of our functional dispositions and dynamics to sustain us as they once did. The decrease of functional dominance may leave us feeling empty. We rely as never before on the Mystery to help us. We want to be under the sovereign direction of the Spirit. We know that this grace can only be ours through decreased domination of functional-transcendence. Painful as this purification is, it begins to disclose, at this midpoint of the cave trial, an illumination van Kaam associated with intimate self-communications of the

---

39. Ibid., 235, 237.
40. Ibid., 237.
41. Ibid., 236.
42. Ibid., 235–37.

Mystery hidden in the ravines of our heart.[43] We experience the truth that our sociohistorical, vital, and functional dimensions, with their strivings and expressions, must once and for all be at the service of the transcendent.

Along with this graced realization comes an exiting of the cave that points, in van Kaam's teaching, to transcendent-functional transformation. The metaphors of transcendent water and light now give way to that of transcendent fire ignited by the Mystery of transforming love.[44] Thanks to the gift of radical reformation, and thanks to our faith in the Mystery, we begin to feel liberated from the pretenses of autarkic self-actualization. Most of all, we want to live in renewed fidelity to the Mystery in the "valley of daily existence."[45] Grace has readied us for the culminating phase of transcendent and post-transcendent living.

Transcendent and Post-Transcendent Phase

Having experienced more profoundly than ever that our life has been released from the domination of functional-transcendence, and that grace has led us through the cave trial to transcendent-functional living, we stand on the threshold of a more integrated, transcendent, and post-transcendent phase of life. Although the transcendent dimension has become the integrating instrument of our presence to life and world, the danger of our falling back into unpurified and unreformed habits of being has not gone away. The challenge of this post-transcendent phase of unifying transformation is to recognize and resubmit to purifying formation and illuminating reformation, what for van Kaam are coercive dispositions so deeply engrained in our core form by the pride form that they can be triggered when we least expect it. We are so grateful to God for deigning to bestow upon us some experience, however slight, of unifying transformation, that it is shocking to witness how easily we still get upset and disturbed by our own useless worry or the difficulty we may be having in a relationship.

Van Kaam offers four features of the post-transcendent phase. First comes the preeminence of confidence in something more than we are. To quote van Kaam: "Our post-transcendent state of life should be marked by faith in the embracing love of the Mystery, even if we do not feel the sensation of intimacy."[46]

---

43. Ibid., 236.
44. Ibid., 236–37.
45. Ibid., 4.
46. Ibid., 240.

The second feature of post-transcendent living is wisdom of the heart. Of this wisdom he reflected,

> The transcendent knowledge of higher reason, the wisdom of the heart, the perceptiveness of our senses as transformed by the human spirit, the treasures of classical traditions became less and less appreciated [in the industrialized, "Western" world] . . .
> We need personally and as a people to pay more attention to the transcendent-functional phase of the human journey. We need to know the conditions of the post-transcendent formation of those who participate in the public life of a functionalistic society.
> Transcendent peace and effectiveness depend on our tuning in to all spheres of our field of life. The radiating center of this field is the mystery, which is at the heart of our daily actions and interactions. This field itself involves our being faithful to our inner personal-communal life call. It suggests reasonable compatibility with the people around us, with our environmental life situation as well as with our wider global and cosmic surroundings.[47]

A third facet of this phase of living is a keener awareness of the direction our attention takes. Van Kaam counseled that to cope with the danger of coercive and depreciative dispositions, we have to become prayerfully aware of the direction our power of attention tends to take. Is our neuroform secretly directing us to dissonant projects that diminish our presence to the Sacred? Are we still inclined to plunge into our work-a-day world without abiding in awe-filled attention? How do we handle what happens when pretranscendent neuroformational coercions get the best of us?

The fourth feature of the post-transcendent phase is transcendent effectiveness. There is that in us that demands that we try to reform our neuroform and its pre-selective appraisals.[48] If we do not effectively reign in the avalanche of sensual impressions that may rush upon us already at the beginning of the day, we cannot expect to be effective servants of the Mystery. This feature of post-transcendent living points to the fact that we need to rearrange the input of our neuroform into a serviceable constellation of stimuli more consonant than dissonant with our transcendent life direction. This is why many Christian spiritual writers consider the work of purification, illumination, and union to be ongoing over a lifetime.

---

47. Ibid., 244–45.
48. Ibid., 248–49.

Van Kaam identified seven challenges we must face on the way to post-transcendent living. The first is to acknowledge the fact that the Mystery has weaned our senses and our spirit away from many of the coercive attachments that prevented us from becoming spiritually mature, and that we have been set now on the path of implementing what we have learned about fully integrated transcendent presence and action.[49]

The second and perhaps greatest challenge we face is the new use of our neuroform. Feelings of alienation, threat, or severe anxiety may come upon us when we least expect them. Our great task at this post-transcendent phase is to allow the reformation and transformation of these coercive neuroformational dispositions. According to van Kaam, This

> change in our neuro-formation can only happen through a change in both our focal and prefocal regions of dispositional attentiveness. They have to be inspired by epiphanic love. Such love has about it the miraculous quality of deepening beneficial purgation that makes reformation and transformation possible for us. At the same time, it fills our hearts with a peace and joy that surpasses any pretranscendent understanding.[50]

We are not at the mercy of a neuroform that had been programmed coercively during the earlier phases of life.[51] Even those coercive attention dispositions can be transformed in this phase on the condition that we foster the remaining features of post-transcendent living.

A third challenge is to see wisely and clearly that we have been granted the grace to reform coercive dispositions that had become, as it were, second nature to us. We acknowledge, in humility, that the pride form had made these coercions more powerful than we thought and had at times severely blocked our free formation flow.

A fourth challenge, simply put, is to remember who we are. We are more than our current form and our apparent form. We are people deeply loved by the Mystery, who have been given every chance to align our core form with our founding life form. This sublime disclosure is a continual reminder that our deepest identity is not functional, but transcendent. It is not about what we do, but who we are.

The fifth challenge van Kaam identified is to handle failure in the light of where we are now and not where we used to be. We may fail, here and there, to submit to reformation our deeply rooted coercive dispositions, which may have been part of our childhood. We may find ourselves

---

49. Ibid., 252–53, 263–64.
50. Ibid., 251.
51. Ibid., 264–66.

encapsulated in the demands of pretranscendent functionalism, vitalism, or sociohistoricism. We must accept that what happens, then, is not merely a chastisement of the Mystery, but a learning experience.[52] It humbles us to notice how deeply some coercive dispositions have embedded themselves in our neuroform. The challenge is to see them as invitations to grow day-by-day in spiritual maturity.

Aiding us in this regard is what van Kaam named as the sixth challenge "instant appreciative abandonment."[53] He said that the key to coping with coercive dispositions is to abandon ourselves as soon as possible to the love and mercy of the Mystery, as well as to identify each obstacle on our path as a formation opportunity. Unless we practice instant appreciative abandonment, we risk triggering more coercive dispositions, because with them our neuroform sends a flood of depreciative information to our powers of attention. Overwhelmed by anxious depreciation, we focus attention on signs of danger, threat, anxiety, suspicion, and alienation. This avalanche of depreciative abandonment interferes with the flow of transcendent epiphanic love, joy, and peace the Mystery asks us to radiate into the world.

Moments of inner vacation and recollection are the seventh and final challenge in this post-transcendent phase.[54] Van Kaam recommended that we take repeated "inner vacations or periods of recollection," especially in the midst of our busiest days.[55] This practice helps us to distance ourselves from, and to appraise, reemerging coercive dispositions. Our life needs to be permeated by vacation moments of quiet meditation and contemplative presence the moment coercions are triggered by the daily struggles in which we inevitably find ourselves.

In addition to naming challenges to post-transcendent living, van Kaam provided for our guidance four facets of peace preservation that keep us on the path of post-transcendent living.[56] One of the common invitations we experience is liberation from coercive dispositions.[57] We experience, first, the disclosure of remaining coercive security directives that despoil our peaceful presence to God. We learn to welcome events of daily life as occasions to shed light on and purify such coercions.[58] A major facet of the post-transcendent phase is to disclose "these hidden land mines in our

---

52. Ibid., 245–46.
53. Ibid., 260.
54. Ibid., 260–61.
55. Ibid., 261.
56. Ibid., 268–70.
57. Ibid., 268–69.
58. Ibid., 257–59.

field of life" along with "detonat[ing] their explosive power."⁵⁹ What we learn from facing these coercions and reappraising them helps us to grow in consonance with God's will for our lives. This transformation is led by love, never driven by guilt. We are invited by God to let go of these coercions and to accept that our sins, failures, and faults are forgiven.

A second dynamic of peace preservation is that of being present to events in the light of our having been called by the Mystery to appraise their formative meaning.⁶⁰ We recognize that even an event that at first glance appears to be ordinary, is an invitation to ponder God's providential plan for our lives. Van Kaam noted that we humans have a "potency-to-praise [the Mystery] . . . in the thick of overwhelming odds, displeasures and dissatisfactions."⁶¹ The more we live in praise, the more likely it is that we will be present to events in a joyful, serene, and courageous manner.

The third dynamic of peace preservation relates to the interformative sphere of our formation field. In congeniality, compatibility, compassion, and competence, we celebrate together the gifts of post-transcendent transformation we have received. We learn alone and together how to be more faithful to our unique-communal life-call. We welcome the opportunity to explore its dynamics with people we trust. We respect and care for one another. In this post-transcendent phase of life, our interformation is characterized by self-giving, rather than selfishness.⁶²

The fourth dynamic of peace preservation calms our vital excitement and our restless functional meandering.⁶³ The pretranscendent dimensions of our human life form are no longer the main sources of our thoughts, feelings, attentions, and actions.⁶⁴ This phase reveals that the true foundation of our life is our union and communion with the Mystery and its manifestations. All pretranscendent dimensions place themselves at the disposal of our presence to the Divine Presence, granted to us undeservedly. All that we are and do becomes increasingly open to unifying transformation and its disclosures of peace and joy.

---

59. Ibid., 248.
60. Ibid., 269.
61. Ibid., 249.
62. Ibid., 269–70.
63. Ibid., 270.
64. Ibid.

Conclusion

In this chapter we have traced the path leading to transcendent-functional and post-transcendent living. We have been restored to a vision of the intrinsic splendor of the Mystery, purifying, illuminating, and transforming the shadowy contours of our fallen world. We have beheld with awe the epiphanic splendor of God's glory shining forth in us personally and through creation. Our longing for the More Than manifests the fact that we seek liberation from confinement in any pretranscendent dimension of life as if it were ultimate. Our innate orientation to wholeness does not let us find lasting peace and joy by fixating our thoughts exclusively on any partial mode of fulfillment. We have learned that substitutes for the transcendent may appear to satisfy us at certain moments of life, but they are incapable of addressing the deeper hunger and thirst that animates us. We are, and will always be, "pilgrim souls endowed by the Mystery with a transcendence dynamic."[65]

It is our hope that by being introduced to the life's work and legacy of Adrian van Kaam, our readers find themselves better equipped to understand, appreciate, and yield in reverence to the wonder of the formation journeys to which they have been called by the Mystery.

Reflection Questions

1. Understanding Our Story: Reflecting on Themes of Christian Maturity

    In this chapter, we learned about some of the touchstones of Christian maturity that van Kaam identified in what he called transcendent and post-transcendent living: living with ever-increasing abandonment to God and in grace-filled discernment and responsiveness to the invitations of God's Spirit in everyday life. Van Kaam identified four themes pertaining to the invitations of the Spirit to grow in post-transcendent peace preservation: liberation from coercive security directives; living in awe and praise-filled presence to each event in our lives; increasing awareness of and love for the interconnectedness of our formation with that of all other persons; and greater faithfulness to and integration in consonance with God in all facets of our formation field.

    Allow God to be present to you as you reflect on the following questions: Gently reflect on ways in which you perceive God's Spirit to

---

65. van Kaam and Muto, *Essential Elements*, s.v. "Manifestation of the Transcendence Dynamic."

be at work in you during this season of life. In what areas of your life (consider your entire formation field with all its spheres, dimensions, and integrating structures) do you sense the focus of reformation to be? Why do you believe this is the case?

To which (if any) of van Kaam's four themes of post-transcendent peace preservation do you find yourself drawn? Take some time to review the sections of this chapter that relate to any relevant theme and reflect on how it might apply to your situation. Describe any desires, hopes, or insights that come to you as you do this. How has the Holy Spirit inspired you to identify obstacles to transcendent and post-transcendent living? How have you been inspired to identify conditions that facilitate receiving greater formation freedom and walking in peace preservation?

2. Understanding God's Story: Reflecting on Phases of Formation in a Bible Character

This chapter reviewed van Kaam's concept of phasic formation, the way people's formation dimensions are connected with transitions from one phase of life to another (sociohistorical, vital, functional, functional-transcendent, transcendent-functional, and transcendent and post-transcendent phases). He identified both gifts and challenges that are a part of phasic formation, which in turn influence our fidelity to our unique-communal life-call.

Choose one of your favorite Bible characters about whom much of the unfolding of their life is recorded (examples include: Abraham and Sarah; Jacob, Leah, and Rebecca; Samuel and David; Ruth and Naomi; Mary Magdalene; and the Apostles Peter and Paul). Consider the unfolding of their phasic formation for as many of the phases that you can identify (note: not all characters reach transcendent and post-transcendent living, though some do), describing how the gifts and challenges of each phase manifested themselves in the character's life.

As you continue to reflect, describe any observations and insights that come to you about the role of phasic formation in this character's life, including the role of the various spheres of the character's formation field during crucial transitions from one phase of formation to another.

As you conclude your reflection, take time to notice what stirs in your own heart and mind as you reflect in this way on this person's life. Describe any ways in which you find yourself responding to or perhaps resisting the unfolding story of this character's phasic formation.

Epilogue
Adrian van Kaam's Legacy

THE EPIPHANY CERTIFICATION PROGRAM (ECP), cofacilitated by Father Adrian and Doctor Muto for a number of years, is now flourishing in Pittsburgh under the teachers they trained. The goal of the Epiphany Academy of Formative Spirituality is to continue to advance the pioneering work begun by van Kaam in the Netherlands. Essential to his overall project and completed before his death were the four volumes in Christian formation theology, coauthored with Doctor Muto. This series, validated authoritatively as a *Summa Forma Theologica*, is a true treasure in the corpus of his work.[1] It complements his seven-volume series on the science and anthropology of formation and allows readers to follow his theory from its initial phases to its continuing significance. The latest findings of formative spirituality and evidence of its growing influence on scholars and readers worldwide continue to be published under the watch of Dr. Susan Muto, dean of the academy. Colleagues and students the world over concur with the truth that this body

---

1. Shortly after his ordination to the priesthood in 1946, van Kaam was assigned to teach in his seminary the works of the thirteenth-century theologian and spiritual master, Thomas Aquinas, OP. As a professor of philosophical anthropology, van Kaam noted that Aquinas, an outstanding Dominican priest, could not ignore in his time the findings of the pagan philosophers Plato and Aristotle, whose works were permeating the philosophical-speculative intellectual atmosphere of his own University of Paris as well as other institutes of higher learning in Europe. In response, Aquinas posited as the two wings of truth reason and faith, thereby holding philosophy and theology in respectful and creative dialogue. Van Kaam himself shared the conviction that it was vital to attend to the empirical-experiential findings of contemporary thinking. He saw quite clearly that students in the twentieth century would be less informationally and more formationally oriented. He intuited the wisdom of following the Aquinas method of devising a pre-theological philosophy to serve the unfolding of a systematic doctrinal theology. In his case, he set out to develop, in consultation with the to-date formationally relevant arts and sciences, a pre-theological formation science and anthropology. These two new fields of study serve as the "handmaidens" of his systematic and systemic formation theology, articulated in his *Summa Forma Theologica*.

of work touches the hearts of people at every level of scholarly and social life. It remains the mission of the Epiphany Association to provide an antidote to the functionalism that pervades contemporary American culture, which tends to underestimate the spiritual needs of people.

Epiphany formation sessions are reminiscent of the gatherings of the spiritually starved citizens eluding the Nazis many years ago. They offer people needed sustenance, drawing participants from diverse backgrounds, churches, and denominations. All come together to deepen their awareness of how to integrate worship and work, presence and participation, contemplation and action. In an atmosphere of trust and mutuality, participants form a "little epiphany" supportive of one another, sharing their stories and revealing the longing in each one's soul for the More Than. Tensions melt away as participants grow in awareness of their shared humanity through small group experiences, in-depth direction, and formative reading of Scripture and the Christian classics. Time and again, it has been shown through experiences of people at the Academy that van Kaam's work has the potential to heal the hostile divisions caused by the ethnic and religious rivalry that threatens to tear apart the fabric of culture and civilization whether in Europe, Asia, Africa, North and South America, or the Middle East.

One of the challenges formative spirituality addresses is the distinction between people's way of life (their formation tradition) and the religious faith convictions they profess (their faith tradition). In many of the most violent conflicts, people share customs (formation traditions) that are almost identical. Yet because some are Christian, for example, and others Muslim, they grow up in opposition to one another. Is there not less likelihood of demonizing a faith tradition other than one's own when we perceive that, although our beliefs may differ, we recognize that we share common universal longings for the More Than, which all humans strive to express in their own ways? To be moving toward a shared goal is to be companions on a journey of formation despite the fact that we may belong to a variety of faith traditions.

Van Kaam envisioned that formative spirituality belongs in any global dialogue about world peace, since it highlights, in deep respect, our shared human spirit and its longing for meaning and relationship with the Mystery. The efficacy of van Kaam's ideas has proven itself over decades. Followers of his teaching validate it in the work they do to serve abandoned souls across the globe, from Australia to North America, from South Korea to Canada, from East and West Africa to Western Europe and India. Their dedication is a tribute to the fact that van Kaam offered to all who came in contact with him a fresh opportunity to engage in both ecumenical and interfaith dialogue about human living and spirituality. His experiences in war-torn

Europe would not allow him to settle for a simplistic hybrid like "theo-psychology" or "psycho-theology."[2] Rather, he followed the harder route of creating a new, comprehensive science of meaning, a formation science that posits from the start that the distinctive mark of our humanness is our transcendence dynamic. By placing the Mystery of formation at the center of our field of life, he challenged us to explore our own sociohistorical, vital, functional, and transcendent dimensions not in piecemeal fashion, but as a whole in dialogue with our inner- and inter-relational experiences, our immediate situation, and the wider world. And he did all of this with respect for his own theological roots. As a deeply committed Christian, a Roman Catholic priest, and a man of God of the highest caliber, it is our hope that he will be remembered, among other accolades, as the main bridging figure in the West between what we profess to believe (our faith tradition) and how we live these creeds with integrity and humility (our formation tradition).

As this book has shown, van Kaam based his vision of life on an anthropology of the person as essentially "formable" and "forming." He never deviated from the necessity of looking at who we are in the light of what it means to tell our story from a transcendent perspective. His scientific and anthropological description of the essential characteristics of human life and its emergence serve in turn the systematic and systemic articulation of formation theology.

From a Christian perspective, the transformation of nature by grace does not represent a destruction of but rather a healing and elevation of our

---

2. The didactical-consultative rigor of van Kaam's thinking prevents his system from in any way being "self-referential" or "closed" and hence difficult to penetrate. His seven volumes on formative spirituality, which detail both the roots of the science and anthropology of formation and the fruits they have yielded among a growing body of researchers, and his four coauthored volumes on formation theology, offer extensive bibliographical references revealing the width and breath of his approach. In fact, consultation—with an eye toward what may need to be modified or corrected in his own and others' thinking—plays a significant role in the methodology and metalingual precision of formation science. As outlined in volume four of his Formative Spirituality series (*Scientific Formation*, 92), these main methods are: dialogical articulation, elucidation, consultation, and application, with three auxiliary methods: dialogical translation, transposition, and integration. Several chapters in this book are devoted to an explanation and illustration of these methods, notably chapter 21 on consultation. The result is a theoretical-integrational model of study and application invaluable to anyone interested in an in-depth understanding of human and Christian formation as intellectual, spiritual, and pastoral. In his prodigious efforts to craft these intertwining fields of study, he needed to develop, as all original theorists do, a metalanguage, which has to be absorbed with fresh eyes. One must take time, as with any other theory, to understand this one as a whole. Only then will it become clear that his syntheses and formulations remain compatible with the testimony of ancient, medieval, and modern spiritual masters and experts in every branch of spirituality.

created, distinctively human being and becoming. Due to what tradition identifies as the Fall of Man, our understanding of our deepest identity has been veiled and obscured. By the same token, our powers of formation have been rendered vulnerable and weak. It would be impossible for us to attain the ideal-form to which we are called by virtue of our creation without the grace of revelation and redemption. While formation anthropology provides integrative descriptions of the phases of maturation we undergo from conception to natural death, it has to be complemented by a formation theory of personality that offers researchers a comprehensive way of explaining and understanding how and why we act as we do. Here, too, the Mystery of grace in the formation-deformation-reformation-transformation process of believers and sincere seekers can never be overlooked, but neither can we ignore the relevance of the insights and findings offered by the arts and sciences.

In the van Kaamian approach, our essence in the Mystery is primordial; it becomes manifest in personal existence. In this way, van Kaam countered the "existence precedes essence" assumption of an atheistic thinker like Jean-Paul Sartre. Our essence or founding life-form comes into existence as a unique-communal life-call in interformation with family, church, and society, with a vast array of lingual and cultural traditions. Our essence as believers discloses itself above all in interformation with the Eternal Trinitarian Formation and Interformation Event of Father, Son, and Holy Spirit. This calling by grace precedes its implementation in our everyday existence or field of life. In other words, consonant formation never occurs in a vacuum; it always includes a concern for society embodied in practical directives that respect the dignity of life from its natural beginning at conception to its natural ending at death.

This book has shown that our story cannot be contained within the inner life alone; it involves our entire formation field in interaction with our here-and-now situation, our relationships, and the world in which we live under global and cosmic influences. The center of the van Kaamian model of full field formation is after all not the self as an end in itself but the Mystery "in whom we live and move and have our being."[3] This Mystery always calls a person to further formation, reformation, and transformation.

Each person, consciously or unconsciously, assumes a stance of feeling abandoned by or abandoned to the Mystery. This underlying choice affects our perceptions, feelings, thoughts, and actions. When we opt for appreciative versus depreciative abandonment, several consequences occur. We are better able to accept as a formation opportunity any obstacle on our path.

3. Acts 17:28.

We worry less about what we look like in the eyes of others. We cease focusing on how to wreak vengeance on those who seem to be persecuting us. No wonder the Son of Man asked, "Why do you notice the splinter in your brother's eye, but do not perceive the wooden beam in your own?"[4]

If our heart is ready to move from condemnation through forgiveness to compassion, we can help others do the same despite the misunderstanding we and they may have to endure. Such reformation raises us to new heights of faith, hope, and love. As disciples of a gracious Master, we believe in faith that what is happening to us has a definite purpose. We trust in hope that the meaning of persecution will become clear. We see in love every limit as a challenge to live in union and communion with God and others. Our interrelational or interformative life with family members, authority figures, friends, and foes, influences our outlook as much as the immediate situation in which we find ourselves.

In brief, our lives from their earliest days to the closure of our earthly window are an invitation to integrate the truths of informational (what we believe) and formational (how we live) theology. To become fully human and truly committed, love has to be "chastened" or "purified" of self-centered passions and purposes, anxious needs, and over-dependent demands; only when love is chastened can we diminish the tendency to use and abuse ourselves or others as commodities for pleasure, as sources of need fulfillment or excuses for ego-enhancement. Chastened or purified love expresses a commitment never to violate the God-given integrity of self and others. To imagine and then to image in word and deed how to live chastely and lovingly takes a lifetime since, despite our best efforts, we often mistake dead-ends for the open road to human and Christian maturation.

Through formative reading of Holy Scripture and classic and contemporary masters of Christian spirituality, we open ourselves to God's grace alive and at work in us and others. We learn that this passing world cannot offer us the keys to lasting peace nor quell the restless yearnings of the human heart. In a spirit of praise and thanksgiving, we rejoice in the limited goodness, truth, and beauty of this world; we see such epiphanic disclosures as pointers to what awaits us in the life to come.

Highlighted in this book have been in-depth views of the life's work and legacy of Adrian van Kaam. It has presented, in fidelity to his theoretical insights and practical findings, the tools we need to comprehend our life as a journey from purifying formation, through illuminating reformation, to unifying transformation. This transformation by God enables us to acknowledge with docility the need to detach ourselves from the illusory

---

4. Luke 6:41.

powers, pleasures, and possessions that prevent us from growing into participative likeness with the Mystery at the center of our life and world. In the end, it is the gift of transforming love that makes it possible for us to let go of our own agendas and allow ourselves to be led by grace to wordless union and communion with the love-will of Father, Son, and Holy Spirit.

If there were one word by which to summarize the life's work of Adrian van Kaam from its inception to its culmination, that word would be *fidelity*. To find and follow God's will and to lead others to do the same became the chief motif in a symphony of awe and application begun in postwar Europe and still unfolding today.

Glossary

abandonment option. See primordial abandonment option.

abiding in awe-filled attention. The first of the A's of appraisal, to position oneself in trust and awe before the Mystery in order to nurture receptivity to the leading of the Holy Spirit (see also: apprehension, acknowledge the dissonance, argumentation/assessment, appreciative abandonment, affirmation of formative option, application of our yes).

absolutize (synonym: ultimize). To make ultimate or absolute in one's life; to identify something or someone as the final measurement of value and meaning; when not applied to the Holy Trinity, to absolutize is to idolize.

accretion. A formation tradition that may be changed without compromising the faith tradition that it expresses; a formation tradition that is not foundational.

accretional. Non-foundational (see also: foundational).

acknowledge the dissonance. One of the A's of appraisal, an honest attention to and courageous naming of dynamics of dissonance that are entailed in the appraisal of a directive (see also: abiding in awe-filled attention, apprehension, argumentation/assessment, appreciative abandonment, affirmation of formative option, application of our yes).

acquired disposition. A descriptor for those dispositions that we gain through interformation with our formation field and life events; acquired dispositions are sourced most often through consistently repeated acts.

actual form (synonyms: actual life-form, secondary foundational life-form). An empirical integrating structure of our human life form that integrates the core, current, and apparent forms of life; the actual form serves as the present-moment integration of our entire formation field (see also: neuroform).

actualized consciousness. A facet of formation consciousness that results when the potentials of fundamental human consciousness interact with people and events in our formation field and thereby become appropriated and personalized by us.

affirmation. In relation to maintaining our call efficacy, affirmation is an act of the intrasphere of personally and freely affirming a directive that we have appraised as consonant with our life-call (see also: confirmation).

affirmation of formative option. One of the A's of appraisal, the act of engaging the human will to say "yes" to a consonant or "no" to a dissonant directive (see also: abiding in awe-filled attention, apprehension, acknowledge the dissonance, argumentation/assessment, appreciative abandonment, application of our yes).

ambition. The expression of our striving to fulfill functional projects.

apparent form (synonym: apparent life-form). An empirical integrating structure of our human life form, grounded in the intersphere; the apparent form integrates all the ways in which we are disposed to appear to ourselves (inwardly) and to others (outwardly) through roles that we take up in dialogue with our formation field (see also: core form, current form, actual form, neuroform).

application of our yes. One of the A's of appraisal, the act of tentatively giving concrete form to a directive that has been appraised as consonant for one's life, with the intention of yielding the results of this act to further appraisal (see also: abiding in awe-filled attention, apprehension, acknowledge the dissonance, argumentation/assessment, appreciative abandonment, affirmation of formative option).

appraisal. Disposition in everyday life that seeks to apprehend and respond to directives as either consonant or dissonant with our formation field (see also: appraisal process, full field appraisal).

appraisal process. Full field appraisal that is focal and sustained over time beyond the normal practice of appraisal as a disposition in everyday life; the appraisal process is especially important in the context of transcendence crises, or other circumstances requiring major life decisions; the appraisal process intentionally includes all the A's of appraisal.

appreciative abandonment. As one of the A's of appraisal, the choice to trust oneself to the care of the Mystery; also used as a synonym for the appreciative abandonment option (see also: abiding in awe-filled attention, apprehension, acknowledge the dissonance, argumentation/assessment, affirmation of formative option, application of our yes).

appreciative abandonment option (synonym: appreciative abandonment). The choice to believe that one can abandon oneself to the care of the Mystery; a basic inclination or disposition to strive for consonance with the Mystery, which is fostered by (and in turn fosters) a conviction that ultimately one is cared for by the Mystery (see also: depreciative abandonment option, primordial abandonment option).

apprehension. One of the A's of appraisal, the selection of something for sustained focal attention and appraisal; apprehension connotes both understanding as well as fear of the unknown (see also: abiding in awe-filled attention, acknowledge the dissonance, argumentation/assessment, appreciative abandonment, affirmation of formative option, application of our yes).

argumentation/assessment. One of the A's of appraisal, the act of using the rational mind to distance oneself somewhat from a directive that is under consideration, so as to move from reactive impulsivity toward full field appraisal (see also: abiding in awe-filled attention, apprehension, acknowledge the dissonance, appreciative abandonment, affirmation of formative option, application of our yes).

arrogance. The opposite of awe, since it disposes us to lose respect for the Mystery and its epiphanies in people, events, and things (see also: awe, full awe, diffused awe, inverted awe, refused awe).

articulation. One of the six skills needed for one-on-one spiritual direction, articulation is the skill used by spiritual directors to guide directees beyond mere introspection toward full field appraisal and a transcendent, pneumatic-ecclesial vision of their lives, and to name possible obstacles and facilitating conditions directees may be experiencing in relation to where they may be being drawn by the Holy Spirit (see also: consultation, description, elucidation, reflection, translation).

A's of appraisal. A mnemonic for the seven facets of a process of full field appraisal (see also: abiding in awe-filled attention, apprehension, acknowledge the dissonance, argumentation/assessment, appreciative abandonment, affirmation of formative option, application of our yes).

aspiration. The expression of our striving to fulfill transcendent ideals.

assessment. The act of gathering as much information as possible about a directive under consideration, including identifying and naming various feelings and other formative dynamics that the directive either evokes or masks; assessment is one facet of argument/assessment, one of the A's of appraisal.

attention. Becoming aware of directives and dynamics of formation as they emerge from prefocal to focal consciousness.

autarkic. Descriptor of the quality of considering oneself as utterly self-sufficient and independent.

avocation. The vast array of gifts, skills, and talents that one draws upon over a lifetime in service of one's unique-communal life-call and vocation.

awe. The central, primordial predisposition and disposition of the spiritual life; both the gifted experience of and the orientation toward one's presence in ultimate reverence to the Mystery.

call disclosure. See life-call disclosure.

call efficacy. The effective expression of our awed appreciation of the presence of the Mystery at the center of our formation field.

cave trial. A purgative experience that shakes the very foundations of what we have understood thus far about the Mystery and ourselves (especially what we understand of our unique-communal life-call); an invitation, often in the midst of a transcendence crisis, to transition from the functional-transcendent phase of formation to the transcendent-functional phase and transcendent and post-transcendent phases of formation.

Christ form (synonyms: Christ-form, unique-communal Christ-form). Our essence as redeemed by Christ from the woundedness inflicted by the counterfeit pride form; the Christ form counters the effects of the pride form of life, reorienting the founding form that has been distorted by sin to a right relationship with the Mystery of the Trinity at the center of our formation field, thereby inviting us in all that we are and do to become more like Christ.

Christian formation conscience. See transcendent Christian conscience.

closure. The fifth of six components of a direction-in-common session, closure is a time during which members other than the facilitator of the group may add or highlight any additional common themes that they recognized during the session; it is also the time when the facilitator may clarify any needed information regarding upcoming sessions.

coercive disposition. A disposition rooted in our neuroform that is not consonant; it automatically triggers coercive security directives before we can submit them to focal appraisal; because these dispositions are embodied in our biological, neurological makeup, they are extremely resistant to reformation.

coercive security directive. An ultimized directive emerging from a coercive disposition; such directives are rooted in our neuroform; they are most often triggered before we are focally aware of them.

coform. To mutually influence and be influenced by.

coformant. A facet of our formation field that in some way both influences us and is influenced by us.

commitment. The sixth of six components of a direction-in-common session, during which the facilitator sends the group forward, until they meet again, with a renewed sense of love and service (see also: transcendent commitment).

communion. (1) A formation disposition that fosters an orientation toward community and communication, thus enabling freely formed bonds of intimacy among people (see also: privacy); (2) the fourth of six components of a direction-in-common session, during which a facilitator summarizes themes that have been shared in order for them to be appraised in the context of each participant's life and world.

compassion. A disposition of the C's of consonance, closely linked with our intersphere, that enables us to express heartfelt mercy and to suffer with our own and others' vulnerability.

compatibility. A disposition of the C's of consonance, closely linked with our situational sphere, that enables us to express patience with the limits always present in our here and now life and world.

competence. A disposition of the C's of consonance, closely linked with our world sphere, that encourages us to use to the full our gifts, talents, and skills to make concrete and necessary contributions, with courage and candor, to the betterment of our shared formation fields.

conference. The second of six components of a direction-in-common session, during which a facilitator introduces the text upon which the session will focus, and shares his or her own experience of it, thereby evoking experiential sharing on the part of the group.

confirmation. In relation to maintaining our call efficacy, confirmation is the necessary expression offered by significant others in support of the direction our life is meant to take (see also: affirmation).

congeniality. A disposition of the C's of consonance, closely linked with our intrasphere, that enables harmony between our founding form and its expression in our unique-communal life-call.

consecration. A profound awareness that beyond our calling in Christ and our commitment to Christ, we have been set apart by the grace of God for a life of loving, and perhaps even sacrificial, service to whatever the Spirit asks of us in obedience to the Father's will.

consonance. The central disposition at the heart of our formation field; it enables us to "sound together with" the Mystery and to maintain harmony between that center and all spheres of our formation field; from the perspective of formation theology, consonance is understood as a love relationship with God (see also: foundational dispositional triad, integration).

consonant. Descriptor of being in consonance.

consultation. One of the six skills needed for one-on-one spiritual direction, consultation is the skill used by spiritual directors to draw upon Scripture passages, spiritual writings, and other resources relevant to what is happening in directees' lives, in order to help directees feel less isolated and more in the company of other sincere seekers of God, past and present (see also: articulation, description, elucidation, reflection, translation).

contemplation. The first of the six components of a direction-in-common session, contemplation is when the group gathers quietly together, stills their hearts before the Mystery, and intentionally dwells in awe and reverence.

conversation. The third of six components of a direction-in-common session, conversation is when all members of the group share the movements and reflections in their hearts in relation to the text under consideration; this component encourages experiential give-and-take with respectful pauses that fosters the right balance of privacy and communion.

core form (synonyms: heart, core life-form). The main empirical integrating structure of our human life form, grounded in our intrasphere, which gathers together the continuous lasting dispositions, dynamics, and directives of our inner life (see also: current form, apparent form, actual form, neuroform).

cosmic epiphany. The Mystery disclosing itself as a never-ending dance of rising and falling forms in the cosmos (see also: human epiphany, transhuman/transcosmic epiphany).

crossover phase (synonym: cross-over phase). A transformation in one's life that moves one from a primarily self-initiated, self-resourced way of living, through a purgative experience, to a God-initiated, God-resourced way of living; it is the bridge from the functional-transcendent to the transcendent-functional phase of formation (see also: cave trial).

C's of consonance. A mnemonic for the four continuous, lasting dispositions of the heart that facilitate, with courage and candor, the process of full field appraisal of consonance (see also: congeniality, compatibility, compassion, competence).

current form (synonym: current life-form). An empirical integrating structure of our human life form, grounded in the situational and world spheres of our formation field, that articulates how we give and receive form here-and-now (see also: neuroform, actual form, apparent form, core form).

deformative. Exerting or experiencing influences contrary to the dynamics, dispositions, and directives of our unique-communal life-call, resulting in dissonance with the Mystery at the center of our formation field (see also: formative).

depreciative abandonment option (synonym: depreciative abandonment). (1) The choice to believe that we have been abandoned by a malevolent, indifferent, and perhaps nonexistent God, and therefore that we cannot surrender ourselves to an ultimately benevolent God; (2) a basic inclination to see life as ultimately meaningless, not meaningful, thus arousing in one a sense of hopelessness (see also: depreciative appraisal, appreciative abandonment option, primordial abandonment option).

depreciative appraisal. A disposition that is fostered by continually rationalizing away any manifestations of life as potentially meaningful; it is the fruit of continually choosing the depreciative abandonment option.

description. One of the six skills needed for one-on-one spiritual direction, description is the skill used by spiritual directors to help directees identify and describe the formative event that has brought them to seek spiritual direction (see also: articulation, consultation, elucidation, reflection, translation).

detachment. The act or process of letting go of our fixation on anything or anyone as the ultimate definer of meaning and direction in our lives.

detection. One of the five dispositions for the mode of one-on-one direction, detection is the disposition of spiritual directors to help directees to find and follow divine directive disclosures emerging in their lives (see also: embodiment, expression, inquiry, receptivity).

differentiation. A movement that seeks to distinguish particular facets of the spheres, dimensions, and dynamics of our formation field so that we can better understand their functions in the emergent story of our unfolding (see also: integration).

diffused awe. Remnants of a full awe experience that continue to permeate our everyday engagements (see also: awe, full awe, inverted awe, refused awe, arrogance).

dimension. An aspect of the formation field that represents modes of human presence and their dynamics, strivings, and expressions (see also: vital dimension, functional dimension, transcendent dimension, pneumatic-ecclesial dimension).

dimensions of consciousness (synonyms: levels of consciousness, regions of consciousness). A holistic understanding of human awareness as focal, prefocal, infrafocal, intrafocal, interfocal, and transfocal; these dimensions of consciousness, when we are open to them, enable us to live more harmonious and productive lives.

directee. In the context of one-on-one spiritual direction, a person who seeks the assistance of a spiritual director in appraising a transcendence crisis or other critical period of divine directive disclosures.

direction-in-common. One of three modes of spiritual direction that utilizes six components (contemplation, conference, conversation, communion, closure, and commitment) to enable a group of people to discern together, and obediently respond to, Spirit-inspired directives that at once appeal to each person and to the group as a whole (see also: spiritual self-direction, one-on-one direction).

directive. An expectation, a command, or an implied action linked with a faith tradition (see also: divine directive disclosure).

disposition. See formation disposition.

dissonance. Dissonance creates a climate of inner turmoil that prevents us from living in harmony with the Mystery; though dissonance tempts us to resist the way in which the Mystery beckons us to live in consonance, it can paradoxically invite us to realign our life with the Mystery (see also: insulation, exaltation, consonance).

dissonant. That which is out of tune with and resistant to the Mystery.

divine directive disclosure. A directive that is disclosed to us by the Mystery.

Divine Forming and Preforming Mystery (synonyms: Mystery, Eternal Trinitarian Formation and Interformation Event). The term used by formation science and formation anthropology that, from the perspective of formation theology, refers to the Holy Trinity.

ego guilt. Guilt that arises from conscience directives that are appraised only by the pride form from a functional perspective that excludes any influence of the Holy Spirit (see also: spiritual self-guilt, ego self-guilt).

ego self-guilt. Guilt that results from the recognition that one's formation traditions are dissonant with one's foundational faith traditions and one's unique-communal life-call; ego self-guilt can be experienced as an invitation to repentance and more faithful living in consonance with the will of God (see also: ego guilt, spiritual self-guilt).

elucidation. One of the six skills needed for one-on-one spiritual direction, elucidation is the skill used by spiritual directors to help directees bring to light dynamics and motivations behind the event or crisis with which they are struggling (see also: articulation, consultation, description, reflection, translation).

embodiment. One of the five dispositions for the mode of one-on-one direction, embodiment is the disposition of spiritual directors to express through voice, gesture, comportment, and other body language their sincerity, gentleness, and prayerful acceptance of directees (see also: detection, expression, inquiry, receptivity).

empathic conscience. That aspect of formation conscience that resonates with directives acknowledged by faith traditions that point to the interconnectedness of all creation (see also: vital formation conscience, parental formation conscience, social formation conscience, functional conscience, transcendent Christian conscience).

epiphany. Any manifestation of the Mystery that reveals itself in daily life (see also: cosmic epiphany, human epiphany, transhuman/transcosmic epiphany).

erratic heroism. Unrealistic, fantasy-based exaltations of what our involvement in life should be like; dispositions and actions that result from inspirations and aspirations that have been ultimized or unappraised in relation to our overall formation field.

essence. Our deepest identity, preformed from all eternity in the loving mind and heart of God.

Eternal Trinitarian Formation and Interformation Event (synonyms: Mystery, Divine-Forming Mystery, Divine Forming and Preforming Mystery). The term used in formation theology for the Holy Trinity.

exaltation. The human proclivity, rooted in the pride form, to treat a limited facet of life as ultimately important (see also: insulation).

executive will. See functional will.

existence. The embodiment of our preformed essence in our whole field of formation, more or less in fidelity to our unique-communal life-call.

expression. One of the five dispositions for the mode of one-on-one direction, expression is the disposition of spiritual directors to avoid communicating abstract information and instead to draw directees toward experiential, formative disclosures of where they find themselves and where they believe God may be leading them (see also: detection, embodiment, inquiry, receptivity).

faith. The conviction, in confidence and trust, that we are moving toward that which is infinitely more than we are, a truth, not necessarily provable by logic alone; from a Christian perspective, faith is a theological virtue.

faith conscience. That aspect of human conscience development that points to the ultimate beliefs and directives implemented by us in everyday life.

faith tradition (synonym: faith and formation tradition). An ultimate belief or set of beliefs to which we adhere, and from whence we derive the meaning and purpose of our existence.

Fall, the. From the perspective of formation theology, this term refers to the marred outcome of the Genesis story, in which God's desires for humankind and the cosmos were thwarted by the entry of sin into the world.

firmness. A continuous, lasting disposition of the heart characterized by perseverance, which enables us to respond to, and cope with, the burdens and blessings of life; it fosters a healthy decisiveness to pursue consonant versus dissonant directives without rigidity (see also: gentleness).

focal (synonym: focal-vocal). That which is easily accessed and able to be explicitly expressed; when something focal is vocalized, it is termed vocal (see also: focal consciousness, vocalization).

focal consciousness. A region of our consciousness in which are embedded ideas, images, desires, and feelings that are easily accessed and actualized so that we can straightforwardly verbalize or explicitly express them; one of four refinements of interconsciousness and intraconsciousness (see also: prefocal consciousness, infraconsciousness, intraconsciousness, interconsciousness, transfocal consciousness).

form. To influence, shape, give meaning to; to move in tandem with one's unique-communal life-call in God.

form donation. The potential and dynamic of contributing form to some facet of our formation field (see also: formability).

form reception. The potential and dynamic of receiving form from some facet of our formation field (see also: formability).

form tradition. See formation tradition.

form tradition pyramid (synonyms: form traditional pyramid, formation pyramid). A construct utilizing a pyramid-like diagram to enable us to identify the faith and formation traditions that exercise the most influence upon us (see also: pre-conversion pyramid, post-conversion pyramid).

formability. One of the five infrastructural principles of formative spirituality, the potency to give and receive form (see also: ongoing formation, formation field, maintenance of form potency, traditional formation).

formation. The receiving, giving, expressing, and maintaining of form in our life and world.

formation anthropology. In service of a comprehensive understanding of formative spirituality, formation anthropology articulates and elucidates in detail the transcendence dynamic presented as part of the holistic theory of personality presented in formation science; both the science and the anthropology of formation were designed by their initiator, Adrian van Kaam, to be from the beginning conducive to and compatible with the Judeo-Christian revelation, which is the basis of formation theology (see also: formation science, formation theology).

formation conscience. That facet of human conscience that ought to implement the truths embedded in faith and formation traditions that define the directives of our moral conscience (see also: vital formation conscience, parental formation conscience, social formation conscience, functional conscience, empathic conscience, transcendent Christian conscience).

formation consciousness (synonyms: formative consciousness, seminal human awareness). The empirical implementation of the potential modes of awareness embedded in our fundamental human consciousness.

formation crisis. See transcendence crisis.

formation disposition (synonym: disposition). A life orientation that describes our distinctive, relatively long-lasting habits of being and acting.

formation field (synonym: van Kaamian Formation Field Model). One of the infrastructural principles of formative spirituality that depicts a foundational construct of van Kaam's holistic theory of personality; the center of the formation field is not "me, my, or mine," but the Mystery; surrounding the Mystery, and always in relationship to it, are the four spheres or quadrants of our distinctively human personhood, named by him as: the intrasphere, intersphere, immediate situational sphere, and world sphere (see also: formability, ongoing formation, maintenance of form potency, traditional formation).

formation freedom. The human potential that frees us from entrapment in biological determination; it enables us to receive and respond to directives emerging from our Christ form, and to develop, with the help of grace, the dispositions and actions that, to the best of our ability, may bring them to fulfillment.

formation science. In service of a comprehensive understanding of formative spirituality, formation science crafts a holistic theory of personality that explicitly names as central our distinctively human transcendence dynamic; this science articulates and elucidates constructs, models, and metalingual terms that offer us a unique view of the human condition and all of creation as centered in the Mystery (see also: formation anthropology, formation theology).

formation theology. A systematic and systemic complement to informational theology; it presents a comprehensive understanding of the foundations of Christian formation, the formation of the Christian heart, the Christian articulation of the mystery of the Holy Trinity, along with a way to live to the full our Christian faith and formation traditions; from the beginning, van Kaam developed his pretheological formation science and anthropology as servant sources designed to be conducive to and compatible with the Christian revelation (see also: formation anthropology, formation science).

formation tradition (synonyms: form tradition, tradition). A distinctive overall pattern of receiving, expressing, and giving form in our life and world; faith traditions express what we believe, formation traditions point to the way we live these beliefs in everyday life; to the degree that this integration of faith and formation does not occur, we face the danger of a formation tradition becoming an end in itself, and thereby posing as a quasi-foundational faith tradition.

formative. Exerting or experiencing influences aligned with the dynamics, dispositions, and directives of our unique-communal life-call, resulting in consonance with the Mystery at the center of our formation field (see also: deformative).

formative action pattern (synonym: from-through-to movement). A description of the observed pattern that occurs in formative events, whereby one moves from a current life form that is no longer adequate, through a transcendence crisis, to a new current form that is more congenial with one's unique-communal life-call.

formative anticipation. One of the three incarnational sources, rooted in our transcendent and functional mind and will, that enables us to dwell upon (versus to predict) concrete images and symbols that may foster fidelity with the will of the Mystery in the future (see also: formative imagination, formative memory).

formative consciousness. See formation consciousness.

formative event (synonym: formation event). A concrete, observable, empirically describable happening of significance in a person's or a community's life (see also: formative action pattern).

formative functional mind. See functional mind.

formative functional will. See functional will.

formative imagination. One of the three incarnational sources, rooted in our transcendent and functional mind and will, that enables us to evoke both formative and deformative images that will affect, for better or worse, the way we think and feel; imagination as formative draws us to live more in harmony with the will of the Mystery for our good; imagination as deformative triggers dissonance with the will of the Mystery; for this reason, van Kaam identified formative imagination as the most significant of the three incarnational sources because both formative anticipation and formative memory draw upon images to function (see also: formative anticipation, formative memory).

formative memory. One of the three incarnational sources, rooted in our transcendent and functional mind and will, that enables us to remember formative and deformative events from the past, as well as effective or ineffective ways in which we applied the directives emerging from these events (see also: formative anticipation, formative imagination).

formative reflection. A dynamic of appraisal that distances us temporarily from the immediacy of the outer spheres of our formation field in order to ask ourselves what an experience means in relation to our intrasphere and to our unique-communal life-call as we understand it thus far (see also: informative reflection).

formative reiteration. A formative experience of reflecting upon and rehearsing whatever fosters growth in insight and commitment to directives received from the Mystery.

formative spirituality (synonym: van Kaamian formative spirituality). (1) An original theory, initiated by Adrian van Kaam, to comprehend and choose to release over a lifetime our inmost identity as having been formed in the image and likeness of God; (2) a spirituality that respects each person's unique-communal life-call, rather than imposing a form from without that may be alien to that call; (3) a way of receiving and giving distinctively human and Christian formation to our life and world.

foundational. That which transcends any particular time and place, and roots us in formative truths that are consistently appraised as consonant with our faith and formation traditions.

foundational dispositional triad (synonyms: foundational formative triad, foundational formational triad). A phrase that points to the dispositions of faith, hope, and consonance (love), grounded in awe for the Mystery.

foundational formational triad. See foundational dispositional triad.

founding form (synonyms: founding life form, founding-life form, soul, soul-form, providential form, providential life form). The pre-empirical base of our empirical integrating structures; the bridge between our essence in God and our empirical existence in time and space.

founding-life form. See founding form.

from-through-to movement. See formative action pattern.

full awe. An experience of awe that inundates our total field of consciousness, a gift that is profound and overwhelming and never forgotten (see also: awe, diffused awe, inverted awe, refused awe, arrogance).

full field appraisal (synonym: appraisal). (1) The formative disposition of abiding in awe-filled attention that prompts us to evaluate the significance of directives in the context of a full field approach to life and world; (2) the process of appraising whether or not received directives are in tune with our unique-communal life-call (see also: A's of appraisal).

functional anticipation. See formative anticipation.

functional conscience. See functional formation conscience.

functional dimension. That dimension of the human life form that embodies the actual gifts, skills, and talents we develop to manage our life and world (see also: sociohistorical dimension, vital dimension, transcendent dimension, pneumatic-ecclesial dimension).

functional formation conscience. That facet of formation conscience that represents the dynamics and directives of appraised and affirmed parental formation conscience and social formation conscience (see also: formation conscience, vital formation conscience, parental formation conscience, social formation conscience, empathic conscience, transcendent Christian conscience).

functional imagination. See formative imagination.

functional memory. See formative memory.

functional mind (synonyms: formative functional mind, functional intelligence). The use of our reasoning powers to appraise and implement directives with an awareness of concrete conditions in our formation field, most formative when it operates as a servant source of our transcendent mind and will and in concert with formative memory, formative imagination, and formative anticipation (see also: transcendent mind).

functional phase (synonym: functional phase of formation). That period of phasic formation during which we acquire lingual skills and exercise a certain degree of management and mastery over our life; in addition to lingual development, this phase emphasizes a fairly high degree of control, discipline, order, and restraint that facilitates the emergence of functional mind and functional will (see also: sociohistorical phase, vital phase, functional-transcendent phase, transcendent-functional phase, transcendent and post-transcendent phase).

functional will (synonyms: executive will, managing will, implementation will, pretranscendent will, incarnational will, secondary will, serve-will, formative functional will). Facet of our formative will that enables us to engage in the many practical decisions that have to be made in accordance with the demands of situations in which we find ourselves; as part of full field appraisal, the functional will decides on and executes what one apprehends and chooses to affirm (see also: transcendent will).

functional-formative sources. Those sources that serve the human spirit in directing the concrete realization of ideals and aspirations in everyday life (see also: functional mind, functional will, formative memory, formative imagination, formative anticipation).

functional-transcendence. A way of living in which one harnesses the energy and aspirations of the transcendent dimension for the sake of functioning more effectively.

functional-transcendent phase (synonym: functional-transcendent phase of formation). That period of phasic formation that represents the bridge between the functional and the transcendent phases of formation; while one is still predominantly rooted in the functional phase, one finds oneself being appealed to by transcendent aspirations, often revealed through discontent with the mere fulfillment of one's ambitions (see also: sociohistorical phase, vital phase, functional phase, transcendent-functional phase, transcendent and post-transcendent phase).

fundamental human consciousness (synonym: fundamental consciousness). A potency shared by all humans for openness to awe as both a predisposition and a disposition, evoking an awareness of who we are that draws us beyond mere instinctive reactions to where we are; points to our distinctively human capacity for creative solutions to problems in consultation with other people (interconsciousness) and in presence to who we most deeply are (intraconsciousness); a sudden "seeing" beyond mere reasoning processes that elevates our openness to the will of the Mystery.

fusion. A process that expresses, often in a deformative way, the human striving for undifferentiated union with another.

gentleness. A continuous, lasting disposition of the heart that expresses respect for what is valuable and vulnerable (see also: firmness).

guilt. Feeling of remorse (false or true) that results from the recognition that one has deviated from a directive emerging from one's formation field.

heart (synonym: core form). (1) The constellation of our character dispositions, serving as the bridge between the human spirit and the other spheres and dimensions of our formation field; (2) the center of our emotional life and its dynamics.

hope. The promise that there is more to life than meets the eye; this disposition helps us to remain hopeful rather than to become hopeless and despairing; from a Christian perspective, hope is a theological virtue.

horizontal interformation. The formative influence of people on one another in the here and now moment (see also: interformation, vertical interformation).

human consciousness. See fundamental human consciousness.

human epiphany. The Mystery disclosing itself in each human life form as created to know, love, and serve God in this world with the promise of being with God for eternity (see also: cosmic epiphany, transhuman/transcosmic epiphany).

human mind. See functional mind, and transcendent mind.

human spirit. See spirit.

human will. See functional will, and transcendent will.

ideal. The expression of our striving to fulfill transcendent aspirations.

idolization. The tendency to make something or someone other than God ultimate (see also: ultimize).

illuminating reformation. Apprehending, with the help of grace, deformations that have alienated us from our unique-communal life-call and availing ourselves of the grace of reforming them (see also: purifying formation, unifying transformation).

immediate situational sphere. See situational sphere.

incarnate. To embody, to enflesh, to make concrete in one's field of presence and action.

incarnational-directive sources. See functional-formative sources.

incarnational sources. Distinctively human capacity to exercise the three powers of formative memory, formative imagination, and formative anticipation in order to incarnate the insights received from our transcendent and functional mind and will; these three sources affect and are affected by what the neuroform responds to or ignores.

informative reflection. A dynamic of appraisal by which we gather and assess information from the outer spheres of our formation field that helps us to effectively handle the situations in which we find ourselves and to appraise wisely what we need to know to make good decisions (see also: formative reflection).

infraconsciousness (synonyms: infra-focal consciousness, infrafocal consciousness, infrafocal region of consciousness). A region of our consciousness in which are embedded as-of-yet unacknowledged, and possibly traumatic, sociohistorical, vital, and other events that still exert influence on our field of formation; this region is always amenable to healing through interfocal counseling and transfocal inspirations (see also: focal consciousness, prefocal consciousness, intraconsciousness, interconsciousness, transfocal consciousness).

infra-focal consciousness. See infraconsciousness.

infrastructural principles (synonym: infra-structural principles). The five basic hypothetical assumptions identified by van Kaam as central to his comprehensive theory of formative spirituality: formability, maintenance of form potency, formation field, ongoing formation, and traditional formation.

infused disposition. A descriptor for those dispositions that signify a pure gift, an undeserved endowment, of the Mystery that has an unwavering, abiding influence on our life (see also: acquired, preformed).

inquiry. One of the five dispositions for the mode of one-on-one direction, inquiry is the disposition of spiritual directors to know when to ask a question that will evoke more self-discovery on the part of directees, as well as when to briefly answer questions directees may pose (see also: detection, embodiment, expression, receptivity).

inspiration. The expression of our striving to fulfill pneumatic-ecclesial invitations.

insulation. An isolating bent toward selfishness, insulation is one of two primary dynamics of dissonance (see also: exaltation).

integrating structures (synonyms: empirical integrating structures, life forms). Empirical life forms by which our essence comes into existence; through these forms, we realize empirically and experientially the directives received from our founding life form (see also: core form, current form, apparent form, neuroform, actual life form).

integration. A dynamic that seeks to wholly and appropriately incorporate all aspects of our formation field into relationship in loving communion with God; integration is one of the two primary dynamics of consonance (see also: transcendence).

inter-apparent form. A subtype of the apparent form that describes how others perceive us; it may be different from the way in which we perceive ourselves (see also: intra-apparent form, outer-apparent form).

interconsciousness (synonyms: inter-focal consciousness, interfocal consciousness). A region of our consciousness that is responsive to the interactions we have with other people, with books and articles we read, and with myriad formation traditions in need of appraisal; it affects the way we perceive ourselves and others (see also: focal consciousness, prefocal consciousness, infraconsciousness, intraconsciousness, transfocal consciousness).

inter-focal consciousness. See interconsciousness.

interform. The way in which we influence and are influenced by the dynamic relationships that occur primarily in the intersphere of our life.

interformation. Formation that happens between us and others, both horizontally and vertically (see also: horizontal interformation, vertical interformation).

intersphere (synonym: inter-pole). The sphere of the formation field that emphasizes the communal aspect of our call; from birth to death, we are always in relationship with others here and now, with those who have gone before us, and even in some way, with those who will come after us (see also: intrasphere, world sphere, situational sphere).

intra-apparent form. A subtype of the apparent form that signifies how we appear to ourselves, whether or not others share this perception (see also: outer-apparent form, inter-apparent form).

intraconsciousness (synonyms: intra-focal consciousness, intrafocal consciousness). A region of our consciousness that gathers together the perceptions, images, traditions, feelings, and experiences that impact our inner life and increase our awareness of who we are and what we are called to do in this life (see also: focal consciousness, prefocal consciousness, infraconsciousness, interconsciousness, transfocal consciousness).

intra-focal consciousness. See intraconsciousness.

intraformation. The way in which the dynamics of our inner life influence the unfolding of the intrasphere of our formation field.

intraformative. Descriptor of the dynamics within the intrasphere of the formation field.

intrasphere (synonym: intra-pole). The sphere of the formation field that gathers together the vast array of personal thoughts, feelings, and decisions that influence how we receive and give form in daily life (see also: world sphere, intersphere, situational sphere).

introspection. A rumination upon what is happening in our life that is so self-centered and closed-off from the transcendent that our reflection becomes increasingly introspectionistic (see also: transcendent self-presence).

inverted awe. An inordinate attachment to our own initiatives that tends to enchant us with our own mechanisms of being in control; a fascination with our own projects of self-salvation (see also: awe, full awe, diffused awe, refused awe, arrogance).

invitation. The expression of our striving to fulfill pneumatic-ecclesial inspirations.

life-call. See unique-communal life-call.

life-call disclosure (synonym: call disclosure). An inspired, often sudden recognition of how to give consonant form to our life in fidelity with the will of the Mystery.

life form (synonym: life-form). See integrating structure.

love. The deepest expression of our longing for intimacy with the Mystery, all the while knowing that from the beginning the Mystery has initiated this love relationship with us; from a Christian perspective, our love for God and God's love for us is a theological virtue.

love-will. See transcendent will.

maintenance of form potency. One of the infrastructural principles of formative spirituality that highlights the human and spiritual propensity to continue throughout our life, however limited we are, to give and receive form (see also: formability, ongoing formation, formation field, traditional formation).

mediated sphere. See world sphere.

moral conscience. The aspect of human conscience development that provides foundational guidelines for distinctively human behavior drawn from, among others, natural law, faith traditions, moral theology, and ethical principles (see also: faith conscience, formation conscience).

motivation. One of three sources facilitating how to spiritualize dispositions; it points to what moves us to attend more fully to the disclosures we receive from our unique-communal life-call (see also: reiteration, participation).

Mystery (synonyms: Holy Trinity, radical mystery, radical formation mystery, Divine Forming Mystery, Divine Forming and Preforming Mystery, Eternal Trinitarian Formation and Interformation Event). The center of the van Kaamian Formation Field Model, in the light of which the other spheres of our field receive their ultimate meaning; van Kaam saw the Mystery as the root of all formation in universe, world, and history; it is the foundational, transcendent, radical, omnipresent source and sustainer of all formation; from the perspective of formation theology, it is the Eternal Trinitarian Formation and Interformation Event.

neuroform. An empirical integrating structure of our human life form that refers to our sensate reality as enmeshed in our vital dimension; it involves our body chemistry, DNA, and autonomic nervous system; while the neuroform cannot be reduced to neurobiology (according to van Kaam, it can be reformed), it serves as the informer, selector, guardian, and executive neuro-hormonal agent that affects, for example, our memory, imagination, and anticipation; deformation of the neuroform gives rise to coercive dispositions and such deformative patterns of behavior as anxiety and fear, which may become embedded in our core form and matching character (see also: core form, current form, apparent form, actual form).

one-on-one direction. One of three modes of spiritual direction that refers to an encounter with a wise, learned, and experienced spiritual guide who assists us with appraising God's will and responding to new life-call disclosures, especially in the context of transcendence crises (see also: spiritual self-direction, direction-in-common).

ongoing formation. One of the infrastructural principles of formative spirituality that highlights the fact that our capacity to give and receive form is never static, but always dynamic; from birth to death, we are in a process of always ongoing formation (see also: formability, formation field, maintenance of form potency, traditional formation).

organismic. Descriptor of our physicality, emphasizing that our vital biogenetic makeup must always be taken into account in the context of living our human and Christian formation.

orientation will. See transcendent will.

outer-apparent form. A subtype of the apparent form that connotes the way in which we choose to appear to others, depending on the circumstances in which we find ourselves (see also: intra-apparent form, inter-apparent form).

outer mediated sphere. See world sphere.

outer mondial sphere. See world sphere.

outer spheres. A comprehensives descriptor of the spheres of our field that are other than instraspheric (that is, the intersphere, situational sphere, world sphere).

parental formation conscience (synonym: parental conscience). That facet of formation conscience interjected by us from our relationships with parents and significant others; the directives we receive from them, if unappraised and not focally affirmed by us, may exert a deformative influence on us; the directives we receive that represent wise counsel ought to be appraised, internalized by us, and passed on to others (see also: vital formation conscience, social formation conscience, empathic conscience, transcendent Christian conscience).

participation. One of three sources facilitating how to spiritualize dispositions; participation is the consistent embodiment of our dispositions in our matching character; it involves the following four facets: 1) participating in the source of all formation dispositions (the Holy Trinity); 2) participating in one's founding form; 3) participating in one's formation field; and 4) participating in one's formation traditions (see also: motivation, reiteration).

periodic form (synonyms: periodic-form, periodic life-form, periodic current form). A descriptor of our current form that is linked specifically to biogenetic changes and developmental phases.

phasic formation. The van Kaamian construct that identifies life form transitions that highlight the influence of the transcendent on our emerging and maturing stages of life; phasic formation is not strictly chronological nor developmental, though some phasic periods may have implicit or explicit links with physical maturation.

pliable. A descriptor of formation dispositions that points to our ability to respond flexibly and dynamically to any and all formative events.

pneumatic-ecclesial dimension (synonym: pneumatic dimension). The distinctly Christian dimension of our human life form; it points to the grace-filled dynamics of our presence to and empowerment by the Holy Spirit and to the gifts of the Church, made available to us through

Jesus Christ (see also: sociohistorical dimension, vital dimension, functional dimension, transcendent dimension).

pneumatic phase of formation. That period of phasic formation, initiated when one becomes a Christian; during this phase, form reception and form donation are transformed by the empowerment of the Holy Spirit; one demonstrates an increasing awareness of one's sinfulness and of one's utter reliance upon the grace of God for spiritual formation, reformation, and transformation.

post-conversion pyramid. A form tradition pyramid that represents the reordered influence of significant faith and formation traditions following a formative event (see also: pre-conversion pyramid).

post-transcendent phase. See transcendent-functional phase.

pre-appraisal process. The gate-keeping function of our neuroform that prefocally filters incoming directives from our formation field.

pre-conversion pyramid. A form tradition pyramid that represents the most influential faith and formation traditions to which we adhered prior to undergoing the from-through-to movement of a formative event (see also: post-conversion pyramid).

predisposition. See preformed disposition.

pre-empirical (synonym: pre-experiential). Descriptor of that which precedes our experience, for example, the gift of our founding form.

prefocal. Descriptor of that rich, creative treasury of ideas, examples, and life events that for the moment may be out of reach of our current attention but are available to it.

prefocal consciousness. A region of our consciousness that is porous enough to receive input from all the other regions of consciousness (see also: focal consciousness, infraconsciousness, intraconsciousness, interconsciousness, transfocal consciousness).

preformed. A descriptor of aspects of our makeup that are given to us by the Mystery, including our sociohistorical origin, our vital-biogenetic makeup, our functional gifts and talents, and, most importantly, our distinctively human transcendence dynamic.

preformed disposition (synonym: predisposition). A disposition connected to the givenness of our vital-biogenetic makeup that especially affects our temperament (see also: acquired disposition, infused disposition, temper form).

pressure. The expression of a pulsation, that is, an expression of a striving of the sociohistorical dimension.

pretranscendent. Descriptor of dynamics inherent in the sociohistorical, vital, and functional dimensions.

pretranscendent dimensions. The sociohistorical, vital, and functional dimensions that function as servant sources of the transcendent and pneumatic-ecclesial dimensions.

pride form (synonyms: pride-form, quasi-foundational life-form, counterfeit form). The counterfeit life form that veils our inmost founding form and makes us susceptible to formation ignorance (ignorance of our true transcendence dynamic), demonic seduction, and inordinate attachments over which we constantly obsess; the pride form isolates and insulates, exalts and ultimizes itself as the sole definer of our existence (see also: autarkic).

primary will. See transcendent will.

primordial abandonment option (synonyms: abandonment option, Foundational Formation Decision, Foundational Formation Option, primordial formation decision, abandonment decision, primary formation decision, primordial alternative, primordial formation alternative). The crucial question of whether, when all is said and done, we have been abandoned by the Mystery or whether, despite so much human suffering, we can abandon ourselves to the Mystery in total trust (see also: appreciative abandonment option, depreciative abandonment option).

privacy. A formation disposition that protects our intrasphere from overexposure; it inclines us to distance ourselves from pressures emanating from the outer spheres of our formation field (see also: communion).

project. The expression of an ambition, that is, the expression of a striving of the functional dimension.

proximate. Immediate, close in time or space.

proximate background. The articulation of the immediate context out of which a formative event has arisen.

pseudogentility. A feigned expression of the disposition of gentleness that pretends to respect another's vulnerability, when in fact one is only pretending to do so.

pulsation. The expression of our striving to fulfill sociohistorical pressures.

pulsion. The expression of our striving to fulfill vital impulses and/or compulsions.

purgation. A descriptor of a spiritual process that frees the soul from entrapment in sin, leading one from over-reliance on self to deeper dependence on God.

purifying formation. The recognition of dissonant and deformative dispositions and directions of our life in need of being purified; a kind of inner "cleansing of the soul" guided by the grace of God (see also: illuminating reformation, unifying transformation).

pyramid. See form tradition pyramid.

quasi-foundational life-form. See pride form.

radical formation Mystery. See Mystery.

radical functional-transcendent reformation. The spiritually, emotionally, mentally, relationally, and physically arduous experience of undergoing a cave trial that exposes our ultimate vulnerability and humbly confirms our reliance upon God.

radical transcendent formation. The process by which God illuminates the deepest meaning of our unique-communal life-call and reveals new ways to live in faithfulness to it.

radical transcendent-functional transformation. See transcendent-functional transformation.

receptivity. One of the five dispositions for the mode of one-on-one direction, receptivity is the disposition of spiritual directors to be open to the directives of the Holy Spirit, as well as to the often private and delicate disclosures of directees (see also: detection, embodiment, expression, inquiry).

recollection. An integrative practice of gathering ourselves together out of the myriad distractions of daily life to reorient our attention more fully to the Mystery.

reflection. One of the six skills needed for one-on-one spiritual direction, reflection is the skill used by spiritual directors to encourage directees to practice spiritual self-direction as they meditate on the insights they have received in one-on-one direction and to apply them in daily life (see also: articulation, consultation, description, elucidation, translation).

refused awe (synonym: repudiated awe). Awe for the Mystery is totally invested in a substitute for the transcendent, such as a sports hero, a movie star, one's career, or possessions (see also: awe, full awe, diffused awe, inverted awe, arrogance).

reiteration. One of three sources facilitating how to spiritualize dispositions, reiteration involves gently and firmly repeating dispositions and acts that sustain our quest for ways to love and serve the Mystery in daily life (see also: motivation, participation).

remote background. The articulation of the general context out of which a formative event has arisen.

responsibility. Our ability to respond to sociohistorical, vital, functional, and transcendent directives in the arena of our formation field; a primary coformant, along with sensibility, of the core form.

routine disposition. An unappraised rote way of going through the motions of functioning, uninspired by any transcendent orientation (see also: spiritual disposition, routinizing disposition).

routinizing disposition (synonym: routinized disposition). A relatively lasting way of functioning that resists appraisal and influence by the transcendent dimension and, unless spiritualized, can become deformative (see also: spiritual disposition, routine).

secondary foundational life-form. A constellation of dispositions that models the directing power of our founding form and makes it more available to our experience.

sensibility. Our capacity to be sensitive to sociohistorical, vital, functional, and transcendent directives in the arena of our formation field; a primary coformant, along with responsibility, of the core form.

servant sources. Dimensions of formation that are pretranscendent but that are understood to be, first and foremost, servants of the transcendent; dynamically speaking, they embody transcendent aspirations and must never be seen as of less importance or as alienated from them.

situational sphere (synonyms: extra-pole, immediate situational sphere). The sphere of the formation field that represents the ways in which our environment and our here and now circumstances influence our human and Christian formation (see also: intrasphere, intersphere, world sphere).

social formation conscience. That aspect of formation conscience that assimilates into one's intrasphere directives received from friends, teachers, and peers; they must be fully appraised to see if they are consonant or dissonant with our unique-communal life-call (see also: functional conscience, vital formation conscience, parental formation conscience, empathic conscience, transcendent Christian conscience).

sociohistorical dimension. That dimension of the human life form that represents the historical, familial, and communal aspects of formation into which we are born and in which we are immersed for a lifetime (see also: vital dimension, functional dimension, transcendent dimension, pneumatic-ecclesial dimension).

sociohistorical phase (synonym: sociohistorical phase of formation). That period of phasic formation related to the ways in which we are influenced by the traditions into which we are born, including familial, cultural, economic, and religious; facets of this phase stay with us, formatively or deformatively, for a lifetime, which is why what occurs to us in this early phase of formation needs to be carefully appraised as we age (see also: vital phase, functional phase, functional-transcendent phase, transcendent-functional phase, transcendent and post-transcendent phase).

sociohistoricism. Exaltation and ultimization of the sociohistorical dimension, with its dynamics and expressions, as the defining facet of one's formation field that gives ultimate meaning and direction in one's life.

soul. See founding form.

sphere. A facet of the formation field that affects us, implicitly or explicitly, depending on the situation in which we find ourselves (see also: intrasphere, intersphere, situational sphere, world sphere).

spirit (synonyms: human spirit, transcendent mind and will, transcendence). The human ability to experience all that we are and do in ways that cannot be measured or exhaustively understood by either our senses or the sciences of measurement; the origin of our distinctively human transcendence dynamic; the gifted disrupter of any complacency that prevents us from becoming spiritually mature.

spiritual. A descriptor for dispositions that are in dialogue with the transcendent dimension and its aspirations, and the pneumatic-ecclesial dimension and its inspirations.

spiritual conscience. See transcendent formation conscience.

spiritual direction. The art and discipline of attending to and appraising Spirit-initiated directives and their implementations in our lives (see also: spiritual self-direction, one-on-one direction, direction-in-common).

spiritual director. A wise, learned, and experienced Christian person who has been trained in the art and discipline of directing people to attend to and to appraise divine directives during transcendence crises and other critical periods of emergent life-call direction, in light of full field appraisal and the treasury of foundational Christian faith traditions.

spiritual disposition. A constellation of attitudes and practices that fosters the consonant unfolding of our unique-communal life-call and that heightens our awareness of transcendent aspirations and pneumatic-ecclesial inspirations (see also: routine disposition, routinizing disposition).

spiritual formation. See formative spirituality.

spiritual self-direction. The ongoing ways in and through which we continue to mature in response to our unique-communal life-call; may in some cases follow the direction process either in one-on-one direction or direction-in-common; the art and discipline of maintaining such practices of faith deepening as: silence, formative reading, meditative reflection, and devotional and contemplative prayer.

spiritual self-guilt (synonym: transcendent guilt). Authentic guilt that results from the recognition that one has been unfaithful to the foundations of one's faith tradition and divine disclosures pertaining to one's unique-communal life-call (see also: ego guilt, ego self-guilt).

spiritualization. A freely chosen decision to respond to, rather than to resist or refuse, the graced invitation of the Spirit to go beyond routine and routinizing dispositions; a readiness and a willingness to open ourselves to the purifying, illuminating, and unifying dynamics of a fully transcendent-functional way of being and doing (see also: motivation, reiteration, participation).

spiritualize. The action of connecting a disposition to our transcendent mind and will, followed by the implementation of this disposition through the exercise of our functional mind and will.

striving. An innate human potential to give and receive form through every dimension of our human life form.

temper form. An expression of our neuro-muscular-hormonal system that takes into account the minimum and maximum rate of speed of our physical makeup, our temperament, and our intellectual acumen, as well as the particular range and intensity of our vital emotions and passions.

tradition. A distinctive overall pattern of giving, receiving, or expressing form in one's formation field; it is distinguishable from a mere personal habit or an instinctive reaction; its nature is relatively enduring, and its tendency is to be passed on intergenerationally (see also: faith tradition, formation tradition).

traditional formation. One of the infrastructural principles of formative spirituality that highlights the fact that since we humans are instinct-deprived, we rely during our entire formation journey on the insights and guidance we receive from the traditions of formation embedded, for example, in language and other symbol systems, in cultural and familial customs, in educational and religious symbols, and in rituals (see also: formability, ongoing formation, formation field, maintenance of form potency).

transcendence. Our longing to go beyond or to go more deeply into what gives meaning to our life and world (see also: transcendence dynamic).

transcendence crisis (synonym: formation crisis). A happening in our life that is so unsettling we can identify it as a formative event; in a crisis, we are invited by grace to move from an old current form of life through many levels of insight and experience to a new current form that is more consonant with our unique-communal life-call.

transcendence dynamic (synonym: the human spirit, transcendence). The distinctive quality of human life; the potential to integrate all levels of our being in the light of the Mystery in the center of our formation field.

transcendence therapy (synonym: transtherapy). A mode of formation counseling with people who may or may not share our faith tradition; not representative of one religion or denomination; distinguished from spiritual direction, which presupposes an encounter between people who share the same faith tradition.

transcendent. Relating to or characteristic of the transcendent dimension.

transcendent and post-transcendent phase (synonym: transcendent and post-transcendent phase of formation). That period of phasic formation that moves us beyond mere functionality to a recognition that our life direction must remain open to more than temporal achievement and success; during this phase we acknowledge our longing for a meaning of life that will carry us beyond the limits of the aging process, and make us more receptive to divine guidance (see also: sociohistorical phase, vital phase, functional phase, functional-transcendent phase, transcendent-functional phase).

transcendent Christian conscience (synonym: Christian formation conscience). That aspect of formation conscience that enables us to affirm, under the guidance of the Holy Spirit, the directives we receive pertaining to our unique-communal life-call; takes into account the values and virtues articulated by our foundational Christian faith tradition with its doctrines and catechesis (see also: vital formation conscience, parental formation conscience, social formation conscience, functional formation conscience, empathic conscience).

transcendent commitment. A purposeful decision to place oneself at the disposal of the Mystery and its disclosures of our life-call, differentiated from basing our life decisions on autarkic self-centeredness; this way of living respects our own judgment, insight, freedom, and responsibility; it resist the temptation to pretranscendent self-centeredness and chooses instead to be directed by the Mystery.

transcendent conscience. See transcendent formation conscience.

transcendent dimension. That distinctively human dimension of our life form that represents our capacity to "go beyond" or "go more deeply into"; it is meant to be served by the pretranscendent sociohistorical, vital, and functional dimensions (see also: sociohistorical dimension, vital dimension, functional dimension, pneumatic-ecclesial dimension).

transcendent formation conscience (synonym: spiritual conscience). That aspect of formation conscience that unfolds under the influence of transcendent aspirations (see also: Christian formation conscience, vital formation conscience, parental formation conscience, social formation conscience, functional formation conscience, empathic conscience, transcendent Christian conscience).

transcendent guilt. See spiritual self-guilt.

transcendent mind. A receptive way of knowing that transcends mere logic and analytical thinking; an orientation of our mind to what is intuitive, integrative, and unitive; a deep knowing that implicitly intuits the presence and calling of the Mystery (see also: functional mind).

transcendent mind and will. See spirit.

transcendent phase. See transcendent and post-transcendent phase.

transcendent self-presence (synonym: Christian consciousness). A meditation on what is happening in our life that is Mystery-centered and open to the transcendent, so much so that our reflection becomes increasingly open to transfocal inspirations and aspirations (see also: introspection).

transcendent will (synonyms: love-will, primary will, orientation will). (1) A unique aspect of the human spirit that complements transcendent mind; as formed and directed by our transcendence dynamic, it makes us more receptive to divine directives; (2) when used in reference to God, it emphasizes the love-will of the Holy Trinity bestowing benevolent graces on all of creation.

transcendent-functional phase (synonym: transcendent-functional phase of formation). That period of phasic formation in which we are primarily oriented toward form reception to the guidance of the Mystery, while at the same time being fully engaged in form donation (see also: sociohistorical phase, vital phase, functional phase, functional-transcendent phase, transcendent and post-transcendent phase).

transcendent-functional transformation (synonym: radical transcendent-functional transformation). A state of being marked by irrevocable detachment from the entanglements of mere self-actualization; by the power of the Holy Spirit, our hearts are so ignited with the fire of God's love that we live our ordinary lives with extraordinary compassion.

transfocal. Descriptor of what transpires in the transfocal region of our consciousness, wherein aspirations and inspirations filter into our prefocal and focal awareness.

transfocal consciousness (synonyms: trans-focal consciousness, transconsciousness). A region of our consciousness open to receiving transcendent aspirations and pneumatic inspirations that can radically change the course of our life (see also: focal consciousness, prefocal consciousness, infraconsciousness, intraconsciousness, interconsciousness).

transformation. See unifying transformation.

transhuman/transcosmic epiphany. The Mystery disclosing itself as beyond any cosmic or human creation (see also: cosmic epiphany, human epiphany).

translation. One of the six skills needed for one-on-one spiritual direction, translation is the skill used by spiritual directors to put into directees' own language and symbol systems insights they have gained during one-on-one sessions; translation draws upon the rich contributions of directees' faith and formation traditions (see also: articulation, consultation, description, elucidation, reflection).

ultimize (synonyms: absolutize, idolize). To make absolute in one's life; to make something or someone the final measurement of one's value and meaning; when not applied to the Holy Trinity, to ultimize is to idolize.

unifying transformation (synonym: transformation). The gift of being detached by grace from our own limited powers, expectations, and perceptions of the meaning of life; glimpsing more fully God's deepest calling to us in Christ; an experience of being freed, through no merit of our own, to participate in the life of union and communion with the Holy Trinity (see also: purifying formation, illuminating reformation).

unique. Descriptor of our life-call that emphasizes the unrepeatable gift of equality in dignity each person is; van Kaam distinguished uniqueness from mere individualism, which emphasizes functional talents and inventiveness, and from mere subjectivism alienated from our transcendence dynamic.

unique-communal life-call (synonym: life-call). The embodiment of our founding form of life in every facet of our existence; a dynamic, ever-beckoning invitation to be faithful over a lifetime to the Christ form of our soul.

van Kaamian Formation Field Model. See formation field.

van Kaamian Formative Spirituality. See formative spirituality.

vertical interformation. The formative influence of parents, teachers, spiritual masters, and others who, though they have gone before us, continue in some way to inspire and direct us here and now; it is imperative that we appraise whether this influence is formative or deformative (see also: interformation, horizontal interformation).

vital dimension. That dimension of the human life form that represents our preformed biogenetic constitution; over a lifetime, it shapes and expresses our physicality and the physiological changes of the aging process; it influences our emotionality; it can degenerate into mere vitalism if it is severed from the transcendent dimension (see also: sociohistorical dimension, functional dimension, transcendent dimension, pneumatic-ecclesial dimension).

vital formation conscience. This early expression of formation conscience is not yet guided by full field appraisal; it responds to the pains and joys of life with sympathy and empathy; when properly guided, it fosters not fusion, but a sense of responsibility to show kindness to others and to care for their well-being (see also: parental formation conscience, social formation conscience, functional conscience, empathic conscience, transcendent Christian conscience).

vital phase (synonym: vital phase of formation). That period of phasic formation during which one shifts from mere vitalistic form reception to a more mature balance of form-giving and form-receiving in service of growth in relational intimacy (see also: sociohistorical phase, functional phase, functional-transcendent phase, transcendent-functional phase, transcendent and post-transcendent phase).

vocalization. A way of expressing verbally, with appropriate words, or nonverbally, with a look or a gesture, what one has received through one's focal consciousness.

vocation. The embodiment of one's unique-communal life-call in a single or marital way of life that may change as the mystery of the call unfolds; for example, if a spouse dies, a married person is suddenly single (see also: avocation).

will. See human will.

world sphere (synonyms: world pole, outer mondial sphere, mediated sphere, outer mediated sphere). The sphere of the formation field that represents the formational dynamics of the wider world, that is to say, the world beyond one's immediate perception; the influences of the world sphere are often mediated to us by means of technology and increasingly sophisticated modes of communication and global transportation (see also: intrasphere, intersphere, situational sphere).

Bibliography

Adler, Alfred. *Social Interest: A Challenge to Mankind.* Translated by John Linton and Richard Vaughn. New York: Capricorn, 1964.
———. *Superiority and Social Interest.* Edited by Heinz Ansbacher and Rowena Ansbacher. Evanston: Northwestern University Press, 1964.
Aelred, of Rievaulx, St. *Spiritual Friendship.* Translated by Mary Eugenia Laker. Notre Dame: Ave Maria, 2008.
Allen, Holly Catterton, ed. *Nurturing Children's Spirituality: Christian Perspectives and Best Practices.* Eugene, OR: Cascade, 2008.
Allport, Gordon. *Becoming: Basic Considerations for a Psychology of Personality.* New Haven: Yale University Press, 1968.
———. *Patterns and Growth in Personality.* New York: Holt, 1961.
———. *Personality: A Psychological Interpretation.* New York: Holt, 1937.
———. *Theories of Personality and the Concept of Structure.* New York: Wiley, 1955.
Ansbacher, Heinz, and Rowena Ansbacher, eds. *The Individual Psychology of Alfred Adler: Systematic Presentation in Selections from His Writings.* New York: Harper and Row, 1964.
Augustine, St., Biship of Hippo. *The Confessions.* Translated by Maria Boulding. Vintage Spiritual Classics. New York: Random House, 1998.
Baab, Lynne M. *Sabbath Keeping: Finding Freedom in the Rhythms of Rest.* Downers Grove, IL: InterVarsity, 2005.
Baille, John. *A Diary of Private Prayer.* New York: Touchstone, 1996.
Barton, Ruth Haley. *Invitation to Silence and Solitude.* Downers Grove, IL: InterVarsity, 2004.
———. *Sacred Rhythms: Arranging Our Lives for Spiritual Transformation.* Downers Grove, IL: InterVarsity, 2006.
———. *Strengthening the Soul of Your Leadership.* Downers Grove, IL: InterVarsity, 2008.
Benedict, of Nursia, St. *Rule of St. Benedict in English.* Edited by Timothy Fry. Collegeville, MN: Liturgical, 1981.
Benson, Robert. *In Constant Prayer.* Nashville: Thomas Nelson, 2008.
Bernard, of Clairvaux, St. *Selected Works.* Translated by G. R. Evans. Classics of Western Spirituality. Mahwah, NJ: Paulist, 1987.
Berry, Wendell. *What Are People For? Essays.* Berkeley: Counterpoint, 2010.
Berryman, Jerome W. *Children and the Theologians: Clearing the Way for Grace.* New York: Morehouse, 2009.

Blythe, Teresa A. *50 Ways to Pray: Practices from Many Traditions and Times.* Nashville: Abingdon, 2006.
Bonhoeffer, Dietrich. *The Cost of Discipleship.* New York: Simon and Schuster, 1995.
———. *Letters and Papers from Prison.* Edited by Eberhard Bethge. Enlarged ed. New York: Simon and Schuster, 1997.
———. *Life Together.* Translated by John. W. Oberstein. New York: Harper, 1954.
The Book of Common Prayer and Administration of the Sacraments and other Rites of the Church. New York: Church Publishing, 1979.
Bouyer, Louis. *Orthodox Spirituality and Anglican Spirituality.* History of Christian Spirituality 3. Minneapolis: Seabury, 1963.
———. *The Spirituality of the Middle Ages.* History of Christian Spirituality 2. Minneapolis: Seabury, 1963.
———. *The Spirituality of the New Testament and the Fathers.* History of Christian Spirituality 1. Minneapolis: Seabury, 1963.
Boyle, Gregory. *Tattoos on the Heart: The Power of Boundless Compassion.* New York: Free Press, 2010.
Brock, Brian. *Christian Ethics in a Technological Age.* Grand Rapids: Eerdmans, 2010.
Brueggemann, Walter. *Sabbath as Resistance: Saying No to the Culture of Now.* Louisville: Westminster John Knox, 2014.
Carmichael, Alexander. *Carmina Gadelica.* Edinburgh: Floris, 2012.
Carr, Nicholas. *The Shallows: What the Internet Is Doing to Our Brains.* New York: Norton, 2010.
Catherine, of Genoa, St. *Purgation and Purgatory; The Spiritual Dialogue.* Translated by Serge Hughes. Classics of Western Spirituality. Mahwah, NJ: Paulist, 1979.
Catherine, of Siena, St. *The Dialogue.* Translated by Suzanne Noffke. Classics of Western Spirituality. Mahwah, NJ: Paulist, 1980.
Celtic Daily Prayer: Prayers and Readings from the Northumbria Community. New York: HarperOne, 2002.
Chautard, Jean-Baptiste. *The Soul of the Apostolate.* Trappist, KY: Abbey of Gethsemani, 1946.
Chittister, Joan. *The Gift of Years: Growing Older Gracefully.* Katonah, NY: BlueBridge, 2008.
Ciszek, Walter. *He Leadeth Me.* San Francisco: Ignatius, 1973.
Clare, of Assisi, St., and St. Francis of Assisi. *Francis and Clare: The Complete Works.* Translated by Regis J. Armstrong and Ignatius C. Brady. Classics of Western Spirituality. Mahwah, NJ: Paulist, 1982.
Conn, Joann Wolski. *Spirituality and Personal Maturity.* Lanham, MD: University Press of America, 1989.
Cross, F. L., and E. A. Livingston, eds. *The Oxford Dictionary of the Christian Church.* 3rd ed. Oxford: Oxford University Press, 1997.
Crouch, Andy. *Playing God: Redeeming the Gift of Power.* Downers Grove, IL: InterVarsity, 2013.
Dawn, Marva. *Keeping the Sabbath Wholly: Ceasing, Resting, Embracing, Feasting.* Grand Rapids: Eerdmans, 1989.
Day, Dorothy. *The Long Loneliness: The Autobiography of Dorothy Day.* New York: Harper, 1952.
Dean, Kenda Creasy, and Ron Foster. *The Godbearing Life: The Art of Soul Tending for Youth Ministry.* Nashville: Upper Room, 2010.

de Caussade, Jean-Pierre. *Abandonment to Divine Providence*. Garden City, NY: Image, 1975.
de Waal, Esther. *Seeking God: The Way of St. Benedict*. Collegeville, MN: Liturgical, 1984.
Dillard, Annie. *Tickets for a Prayer Wheel*. New York: Bantam, 1972.
Doherty, Catherine de Hueck. *Poustinia: Encountering God in Silence, Solitude and Prayer*. Combermere, ON: Madonna House, 2000.
Dreikurs, Rudolf. *Psychology in the Classroom: A Manual for Teachers*. New York: Harper and Row, 1968.
Dreikurs, Rudolf, and Vicki Soltz. *Children: The Challenge*. New York: Duell, Sloan and Pearce, 1967.
Duhigg, Charles. *The Power of Habit: Why We Do What We Do in Life and Business*. New York: Random House, 2012.
Dyrness, William A., and Veli-Matti Kärkkäinen, eds. *Global Dictionary of Theology*. Downers Grove, IL: InterVarsity, 2008.
Earle, Mary C. *Celtic Christian Spirituality: Essential Writings—Annotated and Explained*. Woodstock, VT: Skylight Paths, 2011.
Erb, Peter C., ed. *Pietists: Selected Writings*. Classics of Western Spirituality. Mahwah, NJ: Paulist, 1983.
Erikson, Erik H. *Childhood and Society*. New York: Norton, 1950.
———. *Identity, Youth and Crisis*. New York: Norton, 1950.
———. *The Life Cycle Completed*. New York: Norton, 1998.
Fénelon, Francois. *Meditations on the Heart of God*. Translated by Robert J. Edmonson. Christian Classics. Brewster, MA: Paraclete, 1997.
———. *The Royal Way of the Cross*. Translated by Hal M. Helms. Living Library. Brewster, MA: Paraclete, 1982.
———. *Talking with God*. Translated by Hal M. Helms and Robert J. Edmonson. Christian Classics. Brewster, MA: Paraclete, 2012.
Field, Anne. *From Darkness to Light: How One Became a Christian in the Early Church*. Ben Lomond, CA: Conciliar, 1997.
Fitzgerald, William John. *A Contemporary Celtic Prayer Book*. Chicago: ACTA, 1998.
Foltz, Richard C. *Religions of the Silk Road: Overland Trade and Cultural Exchange from Antiquity to the Fifteenth Century*. New York: St. Martin's Griffin, 1999.
Ford, Leighton. *The Attentive Life*. Downers Grove, IL: InterVarsity, 2008.
Foster, Richard J. *Celebration of Discipline: The Path to Spiritual Growth*. New York: HarperCollins, 1988.
———. *Prayer: Finding the Heart's True Home*. New York: HarperCollins, 1992.
———. *Streams of Living Water: Celebrating the Great Traditions of Christian Faith*. San Francisco: Harper and Row, 1998.
Foster, Richard J., and Gayle D. Beebe. *Longing for God: Seven Paths of Christian Devotion*. Downers Grove, IL: InterVarsity, 2009.
Foster, Richard J., and Emilie Griffin, eds. *Spiritual Classics: Selected Readings for Individuals and Groups on the Twelve Spiritual Disciplines*. New York: HarperCollins, 2000.
Foster, Richard J., and James Bryan Smith, eds. *Devotional Classics: Selected Readings for Individuals and Groups*. New York: HarperCollins, 2005.
Fowler, James W. *Stages of Faith: The Psychology of Human Development and the Quest for Meaning*. New York: Harper and Row, 1981.

Francis, of Assisi, St. *The Little Flowers of St. Francis*. Translated by Raphael Brown. New York: Image/Doubleday, 1958.
Francis, de Sales, St. *Finding God Wherever You Are*. Edited by Joseph F. Power. Hyde Park, NY: New City, 1993.
Goldstein, Kurt. *Human Nature in the Light of Psychotherapy*. New York: Schocken, 1940.
———. *The Organism*. New York: American Book Company, 1939.
González, Justo L. *The Story of Christianity*. 2 vols. 2nd ed. New York: HarperOne, 2010.
Green, Michael. *Evangelism in the Early Church*. Guildford, UK: Eagle, 1995.
Greene, Graham. *The Power and the Glory*. London: Penguin, 1991.
Gregory I, Pope. *Pastoral Care*. Translated by Henry Davis. New York: Newman, 1950.
Gregory, of Nyssa, St. *The Life of Moses*. Translated by Abraham J. Malherbe. Classics of Western Spirituality. Mahwah, NJ: Paulist, 1978.
———. *The Life of Saint Macrina*. Translated by Kevin Corrigan. 1987. Reprint, Eugene, OR: Wipf & Stock, 2005.
Guenther, Margaret. *Holy Listening: The Art of Spiritual Direction*. Boston: Cowley, 1992.
Hammarskjöld, Dag. *Markings*. Translated by Leif Sjöberg and W. H. Auden. London: Faber and Faber, 1964.
Hayes, Diana L., and Charles S. Ndege. *Were You There? Stations of the Cross*. Maryknoll, NY: Orbis, 2000.
Hebblethwaite, Margaret, and Kevin Donovan. *The Theology of Penance*. Theology Today 20. Butler, WI: Clergy Book Service, 1979.
Heschel, Abraham Joshua. *The Sabbath*. New York: Farrar, Straus and Giroux, 1951.
Hillesum, Etty. *An Interrupted Life: The Diaries, 1941–1943, and Letters from Westerbork*. New York: Picador, 1996.
Hilton, Walter. *The Scale of Perfection*. Translated by John P. H. Clark and Rosemary Dorward. Classics of Western Spirituality. Mahwah, NJ: Paulist, 1991.
Hipps, Shane. *The Hidden Power of Electronic Culture*. Grand Rapids: Zondervan, 2005.
Holmes, Urban T. *A History of Christian Spirituality: An Analytical Introduction*. Harrisburg, PA: Morehouse, 2002.
Ignatius, of Loyola, St. *The Spiritual Exercises of Saint Ignatius*. Translated by Pierre Wolff. Liguori, MI: Liguori/Triumph, 1997.
Into Great Silence. DVD. Directed by Philip Gröning. New York: Zeitgeist Films, 2007.
Jacopone, da Todi. *The Lauds*. Translated by Serge Hughes and Elizabeth Hughes. Classics of Western Spirituality. Ramsey, NJ: Paulist, 1982.
James, William. *Habit*. New York: Henry Holt, 1890.
———. *The Principles of Psychology*. New York: Dover, 1950.
———. *The Varieties of Religious Experience: A Study in Human Nature*. New York: Collier, 1961.
Jenkins, Philip. *The Lost History of Christianity: The Thousand-Year Golden Age of the Church in the Middle East, Africa, and Asia—and How It Died*. New York: HarperCollins, 2008.
Job, Reuben P. *A Guide to Retreat for All God's Shepherds*. Nashville: Abingdon, 1994.
John, Climacus, St. *The Ladder of Divine Ascent*. Translated by Colm Luibheid and Norman Russell. Classics of Western Spirituality. Mahwah, NJ: Paulist, 1982.

John of the Cross, St. *The Collected Works of St. John of the Cross*. Translated by Kieran Kavanaugh and Otilio Rodriquez. Washington, DC: Institute of Carmelite Studies, 1991.
Jones, Alan. *Soul Making: The Desert Way of Spirituality*. New York: HarperCollins, 1989.
Julian, of Norwich. *Showings*. Translated by Edmund Colledge and James Walsh. Classics of Western Spirituality. Mahwah, NJ: Paulist, 1978.
Kadloubovsky, E., and G. E. H. Palmer, trans. *Early Fathers from the Philokalia: Together with Some Writings of St. Abba Dorotheus, St. Isaac of Syria, and St. Gregory Palamas*. London: Faber and Faber, 1954.
Keating, Thomas. *Open Mind, Open Heart*. 20th anniversary ed. New York: Bloomsbury, 2006.
Kelly, Kevin. *What Technology Wants*. New York: Viking, 2010.
Kelly, Thomas. *A Testament of Devotion*. New York: HarperCollins, 1992.
Kidd, Sue Monk. *When the Heart Waits: Spiritual Direction for Life's Sacred Questions*. New York: HarperCollins, 1990.
King, Martin Luther, Jr. *I Have a Dream: Writings and Speeches That Changed the World*. Edited by James M. Washington. New York: HarperOne, 1992.
———. *Strength to Love*. Philadelphia: Fortress, 1981.
King, Ursula. *Christian Mystics: The Spiritual Heart of the Christian Tradition*. New York: Simon & Schuster, 1998.
Kopciowski, Elias, ed. *Praying with the Jewish Tradition*. Translated by Paula Clifford. Grand Rapids: Eerdmans, 1997.
Kornfeld, Margaret. *Cultivating Wholeness: A Guide to Care and Counseling in Faith Communities*. New York: Continuum, 2006.
Laird, Martin. *Into the Silent Land: A Guide to the Christian Practice of Contemplation*. Oxford: Oxford University Press, 1986.
Lanier, Jaron. *You Are Not a Gadget: A Manifesto*. New York: Vintage, 2010.
Lawrence, of the Resurrection, Brother. *The Practice of the Presence of God*. New Kensington, PA: Whitaker, 1982.
L'Engle, Madeleine. *Walking on Water: Reflections on Faith and Art*. Wheaton, IL: Harold Shaw, 1980.
Lewis, C. S. *A Grief Observed*. London: Bantam, 1961.
———. *Mere Christianity*. New York: Macmillan, 1943.
Libermann, Francis. *The Spiritual Letters of the Venerable Francis Libermann*. Vol. 3, *Letters to Clergy and Religious (Letters 1–75)*. Edited and translated by Walter van de Putte. Duquesne Studies Spiritan Series 7. Pittsburgh: Duquesne University Press, 1963.
———. *The Spiritual Letters of the Venerable Francis Libermann*. Vol. 4, *Letters to Clergy and Religious (Letters 76–184)*. Edited and translated by Walter van de Putte. Duquesne Studies Spiritan Series 8. Pittsburgh: Duquesne University Press, 1964.
———. *The Spiritual Letters of the Venerable Francis Libermann*. Vol. 5, *Letters to Clergy and Religious (Letters 185–274)*. Edited and translated by Walter van de Putte. Duquesne Studies Spiritan Series 9. Pittsburgh: Duquesne University Press, 1966.
Liechty, Daniel, trans. and ed. *Early Anabaptist Spirituality: Selected Writings*. Classics of Western Spirituality. Mahwah, NJ: Paulist, 1994.
Loder, Ted. *Guerrillas of Grace: Prayers for the Battle*. 25th anniversary ed. Minneapolis: Augsburg, 1981.

Luijpen, William. *Existential Phenomenology*. Translated by H. J. Koren. Pittsburgh: Duquesne University Press, 1969.
Luther, Martin. *Martin Luther: Selections from His Writings*. Edited by John Dillenberger. New York: Anchor, 1961.
MacBeth, Sybil. *Praying in Color: Drawing a New Path to God*. Brewster, MA: Paraclete, 2007.
Maclean, Alistair. *Hebridean Altars: The Spirit of an Island Race*. London: Hodder and Stoughton, 1937.
Malone, Mary T. *Women and Christianity*. 3 vols. Maryknoll, NY: Orbis, 2001–2003.
Mangis, Michael. *Signature Sins: Taming Our Wayward Hearts*. Downers Grove, IL: InterVarsity, 2008.
Marcel, Gabriel. *Being and Having*. Translated by Katherine Farrer. Boston: Beacon, 1951.
———. *The Mystery of Being*. 2 vols. South Bend, IN: Gateway, 1950–1951.
Marcus, Alan I., and Howard P. Segal. *Technology in America: A Brief History*. Orlando: Harcourt Brace, 1999.
Maritan, Jacques. *Approaches to God*. Translated by Peter O'Reilly. New York: Harper, 1956.
———. *The Degrees of Knowledge*. Translated by G. B. Phelan. New York: Scribner, 1959.
Maslow, Abraham. *The Farther Reaches of Human Nature*. New York: Viking, 1972.
———. *Motivation and Personality*. New York: Harper and Row, 1954.
———. *The Psychology of Science*. New York: Harper and Row, 1966.
———. *Religions, Values, and Peak-Experiences*. New York: Penguin, 1970.
———. *Toward a Psychology of Being*. New York: D. Van Nostrand, 1968.
Maslow, Abraham, et al. "The Plateau Experience." *Journal of Transpersonal Psychology* 4 (1972) 107–20.
Maximus, Confessor, St. *Selected Writings*. Edited and translated by George C. Berthold. Classics of Western Spirituality. Mahwah, NJ: Paulist, 1985.
May, Rollo. *The Courage to Create*. New York: Bantam, 1980.
———. *The Discovery of Being*. New York: Norton, 1983.
———. *Freedom and Destiny*. New York: Norton, 1981.
———. *Love and Will*. New York: Norton, 1969.
———. *Man's Search for Himself*. New York: Norton, 1953.
———. *The Meaning of Anxiety*. New York: Norton, 1977.
McIntosh, Gary L., and Samuel D. Rima. *Overcoming the Dark Side of Leadership: How to Become an Effective Leader by Confronting Failures*. Grand Rapids: Baker, 2007.
McMinn, Lisa, and Megan Anna Neff. *Walking Gently on the Earth: Making Faithful Choices about Food, Energy, Shelter and More*. Downers Grove, IL: InterVarsity, 2010.
Merleau-Ponty, Maurice. *Phenomenology of Perception*. Translated by Colin Smith. London: Routledge, 1962.
Metzger, Bruce M. *The Canon of the New Testament*. Oxford: Clarendon, 1987.
Meyendorff, John. *Byzantine Theology*. New York: Fordham, 1979.
Moffett, Samuel Hugh. *A History of Christianity in Asia*. 2 vols. Maryknoll, NY: Orbis, 1992–2005.
Moon, Gary W., and David G. Benner, eds. *Spiritual Direction and the Care of Souls: A Guide to Christian Approaches and Practices*. Downers Grove: IL, InterVarsity, 2004.

Mulholland, Robert. *The Deeper Journey*. Downers Grove, IL: InterVaristy, 2006.

———. *Shaped by the Word: The Power of Scripture in Spiritual Formation*. Nashville: Upper Room, 2001.

Muller, Wayne. *Sabbath: Finding Rest, Renewal, and Delight in Our Busy Lives*. New York: Bantam, 1999.

Murray, Andrew. *Experiencing God through Prayer*. New Kensington, PA: Whitaker, 1981.

Mursell, Gordon, ed. *The Story of Christian Spirituality*. Minneapolis: Fortress, 2001.

Muto, Susan. *Blessings That Make Us Be: A Formative Approach to Living the Beatitudes*. Pittsburgh: Epiphany, 2002.

———. *Celebrating the Single Life: A Spirituality for Single Persons in Today's World*. Makati City, Philippines: St. Pauls, 1990.

———. *Dear Master: Letters on Spiritual Direction Inspired by Saint John of the Cross*. Liguori, MI: Liguori/Triumph, 1999.

———. *John of the Cross for Today: The Ascent*. Pittsburgh: Epiphany, 1991.

———. *John of the Cross for Today: The Dark Night*. Pittsburgh: Epiphany, 2000.

———. *Meditation in Motion: Finding the Mystery in Ordinary Moments*. Pittsburgh: Epiphany, 2001.

———. *Pathways of Spiritual Living*. Petersham, MA: St. Bede's, 1984.

———. *A Practical Guide to Spiritual Reading*. Petersham, MA: St. Bede's, 1994.

———. *Virtues: Your Christian Legacy*. Steubenville, OH: Emmaus Road, 2014.

Myers, Glenn E. *Seeking Spiritual Intimacy: Journeying Deeper with Medieval Women of Faith*. Downers Grove, IL: InterVarsity, 2011.

Nemeck, Francis Kelly, and Marie Theresa Coombs. *The Way of Spiritual Direction*. Collegeville, MN: Liturgical, 1985.

Nes, Solrunn. *The Mystical Language of Icons*. Grand Rapids: Eerdmans, 2004.

Newell, J. Philip. *Celtic Prayers from Iona*. Mahwah, NJ: Paulist, 1997.

Norris, Kathleen. *Acedia & Me: A Marriage, Monks, and a Writer's Life*. New York: Riverhead, 2008.

Nouwen, Henri J. M. *In the Name of Jesus: Reflections on Christian Leadership*. New York: Crossroad, 1989.

———. *Making All Things New: An Invitation to the Spiritual Life*. New York: HarperOne, 2009.

———. *Out of Solitude: Three Meditations on the Christian Life*. Notre Dame: Ave Maria, 1974.

———. *Reaching Out: The Three Movements of the Spiritual Life*. Garden City, NY: Image, 1986.

———. *Return of the Prodigal Son: A Story of Homecoming*. New York: Doubleday, 1994.

———. *With Open Hands: Bringing Prayer into Your Life*. New York: Ballantine, 1972.

———. *The Wounded Healer*. New York: Doubleday, 1972.

Nouwen, Henri J. M., and Walter J. Gaffney. *Aging: The Fulfillment of Life*. New York: Doubleday, 1974.

Nye, David. *Technology Matters: Questions to Live With*. Cambridge: MIT Press, 2006.

Oden, Amy, ed. *In Her Words: Women's Writing in the History of Christian Thought*. Nashville: Abingdon, 1994.

Oden, Thomas. *How Africa Shaped the Christian Mind: Rediscovering the African Seedbed of Western Christianity*. Downers Grove, IL: InterVarsity, 2007.

Pak, Su Yon, et al. *Singing the Lord's Song in a New Land: Korean American Practices of Faith*. Louisville: Westminster John Knox, 2005.
Pauck, Wilhelm, ed. *Melanchthon and Bucer*. Library of Christian Classics. Philadelphia: Westminster, 1969.
Peterson, Eugene H. *The Contemplative Pastor: Returning to the Art of Spiritual Direction*. Grand Rapids: Eerdmans, 1989.
———. *Five Smooth Stones for Pastoral Work*. Grand Rapids: Eerdmans, 1992.
———. *Working the Angles: The Shape of Pastoral Integrity*. Grand Rapids: Eerdmans, 1989.
The Philokalia: The Complete Text. Compiled by St. Nikodimos and St. Makarios. Translated by G. E. H. Palmer et al. 4 vols. London: Faber and Faber, 1979–2007.
Pongracz, Patricia C., et al. *The Christian Story: Five Asian Artists Today*. New York: Museum of Biblical Art, 2007.
Ponticus, Evagrius. *The Praktikos and Chapters on Prayer*. Translated by John Eudes Bamberger. Spencer, MA: Cistercian, 1972.
Porterfield, Amanda. *Healing in the History of Christianity*. Oxford: Oxford University Press, 2005.
Postman, Neil. *The End of Education: Redefining the Value of School*. New York: Vintage, 1995.
———. *Technopoly: The Surrender of Culture to Technology*. New York: Knopf, 1992.
Progoff, Ira, trans. *The Cloud of Unknowing*. New York: Dell, 1957.
Quasten, Johannes. *Patrology*. 4 vols. Notre Dame: Ave Maria, 1950–1986.
Rakoczy, Susan. *Great Mystics and Social Justice: Walking the Two Feet of Love*. Mahwah, NJ: Paulist, 2006.
Ratcliff, Donald, ed. *Children's Spirituality: Christian Perspectives, Research, and Applications*. Eugene, OR: Cascade, 2004.
Ray, Darby Kathleen. *Working*. Minneapolis: Fortress, 2011.
Richard, of St. Victor. *The Twelve Patriarchs; The Mystical Ark; Book Three of the Trinity*. Translated by Grover A. Zinn. Classics of Western Spirituality. Mahwah, NJ: Paulist, 1979.
Ricoeur, Paul. *Fallible Man*. Translated by Charles Kelbley. Chicago: Regnery, 1965.
———. *Freedom and Nature: The Voluntary and the Involuntary*. Translated by Erazim V. Kohák. Evanston: Northwestern University Press, 1966.
Rilke, Rainer Maria. *Letters to a Young Poet*. Translated by Stephen Mitchell. New York: Random House, 1984.
Rogers, Carl. *Client-Centered Therapy*. Boston: Houghton Mifflin, 1951.
———. *On Becoming a Person*. Boston: Houghton Mifflin, 1961.
———. *On Personal Power*. New York: Delacorte, 1977.
Rohr, Richard. *Contemplation in Action*. New York: Crossroad, 2006.
———. *Falling Upward: A Spirituality for the Two Halves of Life*. San Francisco: Jossey-Bass, 2011.
Rolle, Richard. *The English Writings*. Edited and Translated by Rosamund S. Allen. Classics of Western Spirituality. Mahwah, NJ: Paulist, 1988.
Sartre, Jean-Paul. *Being and Nothingness*. Translated by Hazel E. Barnes. New York: Washington Square Press, 1993.
———. *Existentialism and Human Emotions*. New York: Philosophical Library, 1957.
Savin, Olga, trans. *The Way of a Pilgrim and The Pilgrim Continues His Way*. Boston: Shambhala, 2001.

Scheler, Max. *Ressentiment*. Translated by William H. Holdheim. New York: Free Press, 1961.
Sittser, Gerald L. *Water from a Deep Well: Christian Spirituality from Early Martyrs to Modern Missionaries*. Downers Grove, IL: InterVarsity, 2007.
Spyker, Stephen K. *Technology and Spirituality: How the Information Revolution Affects Our Spiritual Lives*. Woodstock, VT: Skylight Paths, 2010.
Stairs, Jean. *Listening for the Soul: Pastoral Care and Spiritual Direction*. Minneapolis: Fortress, 2000.
Stark, Rodney. *Cities of God*. New York: HarperOne, 2006.
———. *God's Battalions: The Case for the Crusades*. New York: HarperOne, 2009.
———. *The Rise of Christianity*. Princeton: Princeton University Press, 1996.
Steindl-Rast, David. *The Music of Silence: Entering the Sacred Space of Monastic Experience*. New York: HarperCollins, 1995.
Street, Gail P. C. *Redeemed Bodies: Women Martyrs in Early Christianity*. Louisville: Westminster John Knox, 2009.
Swan, Laura. *The Forgotten Desert Mothers: Sayings, Lives, and Stories of Early Christian Women*. Mahwah, NJ: Paulist, 2001.
Swenson, Richard A. *Margin: Restoring Emotional, Physical, Financial, and Time Reserves to Overloaded Lives*. Colorado Springs: Navpress, 1992.
"The Teaching of the Twelve Apostles, Commonly Called the Didache." In *Early Christian Fathers*, edited and translated by Cyril C. Richardson, 159–80. Library of Christian Classics 1. Philadelphia: Westminster, 1953.
ten Boom, Corrie, John Sherrill, and Elizabeth Sherrill. *The Hiding Place*. 25th anniversary ed. Grand Rapids: Chosen, 1996.
Teresa, of Avila, St. *The Collected Works of St. Teresa of Avila, Vol. 1: The Book of Her Life*. Translated by Kieran Kavanaugh and Otilio Rodriguez. Washington, DC: Institute of Carmelite Studies, 1976.
———. *The Collected Works of Teresa of Avila, Vol. 2: The Way of Perfection and The Interior Castle*. Translated by Kieran Kavanaugh and Otilio Rodriguez. Washington, DC: Institute of Carmelite Studies, 1980.
———. *The Interior Castle*. Translated by Kieran Kavanaugh and Otilio Rodriguez. Classics of Western Spirituality. Mahwah, NJ: Paulist, 1979.
Thérèse, de Lisieux, St. *Story of a Soul: The Autobiography of Thérèse of Lisieux*. Translated by John Clarke. 3rd ed. Washington, DC: ICS, 1996.
Thomas, à Kempis. *The Imitation of Christ*. Edited by Donald E. Demaray. Staten Island: Alba, 1996.
Thompson, Marjorie J. *Soul Feast: An Invitation to the Christian Spiritual Life*. Louisville: Westminster John Knox, 1995.
Thoreau, Henry David. *Walden, and Other Writings*. Edited by Brooks Atkinson. San Francisco: Internet Archive, 1996. https://archive.org/stream/walden033586mbp/walden033586mbp_djvu.txt.
Tickle, Phyllis. *The Great Emergence: How Christianity Is Changing and Why*. Grand Rapids: Baker, 2008.
Tozer, A. W. *The Pursuit of God*. Harrisburg, PA: Christian Publications, 1982.
Turkle, Sherry. *Alone Together: Why We Expect More from Technology and Less from Each Other*. New York: Basic Books, 2011.
Ulanov, Ann, and Barry Ulanov. *Primary Speech: A Psychology of Prayer*. Atlanta: John Knox, 1982.

Underhill, Evelyn. *Practical Mysticism*. Columbus: Ariel, 1986.
Van de Weyer, Robert, ed. *The Letters of Pelagius: Celtic Soul Friend*. Evesham, UK: Arthur James, 1995.
Vanier, Jean. *Becoming Human*. Mahwah, NJ: Paulist, 1998.
van Kaam, Adrian. *The Art of Existential Counseling: A New Perspective in Psychology*. Wilkes-Barre, PA: Dimension Books, 1966.
———. *Existential Foundations of Psychology*. New York: Doubleday, 1969.
———. *Formation of the Human Heart*. Formative Spirituality 3. New York: Crossroad, 1991.
———. *Fundamental Formation*. Formative Spirituality 1. New York: Crossroad, 1989.
———. *Human Formation*. Formative Spirituality 2. New York: Crossroad, 1989.
———. *In Search of Spiritual Identity*. Denville, NJ: Dimension Books, 1975.
———. *The Life Journey of a Joyful Man of God: The Autobiographical Memoirs of Adrian van Kaam*. Edited by Susan Muto. Pittsburgh: Epiphany, 2010.
———. *A Light to the Gentiles: The Life Story of the Venerable Francis Libermann*. 1959. Reprint, Eugene, OR: Wipf & Stock, 2009.
———. *Looking for Jesus: Meditations on the Last Discourse of St. John*. Denville, NJ: Dimension Books, 1978.
———. *The Music of Eternity: Everyday Sounds of Fidelity*. Notre Dame: Ave Maria, 1990.
———. *On Being Involved: The Rhythm of Involvement and Detachment in Everyday Life*. Denville, NJ: Dimension Books, 1970.
———. *Religion and Personality*. New York: Doubleday, 1968.
———. *Scientific Formation*. Formative Spirituality 4. New York: Crossroad, 1987.
———. *Spirituality and the Gentle Life*. Pittsburgh: Epiphany, 2005.
———. *The Tender Farewell of Jesus: Meditations on Chapter 17 of John's Gospel*. New York: New City, 1996.
———. *Traditional Formation*. Formative Spirituality 5. New York: Crossroad, 1992.
———. *Transcendence Therapy*. Formative Spirituality 7. New York: Crossroad, 1995.
———. *Transcendent Formation*. Formative Spirituality 6. New York: Crossroad, 1995.
———. *The Transcendent Self*. Pittsburgh: Epiphany, 1991.
———. *The Woman at the Well*. Pittsburgh: Epiphany, 1993.
van Kaam, Adrian, and Susan Muto. *Christian Articulation of the Mystery*. Formation Theology 2. Pittsburgh: Epiphany, 2005.
———. *Commitment: Key to Christian Maturity*. Pittsburgh: Epiphany, 1989.
———. "Course I: The Foundations of Human and Christian Formation." Epiphany Certification Program, Unpublished Course I Workbook. Pittsburgh: Epiphany, July 2002.
———. "Course II: The Basics of Formation Anthropology in Service of Formation Theology." Epiphany Certification Program, Unpublished Course II Workbook. Pittsburgh: Epiphany, July 2002.
———. "Course VI: Integrating Contemplation and Action in Daily Living." Epiphany Certification Program, Unpublished Course VI Workbook. Pittsburgh: Epiphany, July 2007.
———. *Divine Guidance: Seeking to Find and Follow the Will of God*. Pittsburgh: Epiphany, 1994.
———. *Dynamics of Spiritual Direction*. Pittsburgh: Epiphany, 2003.

———. *Epiphany Manual on the Art and Discipline of Formation-in-Common: A Fresh Approach to the Ancient Practice of Spiritual Direction*. Pittsburgh: Epiphany, 1998.

———. *Essential Elements of Formation Anthropology and Formation Theology: A Compilation of Complementary Considerations*. Pittsburgh: Epiphany, 2008.

———. *Formation of the Christian Heart*. Formation Theology 3. Pittsburgh: Epiphany, 2006.

———. *Foundations of Christian Formation*. Formation Theology 1. Pittsburgh: Epiphany, 2004.

———. *Living Our Christian Faith and Formation Traditions*. Formation Theology 4. Pittsburgh: Epiphany, 2007.

———. *The Power of Appreciation*. Pittsburgh: Epiphany, 1993.

Vennard, Jane E. *Praying with Body and Soul: A Way to Intimacy with God*. Minneapolis: Augsburg, 1998.

Ward, Benedicta, trans. *The Desert Fathers: Sayings of the Early Christian Monks*. New York: Penguin Classics, 2003.

Watkins, T. Wyatt. *What Our Kids Teach Us about Prayer*. New York: Crossroad, 2005.

Webber, Robert E. *Worship, Old and New*. Grand Rapids: Zondervan, 1994.

Whaling, Frank, ed. *John and Charles Wesley: Selected Writings and Hymns*. Classics of Western Spirituality. Mahwah, NJ: Paulist, 1981.

White, James F. *Introduction to Christian Worship*. Nashville: Abingdon, 1980.

Wiesel, Elie. *Night*. Translated by Marion Wiesel. New York: Hill and Wang, 2006.

Wiesenthal, Simon. *The Sunflower: On the Possibilities and Limits of Forgiveness*. Rev. ed. New York: Schocken, 1998.

Willard, Dallas. *The Divine Conspiracy: Rediscovering Our Hidden Life in God*. New York: HarperCollins, 1997.

———. *Hearing God: Developing a Conversational Relationship with God*. Downers Grove, IL: InterVarsity, 1999.

———. *The Spirit of the Disciplines: Understanding How God Changes Lives*. San Francisco: HarperCollins, 1988.

William, of Saint-Thierry. *The Golden Epistle: A Letter to the Brethren at Mont Dieu*. Translated by Theodore Berkeley. Works of William of St. Thierry 4. Cistercian Fathers Series 12. Kalamazoo, MI: Cistercian, 1971.

———. *On Contemplating God; Prayer; Meditations*. Translated by Sister Penelope. Works of William of St. Thierry 1. Cistercian Fathers Series 3. Kalamazoo, MI: Cistercian, 1977.

Winner, Lauren F. *Mudhouse Sabbath: An Invitation to a Life of Spiritual Discipline*. Brewster, MA: Paraclete, 2010.

Index

A's of appraisal, 122–29, 183–86. *See also* appraisal process.
abandonment, 66, 71, 133; abandonment option, 128, 151–52, 183–84, 189; appreciative abandonment, 44n14, 56, 78, 126–28, 151–52, 155–56, 173, 183–85; depreciative abandonment, 56, 151–52, 173, 189; self-abandonment, 166
abandonment option, 128, 151–52, 184–85, 189, 206. *See also* abandonment, appreciative abandonment, depreciative abandonment, primordial abandonment option.
abiding in awe-filled attention (awe-filled abiding), 67, 123, 138, 140, 171, 183, 185, 197
absolutize, 32, 46, 49, 98–99, 183, 214. *See also* idolize, ultimize.
accretion, 88–89, 183
acknowledge the dissonance (affirm the dissonance), 124–26, 128–29, 183–85. *See also* A's of appraisal.
actualized consciousness, 184. *See also* consciousness.
acquired disposition, 73–74, 183, 186. *See also* disposition.
action, 17, 31, 37, 42, 49, 62n1, 70, 73, 76, 82n3, 88–89, 92, 95–96, 100, 109, 114, 121, 124–25, 129, 135–36, 148, 154, 156–57, 171–72, 174, 178, 180, 190–91, 194, 199, 210
actual form (actual life form), 42, 43n8, 48, 57–58, 63, 65, 183
adolescence, 147
adulthood, 101, 147, 161
affection, 49, 162
affirmation, 70, 98n13, 121n1, 128; of formative option, 128, 184. *See also* call affirmation, self-affirmation.
Allport, Gordon, 6
ambition, 27, 30–32, 34, 50, 69, 98, 104, 106, 110, 113, 134, 137, 144, 184, 198, 206
andragogy, 3. *See also* pedagogy.
Ansbacher, Heinz, 6
anticipation, 31, 55, 105, 116, 168, 203; formative anticipation (formative functional anticipation), 19, 48n36, 76, 110, 113–14, 168–69, 195–97, 199; as an incarnational source, 34, 199; transcendent anticipation, 33n41, 114
apparent form, 42, 48, 51, 53–55, 57, 155, 165, 172, 183–84, 201, 204. *See also* intra-apparent form, inter-apparent form, outer-apparent form.
application, 114, 125n17, 128–29, 143n32, 179n2, 182; of our yes, 128, 184–85

INDEX

appraisal, 8, 19, 26n5, 51–52, 63, 72, 76, 86n14, 88–89, 96–98, 100, 102n30, 111, 122–24, 135, 140, 144, 161, 164, 166, 183, 196, 200–201, 208; deformative appraisal, 150; depreciative appraisal, 189; as a disposition, 34, 49n39, 121–22, 128–29, 184; focal appraisal, 186; full field appraisal, 49, 77, 120–21, 140, 142, 149, 167, 184–85, 189, 197, 210, 214; pre-appraisal process, 205; pre-selective appraisal (of neuroform), 171; as a process, 90, 120–29, 151, 184. *See also* A's of appraisal, C's of consonance.

appraisal process, 90, 120–29, 151, 184. *See also* appraisal.

appreciative abandonment, 44n14, 56, 78, 126–28, 151–52, 155–56, 173, 183–85. *See also* abandonment, instant appreciative abandonment.

appreciative abandonment option, 184, 185, 189. *See also* appreciative abandonment, depreciative abandonment option.

apprehension, 105, 123–24, 163–64, 185

Aquinas (Thomas), 44n15, 177n1. *See also* Thomas Aquinas.

argumentation, 126, 128, 137, 185. *See also* assessment.

arrogance, 67, 74, 137, 185

articulation (related to one-on-one direction), 143, 185; dialogical articulation (as formal method of formation science), 179n2

aspiration, 27, 31–32, 36, 63, 65, 74, 76, 98–100, 102, 107–8, 111–14, 134, 144, 149n13, 163, 166, 185, 191, 198–99, 208–10, 212–13. *See also* transcendent dimension.

assessment, 126, 128, 185–86. *See also* argumentation.

attention, 19, 25, 31, 47, 53, 63, 65, 67, 70, 72, 82–83, 98, 101–2, 104–5, 110n62, 112, 120–23, 127–28, 133, 139, 150, 162, 164, 171–74, 183, 185–86, 197, 205, 207. *See also* abiding in awe-filled attention.

Augustine, Saint, 68, 72–73, 111

autarkic, 46–47, 78, 155, 166–67, 170, 186, 212

authentic guilt, 100, 210. *See also* spiritual self-guilt, guilt.

autonomic nervous system, 55, 203

autonomous, 17, 46

auxiliary source, 19. *See also* incarnational source.

avocation, 38, 102, 132, 156, 186

awakening, 67, 91, 133, 147n3, 162–63, 167

awe, 13, 65–68, 71, 78, 123, 167–68, 175, 182, 185–86, 188, 196, 198, 208; diffused awe, 67n24, 190; as a disposition, 66–68, 186, 196; full awe, 67, 190, 197; inverted awe, 67, 202; as a predisposition, 66–67; repudiated (refused) awe, 67, 208; sustained awe, 67. *See also* abiding in awe-filled attention.

baptism, 48n35, 74
belief system, 2, 21, 77, 84–86, 87n18
Body of Christ, 36, 59
body language, 143, 191
Bonhoeffer, Dietrich, 14, 21, 72

C's of consonance, 65n14, 77, 124, 126, 187–89

call, 30, 36, 101–3, 123–24, 132, 135, 144, 151, 153–56, 163, 167, 184, 186–87, 196, 201, 215. *See also* calling in Christ, life-call, unique-communal life-call.

call affirmation, 154–56, 184
call disclosure (life-call disclosure), 107, 140, 154–55, 186, 202–3
call efficacy, 154–55, 184, 186–87

calling in Christ, 33, 79, 101–3, 129, 144, 155n31, 188. *See also* unique-communal life-call.
catechesis, 99, 212
cave trial, 169–70, 186, 207
character, 5–6, 17–18, 21, 26, 49, 52–53, 55, 68n29, 72, 74, 129, 154, 160n1, 199, 203–4; character formation, 37–38; 65, 76, 77n88, 108, 165, 167
charity, 65, 68, 136
childhood, 52n57, 68–69, 96, 97n8, 99, 116, 147, 154, 161–62, 168, 172; early childhood, 68, 96, 151n17; abuse, 106; education, 89; second transcendent childhood, 168. *See also* infancy.
children, 3, 20, 25–26, 62, 73, 85, 91n33, 96, 106, 121, 162–64
Christ, vii, 12, 33, 36, 38, 44, 47–48, 68, 69n40, 77–79, 85–86, 89, 102–3, 133, 136, 154, 156, 186, 188. *See also* Jesus Christ.
Christ form (life form of Christ), 35, 38, 47–50, 53–55, 57–59, 77, 99, 100, 124, 134, 155–56, 186, 194, 214. *See also* founding form.
Christian consciousness, 212. *See also* consciousness.
Christian doctrine, 99
Christian (Judeo-Christian) faith and formation tradition, 14, 35–36, 37n58, 39, 45, 48n35, 55, 85, 87–88, 93, 167n32, 194, 210, 212
Christian formation, 3, 27, 32, 35–37, 65, 67–68, 70, 78, 82, 108, 137, 160–75, 177, 179n2, 181, 194, 196, 203, 208. *See also* formation, illuminating reformation, purifying formation, transformation, unifying transformation.
Christian formation conscience, 99–100, 186, 212. *See also* transcendent Christian conscience.
Christian (Judeo-Christian) revelation, 8, 12n5, 12n8, 37n58, 44n12, 47, 59, 193, 195
Christian spirituality, 29, 64–65, 71, 74, 78n88, 181
Civil Rights Movement, 70
closure, 138–39, 186
coercion, 37, 56, 64, 76, 171–74
coercive disposition, 29n15, 55–56, 74–75, 77n88, 78, 127–28, 170–73, 186–87, 203
coercive security directive (coercive directive), 55–56, 75, 77–78, 97, 107, 133, 147, 163, 173, 186–87. *See also* directive.
cognition, 162. *See also* functional mind, transcendent mind.
commitment, 4, 89, 91, 99n19, 103, 111, 113–14, 124, 133, 155–56, 165, 181, 188, 196; as component of direction-in-common, 138–39, 187, 190; transcendent commitment, 155–56, 212
communion, as a disposition, 71–72, 187; as component of direction-in-common, 138–39, 187–88, 190; with the Mystery, 78n89, 111, 174, 181–82, 201, 214
community, 11, 14, 20, 27, 30, 54, 72, 83n5, 84, 105n43, 106, 125, 162, 187, 195
compassion, 2, 66, 72, 102, 137, 181, 213; as one of the C's of consonance, 66, 124–25, 129, 174, 187, 189
compatibility, 66, 72, 171, 174; as one of the C's of consonance, 66, 124–25, 174, 187, 189
competence, 72, 102, 174; as one of the C's of consonance, 72, 124–26, 174, 187, 189
compulsion, 27–29, 110, 163, 207. *See also* expression, impulse, pulsion, vital dimension.

conference, as component in direction-in-common, 138, 187, 190
confidentiality, 138–39, 142
confirmation, 99, 154–55, 163, 187. See also affirmation.
congeniality, 72, 77, 174; as one of the C's of consonance, 72, 124, 125n17, 174, 188–89
conscience, 95–96, 100–102, 191; empathic (formation) conscience, 98–99, 191; faith conscience, 95, 192; formation conscience, 55, 95–102, 164, 191, 193–94, 197, 204, 212, 214; functional (formation) conscience, 97–98, 197, 208; moral conscience, 95, 99–100, 164, 193, 202–3; parental (formation) conscience, 96, 197, 204; social (formation) conscience, 22n47, 97, 197, 208; transcendent Christian (formation) conscience, 99–100, 186, 212; transcendent formation conscience (spiritual conscience), 99–100, 212; vital formation conscience, 96, 98n13, 214
conscience development (conscience formation), 95–100, 114, 164, 192, 202
consciousness, 95, 103, 107–8, 110, 115, 138, 152, 197; actualized consciousness, 184; Christian consciousness, 212; dimensions of human consciousness, 190; field of consciousness, 67, 197; focal (vocal) consciousness, 104–5, 122–23, 168, 186, 190, 193, 215; formation consciousness, 184, 194; fundamental (human) consciousness (human consciousness), 13, 103–7, 184, 194, 198–99; infraconsciousness (infra-focal consciousness), 55, 106–7, 124, 190, 200; interconsciousness (inter-focal consciousness), 104–6, 162, 190, 193, 198, 201; intraconsciousness (intra-focal consciousness, intraspheric consciousness), 104–6, 163, 190, 198, 201; prefocal consciousness, 104–5, 107, 129, 143, 150, 167–68, 186, 190, 205; regions of consciousness, 19n37, 104, 107–8, 167, 193, 200–201, 205, 213; transfocal consciousness (trans-consciousness), 99n19, 107–8, 110, 167, 190, 213
consecration, 156, 188
consolation, 3, 37, 133
consonance, 13, 44n11, 60, 68–69, 71, 74, 79, 109, 124, 126, 133–34, 155–56, 174, 188–89, 191, 201; related to appreciative abandonment, 128, 185; related to awe, 66, 68; C's of consonance, 65n14, 77, 124–26, 187–89; and Christ form, 55, 58n86, 60; related to core form, 49–50; related to dissonance, 124, 128–29, 134–35, 150–51, 156, 190; related to founding form, 43n8, 45–46, 124; related to foundational dispositional triad, 68, 151, 196; with the Mystery, 57, 58n86, 65, 67, 79, 129, 143, 152, 167, 185, 188, 195; related to transcendence dynamic, 12n6; transcosmic consonance, 13
consultation, 177n1, 179n2, 198; as needed skill of spiritual directors, 143, 188
contemplation, 29, 178; as component of direction-in-common, 138, 188, 190; as essential discipline for spiritual self-direction, 136, 145
counterfeit life form, 46, 57, 108, 156, 186, 206. See also pride form.

control, 10, 12n5, 14, 31, 38, 56–57, 74, 109, 113, 161, 164–68, 197, 202
conversation, 120; as component of direction-in-common, 138–39, 188, 190
core form, 17–18, 42, 48–52, 54–55, 57, 63n7, 135, 152, 154, 170, 172, 188, 199–200, 203, 208. *See also* heart.
cosmic epiphany, 12, 189. *See also* epiphany.
crisis of transcendence, 149. *See also* transcendence crisis.
current form, 42, 48, 51–53, 57, 121, 148, 172, 189, 195, 204, 211. *See also* periodic form.
custom, 27, 105, 106n43, 125, 161, 178, 211

deformational, 22, 55
deformative appraisal, 150. *See also* depreciative appraisal, appraisal.
denial, 150, 169
depletion, 52n56, 69–70, 150
depreciative abandonment, 56, 152, 173, 180, 189. *See also* abandonment, appreciative abandonment, depreciative abandonment option, depreciative appraisal.
depreciative abandonment option, 152, 185, 189
depreciative appraisal, 189. *See also* appraisal, deformative appraisal, depreciative abandonment.
description, as essential skill for spiritual directors, 143, 148, 189, 195
detachment, 34n48, 65, 78, 135–36, 142, 165, 168, 189, 213
detection, as disposition for spiritual directors, 142, 190
dialogical articulation (as formal method of formation science), 179n2

dialogue, 2, 20, 28, 31, 33–34, 43, 49–51, 62n1, 64, 85, 99, 113, 121, 143, 177n1, 178–79, 184, 209
differentiation, 17, 64–65, 162, 164, 190
diffused awe, 67n24, 190. *See also* awe.
dimension, of van Kaamian Formation Field Model, 11, 15, 18, 23, 25–27, 37, 38–39, 41, 48–51, 75, 77, 122, 147, 154, 160, 190, 199 (*see also* expression, striving); functional, 26–28, 30–33, 41, 50, 65, 69, 92, 98, 102, 109n57, 113, 167–68, 170, 179, 197, 206, 212; functional-transcendent, 35, 165, 168 (dynamics of functional-transcendent dimension, 198); of human consciousness, 107, 190; pneumatic-ecclesial, 26n3, 27, 33n43, 35–36, 38, 41, 64, 92, 97, 103, 204, 206, 209; pre-empirical, 50; pretranscendent, 33n43, 33n45, 65, 85, 165, 174–75, 206 (as servant sources, 208, 212); sociohistorical, 26–28, 33n43, 41, 65, 92, 161, 170, 179, 206, 209, 212; transcendent, 27, 32–35, 41, 63–64, 69, 75, 85, 123, 147n2, 165, 169–70, 179, 206, 208–9, 211–12, 214; transcendent-functional, 35; vital, 16, 27–30, 32, 33n43, 41, 55, 65, 69, 73, 82n3, 96, 169–70, 179, 203, 206, 212, 214
directee, 132, 140–44, 185, 188–92, 200, 207, 213
direction-in-common, 132–33, 136–40, 144, 186–88, 190, 209–10. *See also* one-on-one direction, spiritual self-direction.
directive, 13, 15–17, 21, 27, 31–32, 37, 41, 49, 51–52, 64–65, 69–70, 82n2, 86, 90, 103, 105–6, 109, 111, 114, 120–25, 128, 136–37, 139, 144, 148, 154, 163–64, 166, 168, 180, 183–86, 189–93,

directive (*continued*); 195, 197, 199–200, 204–5, 208; related to Christ form, 38, 48, 100–1, 103, 124, 133, 196; coercive, 74–75, 77–78, 97–98, 100, 103, 107, 133–36, 147, 163, 173, 186–87; related to conscience, 95–103; and core form, 54, 188; divine 75, 103, 108, 128, 132–33, 139–40, 142, 190–91, 196, 207, 209–210, 212–13; related to faith tradition, 85–87, 88n25, 90, 97–98, 105–6, 140
director, 7, 132, 138, 140–44. *See also* spiritual director.
disciple, 60, 85–89, 111, 181
disclosure, 13, 34, 43, 51, 65, 67, 77, 79, 100, 102, 107, 123, 126, 128, 135–37, 139–40, 142, 145, 148n6, 149, 154–56, 172–74, 181, 190–92, 202–3, 207, 210, 212
disposition, 17, 37–38, 49–52, 54–55, 58, 62–79, 82n2, 87, 90, 92, 96, 102, 108, 115, 121–22, 123n6, 127–29, 134–35, 142, 154–56, 168–69, 171, 184–85, 187–92, 194–200, 204–8, 210; acquired, 73–74, 183, 186; coercive, 29n15, 55–56, 74, 78, 127–28, 170, 172–73, 186–87, 203–4; deformative, 18, 77–78, 207; dissonant, 74–75, 207; formation (formative), 62–63, 65, 72, 74, 187, 194, 197, 204, 206 (*see also* spiritual disposition); foundational, 65; prefocal, 121–22; primordial, 67 (*see also* awe); routine, 208; routinizing, 208; spiritual (spiritualized), 63–65, 67n29, 69–72, 75–78, 208–10; unappraised, 64, 73. *See also* disposition formation, dispositional source, dispositional spiritualization, dispositional transformation.

disposition formation (dispositional development), 19n35, 62–65, 73, 76–78, 96, 110n62, 112n69. *See also* dispositional spiritualization, dispositional transformation.
dispositional source, 72–75
dispositional spiritualization, 75–78, 203. *See also* dispositional transformation.
dispositional transformation, 74–75, 77–78. *See also* dispositional spiritualization.
dissonance, 47, 52, 67, 69, 71, 74, 116, 134–35, 150, 152, 189, 190, 195, 200; related to A's of appraisal (acknowledge the dissonance), 124–26, 128–29, 183–85; related to appreciative abandonment, 127–28; related to consonance, 150–51, 155–56, 184, 190
dissonant, 37, 54, 65, 74–75, 92, 96, 99–100, 102, 112, 121, 124, 127–28, 141, 155, 171, 184, 191–92, 207, 209
divine directive disclosure, 190–91. *See also* directive.
Divine Forming and Preforming Mystery, 11, 44, 65, 116, 191–92, 203. *See also* God, Eternal Trinitarian Formation and Interformation Event, More Than, Mystery, Trinity.
Dreikurs, Rudolf, 6
drivenness, 98
Dutch Hunger Winter, 1, 10, 66. *See also* Hunger Winter.
Dutch Life Schools, 3
Dutch Resistance, 152

ego guilt, 100–101, 103, 191. *See also* guilt.
ego self-guilt, 102–3, 191. *See also* guilt.
Elkin, Henry, 6
elucidation, 143, 179n2, 191
embodiment, 31, 34, 36, 50–51, 57, 79, 92, 192, 204, 214–15; as

a disposition for spiritual directors, 142, 191
emotion, 2, 18–19, 28–29, 57, 92, 105, 122, 199, 207, 210, 214
empathic (formation) conscience, 98–99, 191. See also conscience.
empirical integrating structure (empirical structure), 48–51, 55, 58, 99, 183–84, 188–89, 196, 200, 203
empirical life form, 42, 48n36
empiricism, 44
energy, 26, 28, 30–32, 62–63, 82, 112, 162, 198
epiphany, 66, 178, 191; cosmic epiphany, 12, 189; crucifying epiphany, 153; human epiphany, 12–13, 199; resurrection epiphany, 153; transhuman (transcosmic) epiphany, 12–13, 213
Epiphany Academy of Formative Spirituality (Epiphany Academy), vii, 4, 7–8, 41n1, 177–78
Erikson, Erik, 6
erosion, 69, 169
erratic heroism, 102, 191
essence, 12, 14, 43–45, 48, 59, 66, 180, 186, 192, 196, 200
Eternal Trinitarian Formation and Interformation Event, 35, 180, 191–92, 203. See also God, Divine Forming and Preforming Mystery, More Than, Mystery, Trinity.
existentialism, 44–45
expectation, 96, 100, 113, 122, 149n13, 190, 214
expression, 11–13, 16, 18–20, 29, 36–37, 44n15, 50, 53, 56–57, 65–66, 69–70, 79, 87, 96–98, 107, 110, 115, 125, 142, 148, 154, 163–64, 202, 206, 210, 214; of human strivings, 26–29, 32, 36–38, 64, 165, 170, 184–88, 190, 192, 199–200, 202, 206–7, 209; self-expression, 113

faith, 2, 45n17, 65, 67n29, 68, 74, 77–79, 84–89, 95, 97, 99, 107–8, 110–11, 115–16, 128, 133, 136, 140, 142, 151–55, 157, 167, 170, 177n1, 178, 181, 192, 196; faith conscience, 95, 192; faith formation (faith deepening), 7, 136, 138, 210; faith tradition (faith and formation tradition), 8, 11, 21n44, 27n10, 44n14, 65, 77, 82–92, 95, 97–99, 101–2, 106n43, 116, 121n3, 132, 134, 141, 144, 178–79, 183, 190–96, 202, 205, 210–13
faith conscience, 95, 99n19, 192. See also conscience.
faith tradition (faith and formation tradition), 8, 11, 21n44, 27n10, 44n14, 65, 77, 82–92, 95, 97–99, 101–2, 106n43, 116, 121n3, 132, 134, 141, 144, 178–79, 183, 190–96, 202, 205, 210–13; Christian faith and formation tradition, 14, 35, 48n35, 88, 167n32; ideological faith tradition, 83, 85. See also faith, form tradition.
Fall (the Fall), 10, 36, 45, 74, 156, 180, 192
fallacy, of perfectionism, 134; of self-sufficiency, 134
false guilt (inauthentic guilt), 56, 99, 100, 141. See also guilt.
false self, 46n23, 58–59. See also pride form.
fidelity, 114, 140, 170, 181–82, 195, 202; to founding-form or unique-communal life-call, 34, 45, 65, 77, 79, 86, 97, 100, 103, 116, 129, 141, 144, 153, 155, 192
field of consciousness, 67, 197. See also consciousness.
firmness, 70, 80, 192
focal appraisal, 122, 186. See also appraisal.

focal (vocal) consciousness, 104–5, 122–23, 168, 186, 190, 193, 215. See also consciousness.
forgiveness, 115, 118, 142, 157, 159, 181
form, (noun) 13, 15, 17, 22, 25–28, 32, 37, 41n1, 43, 52, 58, 65–67, 71, 87, 88n25, 92–93, 106, 115, 121, 128, 144, 151, 154, 160–62, 165, 168, 180, 184, 189, 193, 196, 202, 200, 211; (verb) 15–16, 27–28, 72–73, 75, 82, 99n19, 110, 121, 167, 178, 193; potency, 15, 58, 75, 77, 161, 162, 165, 200. See also life form.
form donation, 15, 37, 52, 63, 69, 193, 205, 213
form reception, 15, 37, 52, 63, 69, 193, 205, 213
form tradition (formation tradition), 15n19, 20–21, 27n10, 30n24, 34n48, 36, 82–83, 86–92, 97, 102, 105–6, 140, 152, 167n32, 178–79, 183, 191, 193, 195–96, 201, 204
form traditional pyramid, 90, 94, 193
formability, 15, 26n5, 193, 200
formation anthropology, 6, 8–9, 11, 12n5, 33n42, 33n46, 44, 115n79, 180, 191, 193
formation conscience, 55, 95–102, 164, 191, 193–94, 197, 204, 212, 214. See also conscience.
formation consciousness, 184, 194. See also consciousness.
formation field, 10–17, 19–20, 22–23, 25. See also full field model, van Kaamian Formation Field Model.
formation science, 8–9, 11–12n5, 22, 33n42, 44, 88n25, 143n32, 177n1, 179, 191, 193–94
formation theology, 4, 8–9, 11–12n5, 33n42, 44n13, 44n15, 51, 57, 68, 78, 95, 99, 108n56, 115n79, 126n17, 177, 179, 188, 191–94, 203

formative, anticipation, 110, 113–14, 168, 195–97, 199; imagination, 28, 76, 110, 112–13, 195, 197, 199; memory, 110–11, 113, 196–97, 199 ; mind, 109; option, 128, 184; participation, 77; reading, 145, 178, 181, 210 (as discipline of spiritual self-direction, 135); reiteration, 73, 196, 208; reflection, 196
formative action pattern, 148–49, 156–57, 195
formative event, 9, 91, 110n63, 122, 125, 143, 148–49, 189, 195–96, 204–6, 208, 211
formative spirituality, 1, 3, 7–9, 13, 20, 22, 28, 62n2, 129, 148n8, 177–78, 179n2, 193–94, 196, 200, 202–3, 211, 214
foundational, related to dispositions, 65, 68, 90; related to faith traditions, 86, 88–89, 191, 196, 210, 212
foundational dispositional triad, 68, 196. See also disposition.
founding (life) form, 18n34, 42–52, 59, 77, 100, 124, 172, 180, 186, 188, 196, 200, 204–6, 208, 214. See also Christ form, essence, soul.
Francis of Assisi, 86–88
free will, 73
freedom, 13, 53, 55, 73, 88, 100, 105, 108, 144, 151, 155, 162, 166, 194, 212; as situated (relative) 151
from-through-to movement, 6, 148, 195–96, 205. See also formative action pattern.
full awe, 67, 190, 197. See also awe.
full field appraisal, 49, 77, 120–21, 140, 142, 149, 167, 184–85, 189, 197, 210, 214. See also appraisal.
full field model, 10–11, 14, 22, 180. See also formation field, van Kaamian Formation Field Model.

functional ambition, 30–32, 34, 50, 104, 106, 134, 137, 144, 184
functional (formation) conscience, 97–98, 197, 208. See also conscience.
functional dimension, 26–28, 30–33, 41, 50, 65, 69, 92, 98, 102, 109n57, 113, 167–68, 170, 179, 197, 206, 212
functional memory, 110–11, 197. See also formative memory, memory.
functional mind, 19n36, 33n41, 49n36, 109, 169, 197; (functional mind and will, 49n36, 109, 126, 195–97, 199, 210). See also functional memory, functional conscience, mind.
functional phase, 163–64, 197–98. See also phasic formation.
functional will, 19n36, 33n41, 48–49n36, 109, 169, 195–97, 199, 210. See also will.
functional-transcendence, 38, 164, 166, 169–70, 198
functional-transcendent dimension, 35, 165, 168, 198
functional-transcendent phase, 165–66, 169, 186, 189, 198, 209. See also phasic formation.
functionalism, 32, 38, 56, 91, 101, 134, 173, 178
fundamental (human) consciousness, 106, 184, 194, 198. See also consciousness.
fusion, 198, 214

Gemert, 1–3, 114, 157
gentleness, 70–71, 123, 127, 142, 191, 198, 206
God, vii, 7–15, 18, 20, 22, 26, 33, 36, 37n58, 38, 43, 44n12, 44n15, 45–48, 50, 53–54, 56, 58n86, 63–66, 68, 70–75, 78, 84–85, 92, 98–100, 102–3, 107–9, 111, 113, 116–17, 123–27, 129, 132–37, 142–45, 148, 152–57, 166, 170, 173–75, 179, 181, 188–89, 191–93, 196, 199, 201–3, 205, 207, 213–14. See also Divine Forming and Preforming Mystery, Eternal Trinitarian Formation and Interformation Event, More Than, Mystery, Trinity.
God's will, 60, 92, 108, 121n1, 135, 140, 142–43, 174, 182, 203. See also will of the Mystery.
Goldstein, Kurt, 6
grace, 8, 11, 35–36, 38–39, 47, 48n35, 53, 56, 59, 64, 73, 75, 78, 98, 107, 109, 116, 126, 133, 135–36, 141, 143–44, 148, 153, 166–70, 172, 179–82, 188, 194, 199, 204, 205, 207, 211, 213–14; pace of grace, 78, 123, 137
grandparents, 73. See also parents.
gratitude, vii, 28, 153–54, 156
Greene, Graham, 5
guilt, 100–102, 107, 116, 164, 174, 199; authentic guilt, 100, 210; ego guilt, 100–101, 103, 191; ego self-guilt, 102–3, 191; false guilt (inauthentic guilt), 56, 99, 100, 141; spiritual self-guilt, 101–3, 210, 212

habit, 60, 62–63n2, 64, 82, 91, 111, 113, 117, 122, 170, 194, 211
heart, 5, 12n8, 17–19, 49–52, 63n7, 69, 72–73, 75–76, 87, 100–101, 106–9, 116, 121–22, 128–29, 133, 135–36, 138, 142, 151, 153–54, 170–72, 176, 178, 181, 188–89, 192, 194, 198, 199, 213; related to founding form, 48, 50; of the Mystery, 44, 54, 192; related to pride form, 46. See also core form.
Hillesum, Etty, 14
Hitler, Adolf, 83
holistic model of spiritual formation, 10. See also formation field, van Kaamian Formation Field Model.
Holy Ghost Fathers, 1

Holy Spirit, 12n5, 27, 32, 36, 37n58, 38, 45, 48–49, 51, 57, 63–64, 74–77, 78n89, 79, 89, 99, 101, 107, 112, 124, 132–33, 136–38, 140–41, 143–44, 153, 180, 182–83, 185, 191, 204–5, 207, 212–13. See also Spirit (of God).

hope, 2, 5, 10, 47, 68, 100, 117, 127–28, 150–51, 155, 168, 199; related to foundational dispositional triad, 65, 67n29, 68, 74, 142, 151, 181, 196; loss of, 21, 152, 189, 199 (see also depreciative abandonment)

horizontal interformation, 20–21, 27n10, 199. See also interformation, vertical interformation.

human consciousness, 13, 103–7, 199. See also fundamental human consciousness, consciousness.

human epiphany, 12–13, 199. See also epiphany.

human nature, 8, 35

human science, 4, 44

humility, 55, 65, 124, 133, 136, 167, 172, 179

Hunger Winter, 2, 8, 114, 149, 156. See also Dutch Hunger Winter.

ideal, 27, 32, 36, 72, 116, 153, 161, 185, 198–99. See also expression, transcendent dimension.

ideological faith tradition, 83, 85

idolize, 46, 67, 183, 214. See also absolutize, ultimize.

illuminating reformation, 38, 79, 157, 170, 181, 199. See also purifying formation, reformation, unifying transformation.

image of God, 70, 85 (image of Christ, 35, 60)

imagination, 19, 30–31, 34, 48n36, 55, 102n30, 105, 110, 112, 116, 162, 169, 195, 203. See also formative imagination.

impulse, 27–29, 34, 104, 110, 163. See also compulsion, expression, pulsion, vital dimension.

incarnational source, 19, 34, 110, 113–14, 195–96, 199

infancy, 29, 55, 68, 73, 147

informational theology, 95, 114, 194

informative reflection, 200. See also formative reflection, reflection.

infraconsciousness (infra-focal consciousness), 55, 106–7, 124, 190, 200. See also consciousness.

infrastructural principle, 15n19, 82n2, 200

infused disposition, 73–74, 200

inspiration, 27, 35–36, 63, 64–65, 74–76, 98–100, 102, 104, 107–8, 111–12, 114, 116, 124, 134, 138, 144, 154, 163, 191, 200, 202, 209–10, 213. See also pneumatic-ecclesial dimension.

instant appreciative abandonment, 127, 173. See also abandonment, appreciative abandonment, appreciative abandonment option.

instinct, 17, 82, 104, 162, 198, 211

Institute of Formative Spirituality, 6–7

integrating structure, 18n33, 19n35, 41–59, 120, 200, 202 (see also life form); empirical integrating structure 48–58 (see also actual form, apparent form, core form, current form, neuroform); pre-empirical integrating structure, 43–48 (see also Christ form, founding form, pride form)

inter-apparent form, 53–54, 201. See also apparent form, intra-apparent form, outer-apparent form, life form.

interconsciousness (inter-focal consciousness), 104–6, 162, 190, 193, 198, 201. See also consciousness.

interformation, 10, 29–30, 73, 116, 137, 174, 180, 183, 201; horizontal interformation, 20–21, 27n10, 199; vertical interformation, 20–21, 214

intersphere, 20–22, 125, 184, 187, 194, 201, 204. *See also* sphere.

intimacy, 72, 155, 170, 187, 215; with the Mystery, 101, 116, 133, 135, 166–68, 202

intra-apparent form, 53–54, 125n17, 201. *See also* apparent form, life form, self-image.

intraconsciousness (intra-focal consciousness, intraspheric consciousness), 104–6, 163, 190, 198, 201. *See also* consciousness.

intraformation, 10, 168, 201

intrasphere, 17, 19, 21–22, 49, 71, 97, 102, 124, 128, 165, 184, 188, 194, 196, 201–2, 206, 208; emergence of, 162–64. *See also* sphere.

introspective reflection, 115–16

inverted awe, 67, 202. *See also* awe.

invitation, 27, 35–36, 45, 54, 64, 66, 76, 78, 98, 120–21, 124, 127–28, 135, 138, 153–54, 173–74, 186, 191, 200, 202, 210, 214. *See also* expression, pneumatic-ecclesial dimension.

isolation, 22, 34, 67, 77, 147n2

James, William, 5

Jerusalem Council, 88–89

Jesus Christ, 12, 14, 47, 57, 60, 80, 84–85, 89, 93, 111, 132, 205. *See also* Christ.

Jewish faith tradition, 85

Judeo-Christian tradition, 37n58, 44n12, 45

Judeo-Christian theology (Judeo-Christian formation theology), 59, 108n56

Judeo-Christian perspective, 84n8

Judeo-Christian (Christian) revelation, 8, 12n5, 12n8, 37n58, 44n12, 47, 59, 193, 195. *See also* revelation.

King, Martin Luther, Jr., 70

language, 12n5, 18, 90, 143–44, 161, 164, 211, 213; body language, 143, 191; metalanguage (van Kaam's), 4, 9, 17, 67n29, 179n2

Libermann, Francis, 3

life form (human life form), 25–26, 31, 33–35, 39, 42, 51, 55, 62, 110, 112, 125n12, 125n14, 125n16, 139n13, 160–61, 174, 202 (*see also* integrating structure); actual form (actual life form), 42, 43n8, 48, 57–58, 63, 65, 183; apparent form, 42, 48, 51, 53–55, 57, 155, 165, 172, 183–84, 200–201, 204 (*see also* intra-apparent form, inter-apparent form, outer-apparent form); Christ form (life form of Christ), 35, 38, 47–50, 53–55, 57–59, 77, 99–100, 124, 134, 155–56, 186, 194, 214; core form, 17–18, 42, 48–52, 54–55, 57, 63n7, 135, 152, 154, 170, 172, 188, 199–200, 203, 208 (*see also* heart); counterfeit life form, 46, 57, 108, 156, 186, 206; current form, 42, 48, 51–53, 57, 121, 148, 172, 189, 195, 204, 211 (*see also* periodic form); as empirical, 42, 48n36, 200; founding (life) form, 18n34, 42–52, 59, 77, 100, 124, 172, 180, 186, 188, 196, 200, 204–6, 208, 214; neuroform, 29n15, 42, 48, 55–57, 74–75, 96, 117, 122, 162–63, 171, 186–87, 199, 203, 205 (reformation of, 56–57, 75, 117, 127, 171–73, 186–87); periodic form, 52n57, 160, 204; as pre-empirical, 42–43, 48, 50, 59, 196, 205 (*see also* essence, founding form, Christ form, pride form, soul-form);

life form (*continued*); pride form, 45–47, 49–50, 57, 59, 67, 78, 96, 100–101, 108–9, 124, 125n17, 129, 144, 156, 165, 170, 172, 186, 191–92, 206 (as quasi-foundational life form, 46); soul-form, 43n5, 44; temper form, 29, 57, 210
life-call, 30 70–71, 77, 97, 99–100, 112, 125, 128–29, 133, 140–41, 145, 148, 149n13, 154–56, 165–66, 184, 202, 210, 212, 214. *See also* call, calling in Christ, unique-communal life-call.
lingual functionality, 164
love, 12n8, 19n38, 30n24, 53, 65, 67n29, 68, 70, 74, 78, 91, 109, 127, 133, 137, 142, 170, 172–74, 181–82, 187, 196, 199, 202, 213; by the Mystery, 10, 13, 19n38, 44n14, 53, 71, 73, 85, 98, 109, 137, 142, 152–53, 167, 170, 172–73, 188, 202; for the Mystery, 78, 109, 115, 117, 153, 188, 199, 202, 208. *See also* foundational dispositional triad, theological virtue.
love-will (will to love), 19n38, 103, 109, 202, 213. *See also* transcedent will.
Luijpen, William, 5

maintenance of form potency, 15n19, 200, 202. *See also* infrastructural principle.
managerial transcendence, 165–66
managing me, 32, 100, 103, 164
Marcel, Gabriel, 5
Maritain, Jacques, 5
Maslow, Abraham, 6
maternal ambiance, 161, 163
May, Rollo, 6
meaning (meaningful, meaningfulness), 3, 7–8, 10, 15n21, 19, 21, 25, 34, 43n5, 44n15, 45, 50, 66, 68, 76, 82, 84, 87–88, 92, 97n8, 105–6, 110, 116, 121, 123–25, 129, 132, 134, 141, 148, 150–53, 156, 160, 167, 174, 178, 181, 183, 189, 192–93, 203, 207, 209, 211, 214; meaningless (meaninglessness) 84, 150–52, 156, 189; sciences of, 5, 179; transcendent (spiritual, epiphanic), 19, 66, 123
media, 21–22, 99n19
meditation, 76, 141, 166, 173, 212
meditative reflection, 136, 145, 210
memory, 19, 31, 55, 105–6, 110–11, 116, 120, 149, 203; formative memory, 76, 110–11, 113, 196–97, 199 (functional memory, 110–11, 169); as incarnational source, 34, 48n36, 110; transcendent memory, 33n41, 110n60, 111; vital memory, 55, 110
Merleau-Ponty, Maurice, 5
metalanguage, 4, 9, 179n2. *See also* language.
mind, 16–17, 19, 31, 39, 44, 47, 75, 109–110, 112, 121, 123, 126, 133, 162, 185, 192; functional mind, 19n36, 33n41, 49n36, 109, 169, 197 (functional mind and will, 49n36, 109, 126, 195–97, 199, 210, 109, 126, 195–97, 199, 210); transcendent mind, 19n36, 48n36, 108–9, 126, 212–13 (transcendent mind and will, 33n41, 48n36, 49n36, 108–9, 195–97, 199, 210). *See also* incarnational source.
Monica, Saint, 68
monolithic fallacy, 134, 145
moral conscience, 95, 99–100, 164, 193, 202–3. *See also* conscience.
More Than, 2, 12n5, 27, 84, 123, 165, 167, 175, 178. *See also* Divine Forming and Preforming Mystery, Eternal Trinitarian Formation and Interformation Event, God, Mystery, Trinity.

INDEX

motivation, 11, 72, 143, 191; as source of dispositional spiritualization, 76–77, 203. *See also* spiritualization, reiteration, participation.

Muto, Susan, 7–9, 177

Mystery, 10–15, 17, 19, 22, 32, 35, 37–39, 44–46, 51, 53, 56–57, 65–68, 70–71, 73–76, 78–79, 83, 108–112, 116–17, 121, 123–24, 127–29, 133, 135–38, 143–45, 147, 150–57, 160, 166–75, 178–80, 182–86, 188–91, 194–96, 198–200, 202–3, 205–8, 211–13, 215; Divine Forming and Preforming Mystery, 11, 44n11, 116, 191; Trinitarian Mystery, 79, 129. *See also* God, Eternal Trinitarian Formation and Interformation Event, More Than, Trinity.

narrative, 2–3, 5, 10, 85, 105, 143, 148, 156. *See also* storytelling.

Nazi, 21, 83, 152, 178; occupation, 14, 83; Nazism, 2, 83

neuroform, 29n15, 42, 48, 55–57, 74–75, 96, 117, 122, 162–63, 171, 186–87, 199, 203, 205; reformation of, 56–57, 75, 117, 127, 171–73, 186–87

obstacle, 56, 74, 97, 134, 137, 140n23, 141, 143–44, 173, 180, 185

one-on-one direction, 132, 140–44, 190–92, 200, 203, 207, 209–10. *See also* direction-in-common, private direction, spiritual self-direction.

openness, 13, 16, 19, 38, 63, 65, 69, 71, 73–74, 76–77, 83, 98, 100, 108, 116, 126, 133, 135, 154, 161, 167, 198. *See also* receptivity.

outer-apparent form, 53–54, 204. *See also* apparent form, inter-apparent form, intra-apparent form.

outer sphere, 20, 71, 155, 168, 196, 200, 204, 206. *See also* sphere.

pace of grace, 78, 123, 137

parental formation conscience (parental conscience), 96, 197, 204. *See also* conscience.

parents, 15, 20, 29, 62, 68, 73, 79, 96–97, 113–14, 121, 161, 163, 204, 214; grandparents, 73

participation, 11, 35, 37, 106, 136, 178; as source of dispositional spiritualization, 76–77, 204

patience, 64, 133, 135, 187

Paul (the Apostle), 47, 73

peace preservation, 173–74

pedagogy, 3. *See also* andragogy.

perfectionism, 134, 145; self-perfection, 116, 169. *See also* fallacy (of perfectionism).

periodic form, 52n57, 160, 204. *See also* current form.

phasic formation, 52n57, 160, 197–98, 204–5, 209, 211, 213, 215; functional phase, 163–64, 197–98; functional-transcendent phase, 165–66, 169, 186, 198; sociohistorical phase, 160–61, 209; transcendent phase, 168, 198, 212; transcendent and post-transcendent phase, 170–74, 186, 211; transcendent-functional phase, 169–70; vital phase, 161–63, 215

physicality, 27–28, 55, 69, 203, 214

pneumatic-ecclesial dimension, 26n3, 27, 33n43, 35–36, 38, 41, 64, 92, 97, 103, 204, 206, 209

pole, 15n22, 66

post-conversion pyramid, 91, 205. *See also* form traditional pyramid, pre-conversion pyramid.

post-traumatic stress disorder, 106

prayer, 69, 72, 74, 76, 85, 88, 111, 136, 138–39, 141, 210

pre-appraisal process, 205. *See also* pre-selective appraisal, appraisal.

pre-conversion pyramid, 91, 205

pre-empirical, 42–43, 48, 50, 59, 196, 205. *See also* Christ form, essence, founding form, pride form.
predisposition (preformed, pre-given disposition), 26n2, 29, 66, 72–73, 106, 123, 186, 198, 205. *See also* awe.
prefocal consciousness, 104–5, 107, 129, 143, 150, 167–68, 186, 190, 205. *See also* consciousness.
preformed, 16, 17n27, 28–29, 31, 33, 43–45, 59, 121, 147, 192, 205, 214; disposition, 72–74, 205. *See also* essence, founding form, transcendence dynamic, transcendent dimension.
pre-selective appraisal (of neuroform), 171. *See also* pre-appraisal process.
presence, 17–18, 25, 30–32, 37, 41, 49, 62, 65–66, 69–70, 73, 92, 113, 116, 121, 123, 129, 132, 135–36, 144, 170, 172–73, 178, 190, 198–99; of the Mystery, 48, 71, 108, 115, 127, 136, 142, 152, 168, 174, 186; to the Mystery, 66–67, 120, 136, 138, 168, 171, 173–74, 186, 204, 212; of the pride form, 47; transcendent 31, 34, 172; vital (physical), 16, 29–31. *See also* transcendent self-presence.
pressure, 27–28, 38, 112, 155, 163, 206. *See also* expression, pulsation, sociohistorical dimension.
pretranscendent dimensions, 33n43, 33n45, 65, 85, 165, 174–75, 206; as servant sources, 208, 212
pride form, 45–47, 49–50, 57, 59, 67, 78, 96, 100–101, 108–9, 124, 125n17, 129, 144, 156, 165, 170, 172, 186, 191–92, 206; as quasi-foundational life form, 46. *See also* false self.

primordial abandonment option, 68, 157, 206. *See also* abandonment option.
privacy, 71–72, 188, 206
private direction, 132, 140n24, 141n26, 142n27. *See also* one-on-one direction.
project, 27, 30–32, 38, 69, 98, 111, 113, 153, 167–68, 171, 184, 202, 206. *See also* expression, functional dimension.
pseudo-gentility, 70–71
pulsation, 27–28, 34, 50, 106, 110, 134, 144, 206. *See also* sociohistorical dimension.
pulsion, 27–29, 34, 72, 134, 144, 162–63, 207. *See also* vital dimension
purgation, 78n88, 167, 172, 207. *See also* purification.
purification, 47, 153, 166–67, 169, 171. *See also* purgation.
purifying formation, 38, 78n88, 79, 157, 170, 181, 207. *See also* illuminating reformation, reformation, unifying transformation.

quasi-foundational life form, 46, 207. *See also* pride form.

reason (reasoning), 37, 107, 127, 177n1, 197–98
receptivity, 36n57, 71, 76, 183; as disposition of spiritual directors, 142, 207. *See also* openness.
recollection, 56, 173, 207
redemption, 10, 22, 35, 47–48, 180
reflection, 20, 37, 67, 76, 90, 97, 106, 113, 115, 136, 139, 143–44, 148, 188, 196, 202, 210; as discipline of spiritual self-direction, 136, 210; formative, 196; informative, 200; introspective versus transcendent, 115–16; as skill of one-on-one

spiritual directors, 144, 207; transcendent, 115
reformation, 2, 10, 12, 14, 37, 45, 57, 71n53, 74–75, 77n88, 78, 91–92, 137, 161, 168–70, 172, 180–81, 205, 207; of neuroform (coercive security directives), 55–57, 97, 117, 169, 172, 186–87. *See also* illuminating reformation, purifying formation, transformation, unifying transformation.
regions of consciousness, 19n37, 104, 107–8, 167, 193, 200–201, 205, 213. *See also* consciousness.
reiteration, 73, 76, 110, 196. *See also* formative reiteration.
remote background, 208. *See also* formative event.
repentance, 60, 75–76, 100, 103, 116, 155, 191
repudiated (refused) awe, 67, 208. *See also* awe.
responsibility, 140, 155, 212, 214; as coformant of core form, 50–51, 69, 72, 208. *See also* sensibility.
resurrection, 14, 47–48, 154; epiphany, 153
revelation, 12, 74, 84, 101, 141, 180; Christian (Judeo-Christian), 8, 11, 12n5, 35–36, 37n58, 44–45, 47, 59, 114, 193, 195
ritual, 20, 27, 77, 85, 90, 105–6, 110, 211
Rogers, Carl, 6
routine disposition, 208
routinizing disposition, 208

Sartre, Jean-Paul, 44, 180
Scheler, Max, 5
Schouwenaars, Maria, 3
Scripture, 9, 12n5, 73, 117, 132, 136, 141, 143, 178, 181, 188
second transcendent childhood, 168
secondary foundational life-form, 208. *See also* life form.
secular humanism, 4, 11, 13

self-actualization, 14, 116, 134, 166, 168, 170, 213
self-affirmation, 154–55, 163. *See also* affirmation.
self-centeredness, 46, 116, 155, 167–68, 212
self-image, 53, 125n17. *See also* intra-apparent form.
sensibility, as coformant of core form, 50–51, 69, 208. *See also* responsibility.
servant source, 59, 99, 194, 197; dissonance as, 124, 126; pretranscendent dimensions as, 33, 35, 38, 103, 206, 208
silence, 100, 135, 138, 142, 145, 154, 210
sin, 45–47, 85, 186, 192, 207
situational osmosis, 73
situational sphere, 14, 21–22, 125, 187, 194, 204, 208. *See also* sphere.
social formation conscience, 22n47, 97, 197, 208. *See also* conscience.
sociohistorical dimension, 26–28, 33n43, 41, 65, 92, 161, 170, 179, 206, 209, 212
sociohistorical phase, 160–61, 209. *See also* phasic formation.
soul, 2, 18, 48n35, 54, 57, 59, 66, 77, 99–100, 111, 113, 134, 147, 175, 178, 207, 209, 214; soul-form, 43n5, 44. *See also* founding (life) form, essence.
sphere, 10–11, 15–18, 20, 25, 33, 38, 41–42, 48, 49–51, 77, 85, 120, 122, 144, 147, 154, 171, 188, 190, 194, 199, 203, 209; intersphere, 20–22, 125, 184, 187, 194, 201, 204; intrasphere, 17, 19, 21–22, 49, 71, 97, 102, 124, 128, 165, 184, 188, 194, 196, 201–2, 206, 208 (emergence of, 162–64); outer sphere, 20, 71, 155, 168, 196, 200, 204, 206; situational, 14, 21–22, 125, 187, 194, 204, 208; world, 14, 22, 51, 125, 187, 189, 194, 201, 215

spirit (human spirit), 3–5, 12n8, 16–17, 19, 31–36, 37n58, 48, 50–51, 57, 63–64, 66, 75, 83, 99, 103, 112, 133, 144, 147n2, 150, 171–72, 178, 198–99, 209, 213. *See also* transcendent mind and will.

Spirit (of God), 14, 17, 23, 29, 33, 36, 37n58, 45, 47, 60, 64, 73–78, 83, 98–102, 107–8, 116, 128, 133–35, 138–42, 153–54, 169, 188, 190, 210. *See also* Holy Spirit.

spiritual director, 143, 185, 188–92, 200, 207, 210, 213. *See also* director.

spiritual formation, 1, 3, 6, 10–11, 14–15, 18n33, 19–21, 26n5, 30, 32, 45–46, 48n35, 49n39, 52, 68n32, 83, 91, 103, 107, 140n23, 205, 210. *See also* formative spirituality.

spiritual self-direction, 102, 132–35, 140n22, 144, 207, 210. *See also* direction-in-common, one-on-one direction.

spiritual self-guilt, 101–3, 210, 212. *See also* guilt.

spiritualization, 76, 210. *See also* dispositional spiritualization.

stillness, 71, 100, 136

storytelling, 110. *See also* narrative.

striving, 15, 26–27, 37, 105, 167, 190, 198, 210; for consonance, 65, 155; functional striving, 30–32, 165–66, 169–70, 184, 206; pneumatic-ecclesial, 200, 202; sociohistorical 27–28, 169–70, 206; transcendent, 32, 35, 185, 199; vital, 28–30, 72–73, 165, 169–70, 207

submission, 166

suffering, 3, 78, 156, 206

sustained awe, 67. *See also* awe.

symbol, 19–21, 27, 37, 54, 77, 90, 105, 106n43, 107, 112–14, 121n3, 143–44, 164, 169, 195, 211, 213

talent, 27, 31, 37, 135, 186–87, 197, 205, 214

temper form, 29, 57, 210. *See also* life form, temperament.

temperament, 16n23, 27, 29, 57, 205, 210. *See also* temper form.

temptation, 38, 153, 166, 212

ten Boom, Corrie, 14, 21

Teresa of Avila, 72, 111

theological virtue, 67n29, 68, 74, 192, 199, 202

theoretical-integrational framework, 1

theory of consciousness, 103, 107–8, 110. *See also* consciousness.

Thomas Aquinas, 177n1; Thomistic tradition, 147. *See also* Aquinas (Thomas).

Tozer, A. W., 86–87

tradition, 20, 27, 55, 82–83, 89–92, 97, 105–6, 137, 140, 155, 160, 171, 180, 200–201, 209, 211; faith tradition (faith and formation tradition), 8, 11, 21n44, 27n10, 44n14, 65, 77, 82–92, 95, 97–99, 101–2, 106n43, 116, 121n3, 132, 134, 141, 144, 178–79, 183, 190–96, 202, 205, 210–13; Christian faith and formation tradition, 14, 35, 48n35, 88, 167n32; form tradition (formation tradition), 15n19, 20–21, 27n10, 30n24, 34n48, 36, 82–83, 86–92, 97, 102, 105–6, 140, 152, 167n32, 178–79, 183, 191, 193, 195–96, 201, 204; ideological faith tradition, 83, 85

transcendence crisis, 35, 38, 78, 126n17, 140, 147–57, 184, 186, 190, 194–95, 203, 210–11

transcendence dynamic, 16–17, 46, 67, 77, 85, 107, 121, 147–48, 156, 165, 175, 179, 193–94, 205–6, 209, 211, 213–14

transcendence therapy, 211

transcendent, 2, 4–6, 19, 31–32, 35–36, 38–39, 44, 46, 48, 56, 59, 64–66, 76–77, 98, 103, 110–12, 115, 135, 144, 161, 165,

167–69, 170, 175, 179, 202, 204, 208–9, 211–12; character, 37–38; identity (transcendent life-call), 31, 48, 65, 100, 140, 143, 165–67, 172, 185 (*see also* Christ form, founding form, unique-communal life-call)
transcendent anticipation, 33n41, 114
transcendent Christian (formation) conscience, 99–100, 186, 212. *See also* conscience, transcendent formation conscience (spiritual conscience).
transcendent dimension, 27, 32–35, 41, 63–64, 69, 75, 85, 123, 147n2, 165, 169–70, 179, 206, 208–9, 211–12, 214
transcendent formation conscience (spiritual conscience), 99–100, 212. *See also* conscience.
transcendent guilt, 210, 212. *See also* spiritual self-guilt.
transcendent mind, 19n36, 48n36, 108–9, 126, 212–13; transcendent mind and will, 33n41, 48n36, 49n36, 108–9, 195–97, 199, 210. *See also* mind, spirit.
transcendent phase, 168, 198, 212. *See also* phasic formation.
transcendent and post-transcendent phase, 170–74, 186, 211. *See also* phasic formation.
transcendent self-presence, 34, 115–17, 144, 212
transcendent will, 33n41, 48–49n36, 108–9, 126, 195–97, 199, 210, 213. *See also* love-will, will.
transcendent-functional dimension, 35
transcendent-functional phase, 169–70. *See also* phasic formation.
transfocal consciousness (transconsciousness), 99n19, 107–8, 110, 167, 190, 213. *See also* consciousness.
transformation, 2–3, 19n38, 30n24, 36–38, 55–56, 64, 74, 77, 91, 108, 110, 137, 161, 167, 170, 172, 174, 179–81, 189, 205, 207, 213; dispositional transformation, 74–78; unifying transformation, 38, 78n88, 79, 157, 170, 174, 181, 214. *See also* reformation.
transhuman (transcosmic) epiphany, 12–13, 213. *See also* epiphany.
translation, as skill of one-on-one spiritual directors, 144, 179n2, 213
Trinity, 11, 13–14, 16, 19n38, 31, 35–36, 38, 44–48, 68, 77–78, 100–101, 111, 116, 133–34, 136, 154, 156, 183, 186, 191–92, 194, 203–4, 213–14. *See also* Divine Forming and Preforming Mystery, Eternal Trinitarian Formation and Interformation Event, God, More Than, Mystery.
true self, 58, 155. *See also* founding form, Christ form.
trust, 19, 46, 71, 78, 113, 115, 117, 127, 135, 137–39, 142–43, 152, 158, 174, 178, 181, 183–84, 192, 206. *See also* abandonment, abandonment option.

ultimize, 30, 33, 98–99, 163, 187, 191, 206, 214. *See also* absolutize, idolize.
unique-communal life-call, 31, 38, 43, 48n33, 56, 60, 64–65, 75, 77, 79, 86, 96–97, 101, 116, 121, 135, 150, 153–54, 161, 165, 174, 180, 186, 188–89, 191–93, 195–97, 199, 203, 207, 209–212, 214–15; in Christ (life-call in Christ), 33, 44, 70, 77, 79, 99–103, 129, 133, 144, 149n13, 188, 214 (*see also* Christ form). *See also* call, calling in Christ, life-call.
unifying transformation, 38, 78n88, 79, 157, 170, 174, 181, 214. *See also* illuminating reformation, purifying formation, reformation, transformation.

van Kaam, Adrian, vii, 1–8, 19, 177–82
van Kaamian Formation Field Model, 10, 14–15, 25, 28n12, 41, 194, 203. *See also* formation field.
Vatican Council II, 86
vertical interformation, 20–21, 214. *See also* horizontal interformation, interformation.
vital (life) dimension, 16, 27–30, 32, 33n43, 41, 55, 65, 69, 73, 82n3, 96, 169–70, 179, 203, 206, 212, 214
vital formation conscience, 96, 98n13, 214
vital impulse, 29, 32, 106, 207. *See also* compulsion, impulse.
vital memory, 55, 110
vital phase, 161–63, 215. *See also* phasic formation.
vocalization, 215
vocation, 38, 102, 132, 156, 186, 215. *See also* avocation, call, calling in Christ, unique-communal life-call, life-call.

Wesley, John, 73
will, 16–17, 19, 31, 73, 76, 83n5, 109n57, 128, 133, 156, 184, 198–99, 215; functional will, 19n36, 33n41, 48–49, 109, 169, 195–97, 199, 210; transcendent will, 33n41, 48–49, 108–9, 126, 195–97, 199, 210, 213; willfulness, 19 (self-will, 74); willingness, 19, 55, 64, 70, 210 (*see also* openness); willpower, 56; will-lessness, 19. *See also* will of the Mystery.
will of the Mystery (Divine will, will of Christ, etc.), 38, 60, 98–100, 102, 109, 116, 128, 133, 182, 188, 191–92, 195, 198, 202, 213. *See also* God's will.
wisdom, 8–9, 12n8, 27, 44n15, 89, 108, 134, 156, 171, 177n1
wonder, 12, 28, 65–67, 168, 175. *See also* awe.
world sphere, 14, 22, 51, 125, 187, 189, 194, 201, 215. *See also* sphere.
World War II, 5, 22, 83, 152

www.ingramcontent.com/pod-product-compliance
Lightning Source LLC
Chambersburg PA
CBHW050852230426
43667CB00012B/2250